Africa in the
Global Economy

AFRICA IN THE
GLOBAL
ECONOMY

◆

RICHARD E. MSHOMBA

LYNNE
RIENNER
PUBLISHERS

BOULDER
LONDON

Published in the United States of America in 2000 by
Lynne Rienner Publishers, Inc.
1800 30th Street, Boulder, Colorado 80301
www.rienner.com

and in the United Kingdom by
Lynne Rienner Publishers, Inc.
3 Henrietta Street, Covent Garden, London WC2E 8LU

Library of Congress Cataloging-in-Publication Data
Mshomba, Richard E., 1954–
    Africa in the global economy / by Richard E. Mshomba.
      p. cm.
    Includes bibliographical references and index.
    ISBN 1-55587-718-4 (hc : alk. paper) — ISBN 1-55587-443-6 (pb : alk. paper)
      1. Africa, Sub-Saharan—Commerce.   2. Africa, Sub-Saharan—Commercial policy.
3. Africa, Sub-Saharan—Economic policy.   I. Title.

HF3874.M78 2000
337.67—dc21   99-051382

British Cataloguing in Publication Data
A Cataloguing in Publication record for this book
is available from the British Library.

Printed and bound in the United States of America

∞ The paper used in this publication meets the requirements
of the American National Standard for Permanence of
Paper for Printed Library Materials Z39.48-1984.

5   4   3   2   1

For Elaine, Alphonce, and Dennis

Contents

Tables and Figures

Tables

Figures

Acknowledgments

I will bless the Lord at all times; his praise shall be ever in my mouth.
—Psalm 34:2

This book is, in many ways, a culmination of lifelong learning, not just the product of three and a half years of research and writing. I thank my late parents, Filomena and Elias Mshomba, for their vision. Although they did not have any formal education, they worked hard as subsistence farmers to provide the basic needs and instill in their children the value of education. I thank my teachers at all levels of my education and the schools and universities that have supported me.

In researching and writing this book, I received comments, encouragement, and support from many individuals. My families—the Mshombas of Arusha, Tanzania; the Durnings of Glenside, Pennsylvania; and the O'Hallorans of Cary, Illinois—encouraged me throughout and stood by me with their prayers and interest in my progress. So did my friends, far and near.

I am grateful to my colleagues in the Economics Department at La Salle University for discussions on various topics related to the manuscript. My sincere appreciation also goes to La Salle University for a semester research leave. I commend and thank La Salle's reference librarians for their outstanding service. I also wish to thank Ralph Romano of La Salle's Department of Information Technology for his technical assistance.

I owe special thanks to the Lindback Foundation in Philadelphia for a grant that supported my research in New York, Washington,

D.C., Accra, Geneva, and Nairobi. As a result of this support, I was able to obtain information and insights from many individuals, to whom I am also very thankful. These include African ambassadors and commercial attachés in Washington, D.C., and Geneva; officials at the U.S. Department of Commerce and the U.S. State Department, the World Bank, the World Trade Organization, and the United Nations Conference on Trade and Development; and government, business, and association leaders in Ghana and Kenya. I also wish to thank government officials and business leaders in Tanzania for their assistance.

My students were also supportive. My special thanks go to Marc Santugini-Repiquet for reading and editing the manuscript and preparing all the diagrams. Harvey Glickman has helped me tremendously with many discussions on the political economy of Africa. I also wish to extend my gratitude to Stephen O'Connell and an anonymous reviewer for their invaluable comments on the manuscript.

I could not have completed this book without my wife's untiring support. Elaine spent countless hours editing the entire manuscript and discussing it with me. I especially appreciate her attentiveness to organization and detail. It is with pleasure and thanksgiving that I dedicate this book to her and our two sons.

Any errors or omissions are, of course, my own.

—*Richard E. Mshomba*

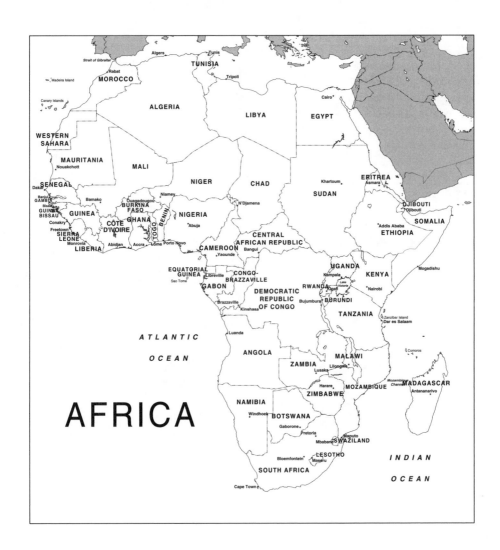

Strait of Gibraltar
Madeira Island
Canary Islands

TUNISIA
Algers   Tunis
Rabat
MOROCCO   Tripoli

ALGERIA   LIBYA   EGYPT
Cairo

WESTERN
SAHARA

MAURITANIA   MALI
Nouakchott

Khartoum   ERITREA
Asmara   DJIBOUTI
Djibouti

SENEGAL   NIGER   CHAD   SUDAN
Dakar
Banjul   Barnako   Niamey   N'Djamena   SOMALIA
GAMBIA   BURKINA
GUINEA   FASO   Ouagadougou   NIGERIA   Addis Ababa   ETHIOPIA
BISSAU
Conakry   GUINEA   CÔTE   GHANA   Abuja
Freetown   D'IVOIRE   CENTRAL   Mogadishu
SIERRA   Abidjan   Accra   Lomé   Porto Novo   AFRICAN REPUBLIC
LEONE   Monrovia   CAMEROON   Bangui
LIBERIA   Yaounde   UGANDA   KENYA

EQUATORIAL   CONGO-   Kampala
GUINEA   Libreville   BRAZZAVILLE   RWANDA   Lake   Nairobi
Sao Tome   GABON   Kigali   Victoria
DEMOCRATIC   Bujumbura   BURUNDI
Brazzaville   REPUBLIC
Kinshasa   OF CONGO   Dar es Salaam
TANZANIA   Zanzibar Island

ATLANTIC   Luanda
OCEAN   Comoros

ANGOLA   MALAWI
ZAMBIA   Lilongwe
Lusaka
Mozambique   MADAGASCAR
AFRICA   Harare   MOZAMBIQUE   Channel   Antananarivo
ZIMBABWE

NAMIBIA   Windhoek   BOTSWANA   INDIAN
Gaborone   Maputo   OCEAN
Pretoria   Mbabane   SWAZILAND

Bloemfontein   LESOTHO
Maseru
SOUTH AFRICA
Cape Town

ONE

♦

Introduction

For someone who travels from a developed country to just about any part of sub-Saharan Africa (SSA), the first impression is that of economic hardship for the majority of the people. If such a traveler is fortunate enough to spend even a few weeks in the rural areas, however, where 70 percent of the region's population resides, the impression of economic poverty will likely be countered by the spiritual richness of a strong community life there. In fact, it can be tempting to ask whether it is really in the interest of African nations to take a greater part in the global economy. One may ask why community-centered Africans should be brought into a world economy that is driven by fierce and cold competition.

This book is not about bringing Africa into the global economy, for Africa has been part of the global economy for centuries. Rural people today may seem concerned only with their personal daily needs and those of their immediate communities, yet most of them are just as closely connected to the world economy as those in the cities who work in the manufacturing sector. About 95 percent of the coffee produced by small farmers is exported to developed countries. Cotton produced by subsistence farmers is mainly for export. Many of the textile firms in Africa, few as they may be, are owned by foreign investors. Used clothes, which compete with the domestic textile and apparel industry, come from developed countries. Thirty-eight of SSA's 48 countries are members of the World Trade Organization (WTO), as shown in Table 1.1.

This book, instead, is about how sub-Saharan Africa has fared in the global economy. More important, it is about the direction that domestic and external policies should take to realize fully and to increase the benefits associated with trade. Countries are integrated into the global economy in many ways, through such means as world

2

Table 1.1   Selected Basic Indicators for Sub-Saharan African Countries

Country	GNP per Capita U.S.$ (1995)	Average Annual Percentage Growth, 1985–1995	Population, mid-1995 (millions)	Members of WTO, 1999
Seychelles	6,620	3.5[a]	0.07	
Gabon	3,490	−8.2	1.10	x
Mauritius	3,380	5.4	1.13	x
South Africa	3,160	−1.1	41.46	x
Botswana	3,020	6.1	1.45	x
Namibia	2,000	2.9	1.55	x
Swaziland	1,170	NA	0.90	x
Cape Verde	960	11.2[a]	0.38	
Lesotho	770	1.2	1.98	x
Congo, Republic of	680	−3.2	2.63	x
Côte d'Ivoire	660	−2.0[a]	13.98	x
Cameroon	650	−6.6	13.29	x
Senegal	600	−0.5[5]	8.47	x
Guinea	550	1.4	6.59	x
Zimbabwe	540	−0.6	11.01	x
Comoros	470	−1.5[a]	0.49	
Mauritania	460	0.5	2.27	x
Angola	410	−6.1	10.77	x
Zambia	400	−0.8	8.98	x
Ghana	390	1.4	17.08	x
Equatorial Guinea	380	2.3[a]	0.40	
Benin	370	−0.3	5.48	x
São Tomé and Principe	350	−0.3[a]	0.13	
Central African Republic	340	−2.4	3.28	x
Gambia	320	1.0[a]	1.11	x
Togo	310	−2.7	4.11	x
Kenya	280	0.1	26.69	x
Nigeria	260	1.2	111.27	x
Guinea-Bissau	250	2.0	1.07	x
Mali	250	0.8	9.79	x
Uganda	240	2.7	19.17	x
Madagascar	230	−2.2	13.65	x
Burkina Faso	230	−0.2	10.38	x
Niger	220	−2.2[a]	9.03	x
Chad	180	0.6	6.45	x
Rwanda	180	−5.4	6.40	x

continues

Table 1.1   continued

Country	GNP per Capita U.S.$ (1995)	Average Annual Percentage Growth, 1985–1995	Population, mid-1995 (millions)	Members of WTO, 1999
Sierra Leone	180	–3.6	4.51	x
Malawi	170	–0.7	9.76	x
Burundi	160	–1.3	6.26	x
Democratic Republic of Congo	120	–8.9[a]	43.85	x
Tanzania (mainland)	120	1.0	29.65	x
Ethiopia	100	–0.3	56.40	
Mozambique	80	3.6	16.17	x
Djibouti	[b]	—	0.63	x
Eritrea	[c]	—	3.57	
Liberia	[c]	—	2.73	
Somalia	[c]	—	9.47	
Sudan	[c]	—	26.71	

Source: World Bank (1997a: 6–9); World Bank (1997b): 214–215; World Bank (1997c: 6–7); WTO Office, Office of the U.S. Trade Representative, Washington, D.C.
  a. These figures are for 1986–1996.
  b. Estimated to be lower middle income ($766 to $3,035).
  c. Estimated to be low income ($765 or less).

health issues, the environment, international relations, immigration and refugee issues, human rights issues, labor issues, foreign direct investment, and especially financial markets and trade. Trade is the focus of this book.

Between 1980 and 1995, world trade (measured in terms of the value of exports) increased by an annual average of about 6.7 percent (World Bank, 1997b). During that same period, SSA (excluding South Africa) experienced negative trade growth on average: an annual average trade growth rate of minus 1 percent. The contribution of SSA (excluding South Africa) to world trade was about 1 percent in the 1990s (UNCTAD, 1997a). One might be inclined to conclude that SSA is not truly integrated into world trade.

What is important in determining to what degree a country is integrated into world trade, however, is the country's level of exports and imports as a ratio of the country's gross domestic product

(GDP). The export/GDP and import/GDP ratios of some sub-Saharan African countries are as high as 50 percent (see Table 2.4). By comparison, the ratios for the United States were about 8 and 11 percent, respectively, in 1995 (World Bank, 1997b).

In addition, one must remember that the value of exports is determined both by the volume of exports and the price of those exports. The price of a country's export goods relative to the price of its import goods is known as the country's terms of trade. A deterioration in the terms of trade is a fall in the price of exports relative to the price of imports, that is, getting less for its exports and paying more for its imports.[1] The terms of trade have been deteriorating for exports from sub-Saharan Africa.

Despite the growth in world trade in general and the degree to which sub-Saharan African countries are integrated into the global economy, African countries are still very poor, and the gap between the poor and rich countries has actually grown.[2] One may therefore question the relevance of trade for Africa. The answer is that although African countries could be better off than they are with the help of an improved trading environment (including better domestic policies in their own countries), without trade they would be worse off than they are.

One reason that trade is important for Africa, as for the rest of the world, is that it allows for an efficient allocation of resources. That is, trade allows production on the basis of comparative advantage. Comparative advantage refers to lower relative opportunity costs. Producers in one country have a comparative advantage if their opportunity cost in producing their good(s) or service(s) is lower, for whatever reason, than that of producers in another country.

Needless to say, comparative advantage is not static. Acquiring new skills, either through formal education or as a spillover from trading with other countries, changes opportunity costs and, thus, comparative advantage. The infant industry argument for restricting trade is based, in part, on the assertion that temporary protection will allow the domestic industry to learn and acquire comparative advantage.

In the 1970s and 1980s, for example, Mauritius had considerable comparative advantage in textiles and apparel because of its cheap and relatively skilled labor. However, in the 1990s it started to lose its competitive edge as a result of increased demand for labor and increased labor costs. In anticipation of these positive changes in labor income and the corresponding loss in comparative advantage in the textiles and apparel industry, Mauritius has been preparing its labor force to move into the second phase of industrialization. This involves diversifying within the clothing industry and moving into service industries and technology-intensive industries. Trade allows this efficient allocation of resources and, thus, provides benefits associated with production.

In addition to the benefits associated with production, trade provides benefits associated with consumption (the exchange of goods). It gives consumers new relative prices that allow them to make changes in their consumption and to consume beyond what the country can produce by itself. Therefore, although a country will benefit more if production adjusts to changes in relative prices, trade is still beneficial from the consumption standpoint, even if production does not change for some reason.

The question then becomes how or even whether these benefits from trade translate into development. Trade can have a role in contributing to economic growth, which in turn may translate into or itself constitute development. Trade can lead to growth through its potential to (1) transmit new ideas and new technology, (2) increase the inflow of foreign direct investment, (3) increase and improve utilization of factors of production, (4) enhance backward and forward linkages, and (5) increase opportunities to take advantage of economies of scale (Haberler, 1964; Hirschman, 1958).

Regarding backward and forward linkages, trade may allow the development of the textile industry, for example, which has a backward linkage to cotton and wool production. Likewise, production of coffee or cocoa has a forward linkage to the commodity processing and packaging industry. Regarding economies of scale, the world market allows even countries with small markets to increase their production and thereby reduce unit costs (the long-run average cost).

The topics discussed so far are only the potential positive impacts of trade. None of these benefits is automatic, and even when they are realized, they may not necessarily translate into development, that is, a better standard of living for the majority of the population. Even though trade may have created many jobs in sub-Saharan Africa during the colonial era, for example, Europeans took land from Africans and, in effect, forced them to take jobs from the Europeans at wages far below the market wage. Moreover, most of the profits accrued from trade were siphoned swiftly out of Africa.

As demonstrated throughout this text, some domestic policies and external factors today also work to limit the realization of benefits from trade and, thus, associated development. For example, as discussed in Chapter 2, interest rate policies of many SSA countries in the 1970s and early 1980s limited availability of capital and the growth of the private sector, thereby reducing the benefits of trade that accrue from the production side. As discussed in Chapter 3, the Generalized System of Preferences (GSP) program may in practice work against the development of industrialization in low-income countries. Chapter 4 describes protectionist policies in countries of the Organization for Economic Cooperation and Development (OECD) in areas such as agriculture and textiles in which sub-Saharan African countries may have the potential for comparative advantage.[3]

Finally, trade is only one piece of the puzzle for bringing development, although it can be an important one. Other components include distribution of the factors of production, access to education and health care, human rights, labor laws, and a political system in which the government is held accountable.

◆　◆　◆

This book concentrates on sub-Saharan Africa. The Arab countries of north Africa are certainly part of Africa, but focusing on SSA makes the study more manageable because the features that SSA countries share (to varying degrees) allow for some cautious generalizations. These features include a primarily rural population, a large agricultural sector, a large public sector, widespread economic poverty, and trade relations most significantly with OECD countries.

Of course, this is not to say that SSA countries are homogeneous. Note, for example, the disparity in GDP per capita among SSA countries, the GDP per capita growth rate, and the population of SSA countries, shown in Table 1.1. In fact, given the number of countries in SSA and their individual salient features, the study at times inevitably makes generalizations. To avoid overgeneralizations, the book focuses on some common trade themes. In addition, specific examples within the chapters have been provided, as well as cases that supplement the chapters.

Since the underlying theme is international trade in SSA, and since developed countries are SSA's major trading partners, special attention is given to both domestic policies and trade policies in OECD countries. About 82 percent of SSA exports and 75 percent of SSA imports are, respectively, destined to and originating from developed countries (UNCTAD, 1997a: 64, 84). See Table 1.2 for the export destination of individual SSA countries. The structure of SSA exports is shown in Table 1.3; it is clear that the agricultural sector is critical in generating export revenue for most countries.

The seven chapters of this book cover the following topics. Chapter 2 considers trade-related policies in SSA, including policies related to private investment, exchange rates, and agriculture as well as overall trade orientation in sub-Saharan Africa. Chapter 3 dis-

Table 1.2 Destination of Sub-Saharan African Exports, 1995 (or latest year available); Value of Exports in U.S. Dollars (millions)

Exporting Country	Total Value	Developed Countries				Eastern Europe	Developing Countries	
		Total	European Union	United States and Canada	Japan		Total	Africa
Angola	3,179	92.5	24.9	64.5	1.3	0.5	7.1	0.1
Benin	45	80.0	55.6	22.2	NA	2.2	17.8	4.4
Burkina Faso	169	60.9	34.5	0.6	2.0	NA	39.1	39.1
Burundi	76	78.6	64.6	7.6	0.5	NA	21.4	20.0
Cameroon	1,365	77.3	61.0	2.6	0.3	1.8	20.9	19.4
Cape Verde	5	66.7	58.3	8.3	NA	NA	33.3	31.3
Central African Republic	79	92.4	87.3	1.3	1.3	NA	7.6	6.3
Chad	261	51.7	42.9	0.8	7.3	0.8	47.5	41.4
Congo	910	97.5	51.5	36.5	NA	0.2	2.3	2.2
Côte d'Ivoire	3,105	65.2	56.6	6.2	1.1	8.0	26.9	25.0
Democratic Republic of Congo	506	84.6	58.7	4.8	6.5	4.5	10.9	5.3
Ethiopia	181	74.9	47.9	4.8	20.0	0.6	24.5	1.9
Gabon	2,474	88.0	48.7	31.8	4.6	3.2	8.8	2.5
Gambia	69	85.5	56.5	1.4	27.5	2.9	11.6	8.7
Ghana	1,152	87.2	61.7	16.1	6.4	3.8	9.0	3.9
Guinea-Bissau	293	38.2	17.7	11.9	7.2	3.8	58.0	1.4
Kenya	1,380	62.5	52.0	4.6	1.3	2.5	35.1	28.1
Liberia	389	79.9	66.8	12.3	NA	1.5	18.5	1.0
Madagascar	262	76.5	49.4	15.8	8.6	6.6	17.0	10.4

continues

Table 1.2 continued

Exporting Country	Total Value	Developed Countries					Developing Countries	
		Total	European Union	United States and Canada	Japan	Eastern Europe	Total	Africa
Malawi	377	76.1	27.3	14.3	11.4	2.4	21.5	14.6
Mali	317	39.1	34.1	3.5	0.9	26.5	34.4	21.1
Mauritania	471	83.0	58.2	4.5	20.4	10.8	6.2	5.9
Mauritius	1,467	92.5	71.3	18.5	0.4	NA	7.5	5.9
Mozambique	161	76.7	35.3	8.6	14.9	NA	14.1	5.5
Niger	416	63.7	53.1	10.3	NA	0.5	35.8	30.8
Nigeria	11,887	89.4	36.6	51.6	0.2	0.5	10.0	7.3
Rwanda	68	79.4	52.9	13.2	5.9	7.4	13.2	5.9
São Tomé and Principe	23	99.8	97.9	NA	NA	NA	0.2	NA
Senegal	705	56.0	53.8	0.3	2.0	0.9	35.0	20.6
Seychelles	24	89.0	81.9	0.3	5.7	NA	10.9	7.7
Sierra Leone	149	80.5	46.3	31.5	1.3	NA	7.4	7.4
Somalia	44	54.5	52.3	NA	NA	NA	45.5	2.3
South Africa	21,002	38.5	20.6	7.5	5.5	0.5	24.0	10.9
Sudan	565	38.4	29.9	2.7	5.1	14.3	47.3	11.3
Tanzania	437	69.1	58.1	2.7	5.0	1.8	29.1	11.0
Togo	261	55.2	38.7	13.8	NA	8.8	36.0	18.8
Uganda	143	89.5	74.1	11.2	3.5	1.4	9.1	7.7
Zambia	1,168	83.0	39.0	2.6	38.5	0.7	16.4	0.9
Zimbabwe	1,321	67.8	34.4	8.3	7.8	1.5	30.8	20.9

Source: UNCTAD (1995a, 1997a).
Note: The commodity classification is in accordance with the United Nations *Standard International Trade Classification (SITC)*: all food items (SITC 0 + 1 + 2 + 22 + 4); agricultural raw materials (SITC 2 – 22 – 27 – 28); ores and metals (SITC 27 + 28 + 68); fuels (SITC 3); and manufactured goods (SITC 5 to 8 less 68).

Table 1.3   The Structure of Sub-Saharan African Exports, 1995 (or latest year available)

Country	Total Value in U.S.$ (millions)	Main Categories of Exports (percentage)[a]				
		All Food Items	Agricultural Raw Materials	Fuels	Ores and Metals	Manufactures
Angola	3,910	0.2	NA	93.5	6.2	0.1
Benin	49	61.8	25.0	4.2	1.1	3.4
Burkina Faso	90	41.3	47.7	0.1	0.1	10.8
Burundi	129	70.5	6.5	NA	5.5	3.7
Cameroon	1,539	27.0	27.5	29.2	8.4	7.9
Cape Verde	4	84.2	1.2	0.3	9.1	5.2
Central African Republic	111	31.0	42.6	NA	0.2	26.2
Chad	72	4.3	80.7	NA	0.1	14.6
Comoros	15	58.7	0.5	NA	14.6	23.8
Congo	949	0.9	12.5	83.4	1.1	2.1
Côte d'Ivoire	2,979	64.2	28.1	2.3	0.2	4.7
Democratic Republic of Congo	2,509	11.0	2.7	8.0	47.3	6.0
Djibouti	25	39.1	4.7	NA	0.2	7.8
Equatorial Guinea	27	87.8	9.5	NA	0.1	2.5
Ethiopia	294	63.3	25.1	6.2	NA	5.3
Gabon	2,391	0.1	8.8	86.6	3.4	1.1
Gambia	36	98.9	0.4	NA	NA	NA
Ghana	942	78.4	3.6	0.4	16.7	0.9
Guinea-Bissau	11	84.9	2.2	NA	0.3	8.2
Kenya	1,021	49.1	5.6	13.1	2.9	29.2
Liberia	597	8.6	29.3	1.2	57.6	1.9
Madagascar	350	69.1	6.0	1.5	6.9	14.4
Malawi	402	92.9	1.9	NA	NA	5.1

continues

Table 1.3 continued

	Total Value in U.S.$ (millions)	Main Categories of Exports (percentage)[a]				
Country		All Food Items	Agricultural Raw Materials	Fuels	Ores and Metals	Manufactures
Mali	330	36.1	62.3	NA	NA	1.6
Mauritania	255	15.5	0.7	NA	83.3	0.4
Mauritius	1,538	28.6	0.7	NA	0.2	70.3
Mozambique	161	66.6	10.5	9.1	1.8	11.3
Niger	580	11.4	0.6	1.1	84.7	2.0
Nigeria	25,058	2.2	0.2	96.9	0.3	0.3
Rwanda	138	81.7	6.7	NA	10.1	0.4
São Tomé and Principe	22	98.8	NA	NA	0.1	1.2
Senegal	783	53.2	2.7	12.3	9.3	22.5
Seychelles	24	98.6	0.1	NA	0.1	1.2
Sierra Leone	302	24.4	1.2	NA	34.2	39.9
Somalia	133	86.7	7.7	4.8	NA	0.5
South Africa	18,438	11.6	4.4	7.4	23.4	53.2
Sudan	584	46.9	50.7	1.0	0.5	0.8
Tanzania	528	58.1	17.5	4.7	5.4	14.1
Togo	268	23.0	21.5	NA	44.7	9.1
Uganda	465	95.6	2.3	0.5	0.5	0.7
Zambia	1,330	1.0	0.5	0.3	82.3	16.0
Zimbabwe	1,895	43.2	6.8	1.0	11.6	37.0

Source: UNCTAD (1997a).

a. The commodity classification is in accordance with the United Nations *Standard International Trade Classification (SITC)*: all food items (SITC 0 + 1 + 22 + 4); agricultural raw materials (SITC 2 − 22 − 27 − 28); ores and metals (SITC 27 + 28 + 68); fuels (SITC 3); and manufactured goods (SITC 5 to 8 less 68). A plus sign means combining together various commodity groups or subgroups. A minus sign means excluding some subgroup from a broader commodity classification.

cusses GSP, a program under which developed countries provide preferential reduction or removal of tariffs on products from designated developing countries. Chapter 4 presents two of the most important trade agreements for SSA—(1) agriculture and (2) textiles and clothing—from the Uruguay Round of the General Agreement on Tariffs and Trade (GATT). Chapter 5 discusses international commodity agreements to raise and stabilize prices of primary products, which are SSA's most important exports. Chapter 6 analyzes regional economic integration as a strategy for trade and development in SSA. Chapter 7 is the conclusion.

Notes

1. For example, suppose Chad must sell ten tons of cotton to buy one tractor. If Chad were exporting only cotton and importing only tractors, we would say that Chad's terms of trade had deteriorated if it now took more than ten tons of the same type and quality of cotton to buy an identical tractor.

2. In 1980 the ratio of GDP per capita for low-income countries in comparison with high-income countries was about 1 to 30. In 1995 that ratio (for the same countries) was 1 to 59 (World Bank, 1997a: 220–221, 236–237).

3. The OECD is an intergovernmental organization whose members are mainly developed countries. It was formed in 1961. The original OECD members were the following countries of Europe and North America: Austria, Belgium, Canada, Denmark, France, Germany, Greece, Iceland, Ireland, Italy, Luxembourg, the Netherlands, Norway, Portugal, Spain, Sweden, Switzerland, Turkey, the United Kingdom, and the United States. Later it was joined, chronologically, by Japan, Finland, Australia, and New Zealand. In the 1990s it was joined by Mexico, the Czech Republic, Hungary, Poland, and South Korea, to bring the total membership in 1998 to 29 countries.

TWO

◆

Trade-Related Policies

The focus in this chapter is on four types of domestic policies that have been important in determining the extent of and the gains from trade: those related to private investment, exchange rate policies, agricultural policies, and overall trade orientation in sub-Saharan Africa. The two cases at the end of the chapter, "The Near Elimination of Pigeon Peas in Tanzania" and "From Coffee to Cut Flowers in Tanzania," illustrate the impact of domestic policies on agricultural production and diversification.

Private Investment and Trade

Private investment refers to new physical capital bought by firms and households that augments future production ability of the economy. The main types of investment are (1) fixed business (nonresidential) investment, such as new manufacturing plants, warehouses, office buildings, restaurants, equipment, and tools; (2) residential investment, including the purchase of new housing or maintenance of housing; and (3) inventory investment, that is, the change in a firm's stock of inputs, unfinished products, and finished products that have not yet been sold.

Owing to the deterioration of old physical capital, some of the new capital simply replaces the old. Thus, there is an important distinction between gross (total) investment and net investment. Net investment is gross investment adjusted for capital depreciation (also known as capital consumption allowance). It is the net investment that really shows whether the economy's capital stock is rising or falling and, therefore, suggests whether the economy's future production potential is growing or declining.

It should be noted, though, that even capital depreciation can offer new opportunities. Even though the depreciation of old machinery and equipment reduces the economy's capital stock, it also allows entrepreneurs to adopt new technology, move to new geographical locations, and/or move from one industry to another. Some physical capital, especially machinery, is industry specific. It may continue to be used in a certain industry in the short run, for its remaining useful life, even when market signals suggest a shift of resources to another industry. In the long run, however, depreciation allows a shift into more profitable industries, as signaled by current prices and expected prices. To make such a move, entrepreneurs need new physical capital and may have to borrow because their own savings may not be sufficient.

Interest rate policies have a direct impact on the availability of loanable funds, which in turn are important for private investment. Any policies that directly or indirectly limit private investment also limit trade and the gains from trade.

Gains from trade accrue in two ways: from specialization in production and from the exchange of goods. They are, therefore, determined by the extent to which both producers and consumers are able to alter their production and consumption, respectively, in response to price signals. Thus, even when production is not flexible enough to take advantage of price signals, a country can benefit from trade through an exchange of goods. A country can benefit more from trade, though, by also allowing production to change, that is, by allowing a relatively more efficient allocation of resources.

As discussed later in more detail, in the 1970s and most of the 1980s many countries in sub-Saharan Africa implemented interest rate policies and other policies that inadvertently or deliberately discouraged resource mobility by limiting private investment. This meant the gains of these countries from trade were less than they could have been.

Table 2.1 gives a general sense of the level and trend of private investment in sub-Saharan Africa and the significant variation between countries. It shows private investment as a percentage of gross domestic fixed investment (PI/GDFI) and gross domestic fixed investment as a percentage of gross domestic product (GDFI/GDP) in eleven countries. Mauritius had the highest GDFI/GDP ratio; Côte d'Ivoire had the lowest. Tanzania saw a sharp decrease in the relative proportion of private investment in the 1980s. For most of the countries, the relative proportion of private investment increased in the early 1990s. This recent trend may be explained, in part, by the eco-

Table 2.1   Private Investment (PI) as a Percentage of Gross Domestic Fixed Investment (GDFI) and Gross Domestic Fixed Investment as a Percentage of GDP

Country		Average 1970–1979	Average 1980–1989	Average 1990–1995
Cameroon	PI/GDFI	47	42[a]	NA
	GDFI/GDP	19.2	23[a]	NA
Central African	PI/GDFI	NA	45	45
Republic	GDFI/GDP	NA	12.8	13
Côte d'Ivoire	PI/GDFI	NA	50	54
	GDFI/GDP	NA	13.7	9.9
Kenya	PI/GDFI	59	58	53
	GDFI/GDP	21.5	19.9	19.6
Malawi	PI/GDFI	37	36	39
	GDFI/GDP	23.7	15	14
Mauritius	PI/GDFI	68	65	68
	GDFI/GDP	27.5	21.4	29.2
Namibia	PI/GDFI	NA	42	60
	GDFI/GDP	NA	19.4	21.4
South Africa	PI/GDFI	52	58	70
	GDFI/GDP	26.9	23.5	17.1
Tanzania	PI/GDFI	59	45[a]	NA
	GDFI/GDP	19.7	16.8[a]	NA
Togo	PI/GDFI	NA	26	47
	GDFI/GDP	NA	17.8	13.3
Zimbabwe	PI/GDFI	61	54[a]	NA
	GDFI/GDP	18.5	18.5[a]	NA

Sources: Bouton and Sumlinski (1996: 19) for all countries except Cameroon, Tanzania, and Zimbabwe, which come from Oshikoya (1994: 575).
    a. Averages for 1980–1988.

nomic reforms taking place in many countries in Africa, under which the role of the private sector has increased.

Figure 2.1 shows the trends of gross domestic investment as a percentage of GDP for sub-Saharan Africa and developing countries (shown as LDCs—less developed countries—in Figure 2.1) as a whole. The gross domestic investment ratio declined in sub-Saharan Africa from an average of about 24 percent in the 1970s to an average of about 15 percent in 1992 and 1993. In contrast, investment in other developing countries has been increasing since the early 1980s. The investment ratios shows in Figure 2.1 are simple averages

Figure 2.1   Gross Investment as a Percentage of GDP

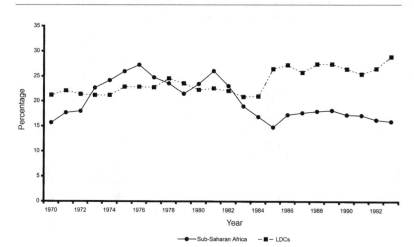

across countries. They are not weighted for the countries' economic size, population, or quality of investment.

There is little argument that investment—that is, appropriate physical capital accumulation—is critical to the economic growth rate in developing countries. Its importance, even to those loyal to the neoclassical growth model, cannot be overstated.[1] However, it is less clear what determines the level of private investment in developing countries. Making such a determination for countries in sub-Saharan Africa is especially difficult because of insufficient or unreliable data and fragmented capital markets.

Current studies suggest that the following variables are important to varying degrees in different countries in determining the level of private sector investment: political stability, macroeconomic stability, public sector investment, exchange rates, the terms of trade, the magnitude of the debt burden, interest rates, and credit availability. The focus here is on the last two variables, which are, of course, interdependent.

To a borrower, interest is a cost of acquiring capital; to a lender, interest is a rate of return on financial capital. Although banks and other financial institutions may provide loans, the ultimate suppliers of financial capital are those who save in or hold assets from financial institutions. It comes as no surprise, therefore, that interest rates play an important role in determining credit availability and, thus, the level of private investment in a country.

Because prices are not constant in any economy, it is important to make a distinction between nominal interest rates and real interest rates. The nominal interest rate refers to the percentage increase in money received by those with deposits in financial institutions. It measures the money receipts and payments in current value. The real interest rate measures the cost or return on a loan in terms of purchasing power; it is the nominal interest rate adjusted for inflation.

Suppose, for example, the nominal one-year interest rate in Ghana is 10 percent. In one year, for every cedi saved, the depositor will receive 1.1 cedis. Now suppose the inflation rate in Ghana is 25 percent. Goods and services that on average cost 1 cedi today will cost 1.25 cedis in a year.[2] This means for each cedi saved today, the purchasing power in a year will be 1.1 cedis/1.25 cedis, which is 0.88. In real terms, there is a loss of 0.12 cedis for each cedi saved. In other words, the real interest rate in this example is negative 12 percent.[3]

$$Real\ interest\ rate = \frac{1 + nominal\ interest\ rate}{1 + inflation\ rate} - 1$$

Theory and intuition tell us there is a negative relationship between the real interest rate and the quantity of loanable funds demanded and a positive relationship between the real interest rate and the quantity of loanable funds supplied. An increase in the real interest rate increases the cost of borrowing. On the other hand, as the real interest rate increases, so does the incentive to save. Where the interest rate is mainly determined by market forces, an equilibrium interest rate emerges (the market-clearing interest rate) that will bring balance between supply and demand.

For most of sub-Saharan Africa, especially in the 1970s and early 1980s, the governments set interest rate ceilings. As a result, real interest rates, especially those received by depositors, were negative in many countries, as shown in Table 2.2. Negative real interest rates create a disincentive to save, which inhibits credit availability. The annual real interest rates shown in Table 2.2 were calculated using the nominal interest rate of a given year and the inflation rate for that year. To the extent that loans that were to be paid back in more than one year were given with a fixed nominal interest rate, and inflation was increasing over time, the actual real lending rates were lower than those shown in Table 2.2.

As shown in Figure 2.2, interest rate ceilings cause a situation in which there can be a positive relationship between interest rates and investment. (Remember that the latter refers to physical investment,

Table 2.2 Average Annual Real Deposit and Lending Interest Rates, 1980–1994

Country	Deposit			Lending		
	1980–1984	1985–1989	1990–1994	1980–1984	1985–1989	1990–1994
Botswana	−2.4	−2.2	−1.8	1.4	0.1	−0.4
Burkina Faso	−1.8	5.1	7.4[a]	NA	NA	16.4[a]
Cameroon	−4.2	1.3	2.4	1.2	7.5	12.2
Cape Verde	NA	−1.6	−3.0	NA	4.0	2.7
Chad	NA	6.7	2.7	NA	12.9	12.6
Central African Republic	−5.2	−0.5	4.9	−0.9	4.0	14.9
Congo	−4.1	4.3	−1.1	−0.1	7.9	8.3
Côte d'Ivoire	−1.0	1.4	7.4[a]	NA	NA	16.4[a]
Ethiopia	NA	3.0	−4.6	NA	3.2	−1.4
Gabon	−2.9	7.0	2.5	1.8	10.9	12.2
Gambia	−2.8	−6.4	4.8	5.8	3.0	17.3
Ghana	−29.8	−6.8	−1.3	−25.3	−2.1[b]	NA
Kenya	−2.7	−1.1	NA	0.1	4.6	2.0
Lesotho	−3.4	−3.4	−2.5	1.4	1.3	3.8
Liberia	3.9	3.6	−1.5	12.9	10.3	4.8
Madagascar	−9.0	−3.0	NA	NA	NA	NA
Malawi	−1.3	−4.6	−1.7[a]	5.9	1.5	4.7[a]
Mauritius	1.0	3.7	2.2	3.5	8.2	8.4
Senegal	−3.6	3.6	7.8[a]	3.4	11.4	16.9
Sierra Leone	−19.0	−33.5	−14.6	−15.7	−29.1	−5.3
South Africa	−1.5	−1.7	1.8	2.5	0.9	5.3
Swaziland	−3.2	−5.1	3.0	1.4	0.6	2.5
Tanzania	−19.8	−13.6	−6.5	−13.4	5.0	5.4
Togo	−2.0	5.7	6.3[a]	5.1	14.1	15.4[a]
Uganda	−26.5	−48.6	0.0	−22.8	−44.7	NA
Zambia	−7.9	−27.6	NA	−4.1	−23.2	NA
Zimbabwe	−4.0	−1.2	−7.4[c]	6.1	2.5	−5.6[c]

Source: Derived using data from various issues of the International Monetary Fund's *International Financial Statistics.*

   a. 1990–1992.
   b. 1985–1988.
   c. 1990–1991.

unless stated otherwise.) The numbers used in Figure 2.2 are only for illustration. The DD line in Figure 2.2 represents the demand for loanable funds in cedis for private domestic investment. The SS line represents the supply of loanable funds in cedis for domestic lending. The market-clearing interest rate is 20 percent. Now suppose an interest rate ceiling is set at 10 percent. Borrowing and investment

Figure 2.2   Demand and Supply of Loanable Funds

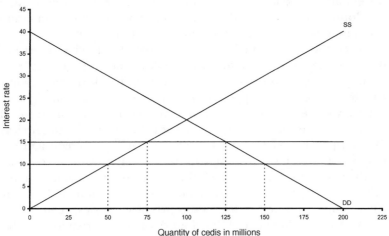

Quantity of cedis in millions

will be constrained to 50 million cedis, even though entrepreneurs are willing to borrow and invest 150 million cedis at that interest rate. (Of course, the quantity of loanable funds demanded is not empirically observable when the interest rate is set below the market-clearing interest rate.) There is a shortage of 100 million cedis. At a higher interest rate ceiling of 15 percent, entrepreneurs would borrow and invest 75 million cedis.

Empirical studies should show a positive relationship between the interest rate and private investment in economies with financial repression, that is, where interest rates are below equilibrium. Under those conditions, private investment is determined by the availability of financial credit and not by the cost of borrowing. This insight was well developed and articulated by McKinnon (1973). Within a short period of his seminal work, a consensus emerged that "in contrast to developed countries, one of the principal constraints on investment in developing countries is the quantity, rather than the cost, of financial resources" (Blejer and Khan, 1984: 386).

Because of insufficient and unreliable data, it has been very difficult to confirm or disprove empirically McKinnon's hypothesis that in financially repressed economies, higher interest rates would increase private investment. A careful study must control for the other major determinants of private investment, such as the relative price of capital, government investment, the GDP gap (i.e., the difference between potential GDP and actual GDP), capital inflows and outflows, political and macroeconomic stability, the substitutability of bank deposits and other assets, retained earnings, and so on. Only a few empirical studies have been done so far on private investment in developing countries, and all of them express some reservation about their results owing to the limitations of their data.

Even though some of these studies could neither support nor disprove McKinnon's hypothesis, available studies in aggregate seem to support the hypothesis. A study of sixteen Latin American countries by Galbis (1979) supported McKinnon's hypothesis in highly financially repressed countries. A study by Blejer and Khan (1984) of twenty-four developing countries (none in sub-Saharan Africa) found a positive relationship between availability of credit and private investment. Oshikoya's study (1994) of eight African countries for the period from 1970 to 1988 also found credit availability "to the private sector is a major determinant of private investment in low-income countries as well as the middle-income countries" (590).[4]

Mataya and Veeman (1996) found a negative relationship between private investment and interest rates in Malawi (1967–1988). Their result, however, does not refute McKinnon's hypothesis because Malawi had managed to avoid financial repression with positive real interest rates in most of the period they studied.

A study by Morisset (1993) on Argentina (1961–1982) suggested that although a rise in interest rates would indeed increase bank credits, this might not necessarily increase private investment. The study warned that the positive impact on private investment of an increase in domestic credit, resulting from higher interest rates, could be offset by a portfolio shift from capital goods and public bonds into monetary assets and an increase in the public sector's demand for credit, thus reducing the amount available to the private sector (Morisset, 1993: 142–143, 148). The crowding out, according to Morisset, does not result from a change in the government's behavior but rather from the reduction in the private sector's demand for government bonds. The crowding out is not necessarily prevented by allowing a simultaneous increase in interest rates on government bonds since that would increase the public debt service on domestic debt and, thus, the public deficit. An increase in the budget deficit would increase the public sector's demand for bank credits and, thus, crowd out the private sector.

Although African governments do not rely on a private market in government bonds to raise financing, Morisset's warning is still valid for all developing countries because of the potential impact of an increase in interest rates on the budget deficit. Governments may need to change their behavior, allowing the increased bank credit to be distributed among the private sector and emphasizing public projects that complement private investment. This may explain why recommendations for financial reforms are usually associated with recommendations to reform the public sector and why implementation of those recommendations usually calls for external assistance.

If low interest rates reduce bank credits and, thus, private investment, and if investment is vital to growth, why did many African countries set interest rate ceilings, thereby maintaining negative real interest rates in the 1970s and 1980s? To pose the question differently, why did countries mostly use nonprice criteria to ration funds when such a system lowers the efficiency and quality of investment?

There are several explanations. It is possible that some countries believed that interest rates are ineffective in increasing saving (Schmidt-Hebbel et al., 1996: 101). Moreover, there are studies showing that most people in sub-Saharan Africa, especially nonurban residents, hold most of their wealth in nonmonetary forms, such as livestock, stored crops, farm machinery, building materials, and radios (Shipton, 1991; Dercon, 1996). In addition, even when people hold their assets in cash, they may prefer to keep the cash at home or with a trusted shopkeeper or relative. In general, many people do not have access to banks and/or do not view them as safe. Some, however, may simply not view banks and the interest rates they offer as worth the trouble of the paperwork involved and other transaction costs.

The interest rate could, indeed, be too low for it to be an important factor in determining savings in financial institutions. In general, however, interest rates would impact the asset portfolio even if they might not affect the overall saving. It would be unrealistic, therefore, to assume that domestic loanable funds are independent of interest rates.

Another ostensible reason for instituting low interest rates may have been to encourage investment. In an effort to speed up the industrialization process, countries wanted to subsidize capital investment, especially public-sector investment. Although the objective may have been noble, the policy to achieve it was not sustainable. As the discussion so far demonstrates, one cannot address the demand (or the need) for loanable funds without taking into account the supply of such funds.

To examine this point further, let us consider who benefits from negative real interest rates. To the depositor, a negative real interest rate is an implicit tax. To the borrower, it is an implicit subsidy.[5]

To illustrate, suppose an economy has an inflation rate of 25 percent a year. An individual borrows 2.5 million cedis, to be paid back in ten years in equal monthly payments. At a fixed nominal interest rate of 25 percent, that is, a real interest rate of zero, the borrower will pay back a nominal total of about 6.8 million cedis, whose real value will be 2.5 million cedis. At a fixed nominal rate of 10 percent, that is, a real interest rate of negative 12 percent[6], the borrower will pay back a total of about 4 million cedis, whose real value will be about 1.45 million cedis.[7] At this negative real interest rate, the borrower has, in effect, been subsidized more than 1 million cedis in real value. For any given loan amount, if the real interest rate is below zero, the smaller the real interest rate and the longer the loan period, the larger the subsidy.

A negative real interest rate is, therefore, a policy to subsidize investment, benefiting borrowers at the expense of depositors. The main borrowers in many countries in sub-Saharan Africa in the 1970s and 1980s were the government and its parastatals. Countries with the lowest interest rates—Ghana, Sierra Leone, Tanzania, Uganda, and Zambia (Table 2.2)—were also the ones who pioneered the growth of the public sector during this period. Because there was a shortage of loanable funds at the government-set interest rates, loans were often only available to government agencies, individuals with political influence, or those who were willing and able to bribe. In other words, nonmarket factors, instead of interest rates, were used to ration loanable funds, thus lowering the efficiency of a given amount of investment. Given who borrowed (and, thus, benefited from) what little credit was available, it is not difficult to understand why governments maintained negative real interest rates, despite the overall ill effects of such policies.

One may ask how banks could and why they would continue to operate in the situation described above, where money repaid to them was worth less in real terms than the money they loaned. The most important factor in explaining this is that in many African countries, the state owned a significant segment of the banking sector. In fact, before the economic reforms initiated in many countries in the late 1980s, the banking industry was under total government monopoly in several countries, including Benin, Gambia, Ghana, Guinea, Guinea-Bissau, Madagascar, Mauritania, Mozambique, Tanzania, Togo, and Uganda (World Bank, 1994a: 234–235). Like other government-run institutions, banks were subsidized. Of course, since the subsidies themselves could not be sustained, the banks' ability to provide credit diminished over time and some banks became insolvent (Caprio and Klingebiel, 1996). Currently all sub-Saharan African countries allow private banks.

The system just described reduces the potential for a country to benefit from trade because it reduces the availability of financial capital. It reduces the ability to move resources from one sector to another in response to price signals or in anticipation of price changes. As noted earlier, some of the benefits from trade come from increasing production in those industries in which the country has comparative advantage.

Other important consequences of negative real interest rates should briefly be noted. Artificially low interest rates can be a disincentive to innovation and to seeking ventures with expected high rates of return. Moreover, people with low-return investment projects may crowd out those with high-yield projects. Since the interest rate is low and, in many cases, independent of the type of proposed projects, financial institutions would favor safer, low-return projects over riskier, high-yield ones. Therefore, in countries with very low interest rate ceilings, increasing interest rates may increase not only investment but also the quality of investment. As McKinnon (1973) said, "high rates of interest for both lenders and borrowers introduce the dynamism that one wants in development, calling forth new net saving and diverting investment from inferior uses so as to encourage technical improvement" (15).

Fry (1993) used a two-sector model to demonstrate how financial repression produces an inefficient mix of investment. In the model, sector 1 is less productive and can finance its investment only by its retained earnings. Sector 2 has a higher return on its investment, some of which can be financed through bank loans. Fry illustrated inefficiency in investment as follows:

> Suppose that economic agents in sector 1 face the choice of holding money balances with a return of 4 percent or investing in physical capital with risk-adjusted return of 5 per cent. Suppose that with these relative rates of return, economic agents in sector 1 allocate $10 to increased money balances and $90 to physical investment. Now, economic agents in sector 2 can borrow $10 from the banks at an interest rate of 6 percent, which they do because their investments yield a risk-adjusted return of 10 percent. They also contribute their saving of $100 to their investment. The average rate of return to the additional stock in this economy is 7.75 per cent: $(5 \cdot \$90 + 10 \cdot \$110)/200$.
>
> Now suppose that deposit and loan rates are raised to 6 and 8 percent, respectively. Rational economic agents in sector 1 increase their money balances by the full amount of their total $100 saving and sector 2 borrows $100 for a total investment of $200. The average return to the new capital stock in the economy rises from 7.75 to 10 per cent. (Fry, 1993: 13)

The old interest rate ceiling of 6 percent was below the market-clearing equilibrium and produced inefficiency in investment.

Negative real interest rates can also be inflationary because they may encourage borrowing for consumption rather than for investment. Increasing interest rates in countries with negative real interest rates, therefore, would improve investment even in an unlikely scenario in which the increased rates do not generate new net saving.

Another possible impact of negative real interest rates is to encourage and support capital flight. Such rates encourage capital flight to the extent that some individuals may decide to move their financial assets to countries where they would earn a positive rate of return. Negative real interest rates also support capital flight to the extent that such rents could enable influential individuals to borrow funds from domestic banks, use the money to buy foreign currency that was typically undervalued, and invest it abroad.

Exchange Rate Policies

Up until the early 1990s, many sub-Saharan African countries had fixed exchange rate systems that overvalued domestic currencies. In theory, under a fixed exchange rate system, the central bank buys and sells foreign currency to maintain the value of the domestic currency within the officially prescribed exchange rate floor and exchange rate ceiling. In practice, however, the exchange rate ceilings were set very low relative to the market rate, and African countries did not have international reserves to sell in order to bring equilibrium. Figure 2.3 is similar to Figure 2.2 and, again, uses Ghana as an example. The vertical axis measures the exchange rate, cedis per dollar, and the horizontal axis measures the quantity of foreign currency, dollars. Again, the numbers are hypothetical and used purely for illustration.

The *DD* and *SS* lines represent demand for and supply of foreign currency, respectively. The location of the demand line is determined by Ghana's demand for foreign goods and services and its demand for foreign currency–denominated assets. The location of the supply line is determined by foreign countries' demands for Ghana's goods and services as well as Ghana's ability to supply them. A decrease in real income in the foreign countries, for example, would cause the supply line to shift to the left, thus decreasing the value of the cedi.

The market equilibrium exchange rate is 20 cedis per U.S. dollar. However, the exchange rate ceiling is set at 10 cedis per U.S. dollar. (That is, the cedi is overvalued.) Notice that this ceiling causes a shortage of 100 million dollars. Theoretically, the central bank of

Figure 2.3   Demand and Supply of Dollars

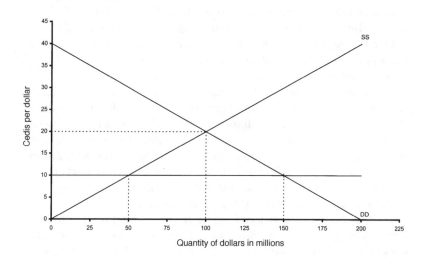

Ghana would have to sell 100 million dollars each period. In practice, an overvalued exchange rate eventually is unsustainable because reserves run out as the shortage persists. This introduces the
dynamic aspect of an overvalued exchange rate. As with loanable
funds, it becomes necessary to use nonmarket factors to ration foreign currency.

Shortages of foreign currencies create parallel markets in which
foreign currencies are exchanged for prices even higher than the
market equilibrium exchange rates. (Thus, the parallel market rate
in Figure 2.3 would be more than 20 cedis per dollar.) A suggestive
measure of the overvaluation of the domestic currency by the official
exchange rate is given by the parallel market exchange rate premium, measured as:

$$\rho = \frac{e_s - e}{e} \times 100,$$

where
ρ is premium;
e_s is parallel market exchange rate (e.g., cedis per dollar);
and
e is official market exchange rate (e.g., cedis per dollar).

050644

Table 2.3 shows the parallel market exchange rate premium for twenty-five individual countries and for Communauté Financière Africaine (CFA) countries, as a group, from 1975 to 1993.[8] The numbers in the table represent the percentage by which the parallel market exchange rate exceeded the official exchange rate. For example, in Angola, in the early 1980s, the parallel market exchange rate exceeded the official exchange rate by more than 2,300 percent.

A number of factors determine the parallel market exchange rate and, thus, the premium. They include the difference between the market equilibrium exchange rate and the official rate, the risk involved in dealing in the parallel market, and the relative demand for foreign currencies by those who are not able to buy them in the official market. The larger the difference between the market equilibrium exchange rate and the official rate, the larger the magnitude of the shortage and, thus, the higher the premium.

An increase in the risk of dealing in the parallel market reduces both the demand for and the supply of foreign currency in that market. The net impact on the parallel market exchange rate would, therefore, depend on the relative magnitudes of those changes and exchange rate elasticities of supply and demand. If the supply is more sensitive to changes in the risk factor than the demand, then an increase in the risk would cause an increase in the parallel market premium. Typically, as long as one used some discretion, the risk in dealing in the parallel market in sub-Saharan African countries was minimal. In some cases, the parallel market operated right beside the government-owned commercial banks.

Since the allocation of foreign currency in the official market is not primarily based on market forces, people who are allocated foreign currency may not necessarily be those with higher demands, that is, those who would be willing and able to pay the most for it. This is especially the case where most of the foreign currency goes to the government and parastatals and also where the official market is infested with corruption, favoritism, and patronage of the state.[9] The parallel premium is higher if the official market favors individuals with lower demands for foreign currency. For insightful cases on parallel exchange rates and their impact on Ghana, Sudan, Tanzania, and Zambia, see, respectively, Ansu (1997), Elbadawi (1997), Kaufmann and O'Connell (1997), and Aron and Elbadawi (1997).

The overvaluation of the domestic currency is often defended, for a number of reasons. One is that it subsidizes imports of important inputs. These inputs, such as spare parts, fertilizers, and physical equipment, are important to economic growth. However, as Figure 2.3 clearly shows, the amount of foreign currency available is less

Table 2.3   Parallel Market Exchange Rate Premium, 1975–1993

Country	1975–1979	1980–1984	1985–1989	1990–1993	1993
Angola	NA	2351[a]	6066	NA	NA
Botswana	NA	15	25	14	16
Burundi	26[b]	24	20	30[c]	NA
CFA countries	3	3	2	2	1
Comoros	4[b]	3	12	8	2
Ethiopia	63[b]	72	161	191	156
Gambia	7[b]	2	18	7	−3
Ghana	320	1321	42	5	3
Guinea	125	514	290	11	21
Kenya	9	19	9	38	32
Malawi	82	73	25	31	32
Mauritania	71	71	158	137	81
Mauritius	NA	NA	5	6	0
Mozambique	507	694	1644	29	12
Nigeria	68	201	122	65	128
Rwanda	NA	NA	33	74	103
Sierra Leone	NA	NA	816	52	17
Somalia	NA	NA	96	NA	NA
South Africa	10	5	10	2	3
Sudan	46	7	92	240	125
Swaziland	NA	NA	13	13	16
Tanzania	112	242	158	43	2
Uganda	768	242	277	29	15
Zaire	209	98	15	61	9
Zambia	140	55	293	75	33
Zimbabwe	NA	95	57	22	23

Sources: Various issues of International Currency Analysis's *Pick's Currency Yearbook* and *World Currency Yearbook.*
  a. 1982–1984.
  b. 1976–1979.
  c. 1990–1992.

than it would be with a market equilibrium exchange rate. In addition, the foreign currency available through the official market may not be allocated according to signals from the world market or according to future potential comparative advantage.

Another argument for overvaluation of domestic currency is to prevent inflation. A flexible exchange rate system will devalue the domestic currency, making imports more expensive and causing inflation. This indeed is true, especially in the short run, because of the low price elasticities of imports and exports. However, the value of a currency cannot be determined simply by will. The value of a currency is determined by the supply of and the demand for goods, services, and assets. A mere declaration of an official exchange rate does not change that fact, as shown by the parallel market exchange rates.

In addition, even though countries with exchange rate controls complemented them with price controls, actual prices adjusted to the parallel market exchange rates, though to varying degrees. The inflationary impact of devaluation, as a country moves from a fixed exchange rate system to a flexible exchange rate system, is often exaggerated by comparing the predevaluation, government-set price ceilings—instead of actual prices—with the postdevaluation market prices. This is inappropriate because in countries where there were price controls, suppliers often avoided the official market, participating in the domestic parallel market or smuggling their goods across the borders where they could obtain better prices. According to the World Bank (1994a: 91), twenty-six sub-Saharan African countries had extensive price controls on goods that were not removed until the late 1980s and early 1990s. The author's experience of Tanzania was that only a very small minority of the ruling class could regularly buy goods at the official prices. The rest of the population had to rely on the parallel markets where prices were significantly higher. Aron and Elbadawi (1997) showed that the uncontrolled prices of manufactured goods in Zambia followed very closely the pattern of the parallel market exchange rate.

Of course, the fear of inflation cannot be totally dismissed. Considering the experiences of Sierra Leone and Ghana, Pinto (1991) pointed out that moving to a flexible exchange rate system would cause inflation if the implicit tax on exports were important in financing the fiscal deficit. "The fiscal deficit is financed by a combination of seignorage (the tax on domestic money) and the implicit tax on exports. With unification [of the official and the parallel market exchange rates], the hidden export tax vanishes. As a result, there is a compensating rise in the tax on domestic money, inflation" (123).[10] Another study by Faini (1994) of Ghana, Kenya, Malawi, Senegal, and Zambia supported Pinto's thesis.

Nonetheless, the fear of inflation may not always be justified. For example, Pinto's conclusion was based on the assumption that the government was a net buyer of foreign currency from the private sector. Under that assumption, unification of the official and the parallel market exchange rates decreases the value of the domestic currency, thus increasing the government deficit and, in turn, inflation. However, as demonstrated by Kaufmann and O'Connell (1997), where the government was a net seller vis-à-vis the private sector, which was the case in some countries, unification might actually reduce inflation.

Yet another argument for a fixed exchange rate system is that by controlling foreign currency, and thus controlling imports, a country can reduce its current account deficit. In reality, the overvaluation of the domestic currency may, instead, increase the current account deficit. Since official importers are subsidized, they may import consumption goods rather than inputs. The policy also discourages domestic production of import competing inputs and goods. More important, there is a close link between imports and exports. Overvaluation causes a shortage of foreign currency and, thus, a shortage of imported inputs. In turn, input prices rise, thereby raising the cost of production of export-producing industries and reducing the revenue generating power of those industries.[11] In addition, the overvaluation of the domestic currency reduces the competitiveness of domestic exports by making domestic goods more expensive to foreign buyers.

Overvaluation of domestic currency generates another form of implicit tax to producers of export goods (most of whom are small farmers who produce export crops), as illustrated in the following numerical example. Suppose the official exchange rate is 200 Tanzanian shillings per U.S. dollar, and the parallel market exchange rate is 440 Tanzanian shillings per U.S. dollar. (This approximates reality in Tanzania in 1991, a year before Tanzania freed its foreign exchange market.) Now suppose the world price of coffee is a dollar per pound, and half of it is passed along to the farmers. Farmers, who are always paid in domestic currency, would receive only 100 shillings per pound. However, since some imports are financed by dollars purchased in the parallel market, consumer prices generally reflect the parallel market exchange rate. Thus, these farmers would end up with approximately half the purchasing power they would have had if the domestic currency were not overvalued. In real terms, then, paying these farmers using the official exchange rate constitutes an implicit tax on them (Mshomba, 1997).

Reduced exports and the widespread use of the parallel market combine to reduce the supply of foreign currency in the official market even further. This leads to underutilization of factories that are dependent on imported inputs and affected by shortages of goods. According to Ghana's Ministry of Trade, capacity utilization in Ghana's textile firms dropped from 70 percent in the mid-1970s to 10 percent in 1982. The decline happened as the government was unable to sustain subsidies to textile firms.

Mbelle and Sterner (1991) showed that in Tanzania a third of all textiles firms operated at more than 60 percent capacity in 1976. Eleven years later, in 1987, no single firm operated at more than 60 percent capacity, and only about 10 percent of the firms operated at more than 40 percent capacity. The explanation for the decline in capacity utilization was determined to be a lack of imported materials. This was the experience of many sub-Saharan African countries in the 1980s.[12]

The situation was so severe in Tanzania, for example, that the government, in desperation, allowed and encouraged anyone able to import to do so with no questions asked about the source of the foreign exchange. At the time, Tanzanian residents were not allowed to hold foreign currency. Although people were initially hesitant, fearing that their goods would be confiscated, reassurances from the government calmed their fears. According to the 1991/1992 budget speech by the Tanzanian minister of finance, 230 million dollars worth of goods were imported in 1988/1989 with foreign currency that was not obtained through the Central Bank of Tanzania. This was approximately 18 percent of total expenditure on imports in 1988/1989. The remaining imports were financed by purchases of foreign currency from the Central Bank of Tanzania (the only legal source of foreign currency for residents of Tanzania) and by external grants and loans to the government (Tanzania, United Republic of, 1991: 4).

By allowing imports by private citizens with no questions asked about the source of foreign currency and keeping the value of the shilling above the market rate, the government essentially endorsed the parallel market for goods and currencies. A significant portion of the foreign exchange used by private citizens was acquired by exchanging the Tanzanian shilling for the U.S. dollar or other major currencies on the parallel market. This situation was not unique to Tanzania.

It may seem unimportant whether it is the government in the official market or private citizens in the parallel market who are buying and selling foreign currency. However, if people know the currency is overvalued, they question the stability of that currency and will be induced to invest in foreign currency. Overvaluation, therefore, ends up causing both legal capital outflows and illegal, or unrecorded, capital outflows, that is, capital flight.

Cuddington (1987) found currency overvaluation to be highly significant in determining capital flight in Argentina, Mexico, Uruguay, and Venezuela. However, his results must be interpreted with great caution for two main reasons. First, as he warns, his sample period was very small; it consisted of only nine annual observations, 1974–1982, inclusive. Second, and more important, these countries were highly indebted. Just as overvaluation breeds fear of future devaluation, indebtedness breeds fear of future tax increases. The capital flight may be explained more by the severe debt problems in those countries than by the overvaluation of the domestic currency. Cuddington's estimating equation did not include foreign debt.

A study by Hermes and Lensink (1992) for six African countries—Côte d'Ivoire, Nigeria, Sudan, Tanzania, Uganda, and Zaire—for 1976–1989 included "debt increasing capital flows" (522) and overvaluation. They found that "capital inflows appear to have a strong positive effect on capital flight" (525).[13] However, they also concluded that "the overvaluation of exchange rate also appears to be an important cause of capital flight for the African countries in this study" (525).

Considering the interest rate policy described above and the overvaluation of domestic currency, one can see how individuals who had access to "government" loans and also to foreign currency in the official market could make a fortune by taking advantage of (i.e., abusing) the system. They could borrow from the government-run banks at a negative real interest rate, use the loan to buy undervalued foreign currency in the official market, invest the foreign currency abroad or sell it in the parallel market, and pay back the loan with a good amount of money remaining.

To conclude, exchange rates that are not in tune with the underlying determinants of supply and demand for foreign currency will distort the allocation of resources, reduce the amount and quality of investment, and in the long run, reduce both imports and exports. As with freeing interest rates, devaluation and floating the exchange rate would achieve better results if they were accompanied by solutions to underlying fiscal problems (Elbadawi, 1997). External assistance, which itself is a function of the credibility of the reform, is also important, especially early on in the implementation.

Agricultural Policies

Agriculture has been and in the foreseeable future will continue to be the backbone of sub-Saharan Africa's economy. This sector employs about 70 percent of the labor force. In 1995, agricultural output accounted for about 40 percent of the nonservice component of the GDP in sub-Saharan Africa (World Bank, 1997b). Agriculture contributes about 25 percent of export revenue to sub-Saharan Africa. Its importance as a source of foreign currency, however, is much higher for many countries. For example, in the early 1990s, food products and agricultural raw materials exports generated over

50 percent of export revenues in twenty-eight of the forty-two sub-Saharan African countries shown in Table 1.3.

Although the focus here is on domestic policies on agriculture and their impact, one must also consider external factors, both past (such as colonialism) and present (such as protectionism in developed countries and the terms of trade), in order to appreciate fully the dynamics of the agricultural sector in Africa. Some of the external factors are discussed in succeeding chapters.

Perhaps nothing has contributed more to the decline of the agricultural growth rate in sub-Saharan Africa in the 1970s and 1980s than the ill-advised, albeit sometimes well-intentioned, policies on agriculture. The average annual growth rates of agricultural output in sub-Saharan Africa for 1965–1973, 1970–1980, and 1980–1990 were respectively 3.1, 1.5, and 1.7 percent (World Bank, 1985, 1993, and 1999).

Following independence, many African leaders proclaimed the importance of agriculture to their nations and promised to provide farmers with credits and subsidies. In actual practice, many of these leaders were more concerned about remaining in power than about the development and welfare of their people (Ake, 1996). Even where leaders had good intentions, as in Tanzania and Zambia, the government failed to develop policies that would effectively help small farmers (Bates, 1981).

In broad terms, the income distribution impact of these policies was to tax small farmers heavily through price controls on their crops. At the same time, the policies subsidized consumption by the people in the cities, few in number but politically powerful. A more detailed examination reveals less consistent income distribution effects, however. The income distribution impact varied between producers and consumers depending on individual producers' production costs, the type of crops they produced,[14] consumption patterns, gender, and geographical location. For example, in Zambia, uniform (panterritorial) pricing of maize (corn), supposedly to equalize farmers' rates of return, "provided a strong relative incentive to producers in surplus areas [of the Eastern Province] and a relative negative incentive to producers in deficit areas [of the Northern Province]" (Jansen, 1991: 282). In other words, the uniform price was higher than the market-determined price for the Eastern Province but lower than the market-determined price for the Northern Province.[15] The emphasis on cash crops also pushed food production into inferior land. As women traditionally cultivate food, their burden also increased (International Labour Organization, 1984: 13).

The degree of government intervention in agriculture varied widely from one country to another. For example, the intervention was relatively minor in Côte d'Ivoire and Zimbabwe. However, the governments of Benin, Burundi, Central African Republic, Gambia, Malawi, Mali, Niger, Nigeria, Sierra Leone, Tanzania, Uganda, and Zambia had total legal monopoly on (1) imports and distribution of fertilizer, (2) setting of producer prices, (3) domestic purchasing, and (4) exports of their major export crops up until 1992. Production of some crops was also under government monopoly; this was the case with the production of sugar in Benin, Burkina Faso, Burundi, Central African Republic, Côte d'Ivoire, Gabon, Guinea-Bissau, Kenya, Madagascar, Mali, and Tanzania.

There were also varying degrees of monopoly in the marketing of food products and milling of wheat and maize (World Bank, 1994a: 232–237). Some countries restricted movement of food products within districts or across districts. For example, in Kenya a permit was required to move more than ten bags of maize (each bag weighing about 60 kilograms) within a district or two bags across district lines (Bates, 1981: 39). My experience in Tanzania was that people were required to get a permit even to move just 20 kilograms (one *debe*) of maize, rice, or wheat across districts. Thus a farmer who wanted to take a present of one *debe* of maize to her relatives who lived in another district had to make a trip to the district government offices first to beg for a permit.

Some of the government intervention just described resulted from cooperative societies or marketing boards established during the colonial era, restructured by governments after independence to increase their monopoly power. In many countries, the marketing board was both a monopoly (the sole provider of inputs) and a monopsony (the only legal buyer of the crop with which it was entrusted). In countries such as Kenya and Côte d'Ivoire, these boards, particularly the ones for export crops, worked relatively well because market forces were still key in determining prices paid to the farmers. In other countries, however, especially those that leaned toward socialism, these marketing boards became convenient tools for governments to tax farmers. Because any profits earned by marketing boards were collected by the government, producer prices, set by the government, were only a fraction of the already declining world prices. The following three examples will illustrate. In Tanzania the producer price of cashew nuts as a percent of the export price dropped from about 70 percent in 1970 to about 40 percent in 1980 (Wilde, 1984: 38). Between 1977 and 1986, the producer price of coffee arabica in Tanzania was, on average, only about 20 percent of the producer price of the same type of coffee in Kenya (Mshomba, 1993).[16] Between 1975/1976 and 1980/1981, the real producer price of cocoa in Côte d'Ivoire dropped by an average of 3 percent per year. In the same period, the real producer price of cocoa in Ghana dropped by an average of 15 percent a year.[17]

Worse still, the marketing boards were notoriously inefficient. Even with a considerable margin, there was scant surplus to be funneled into state expenditure. Questioning why in the late 1970s producer prices in Tanzania had fallen below 50 percent of the world prices, the Bank of Tanzania reported:

> There is ample evidence to suggest that there is abundant scope to reduce operating costs if the [Marketing] Authorities were able to exercise a great degree of financial control to avoid wasteful expenditures, thefts, misappropriation of cash and misdirection of funds. Therefore, while the fall in the grower's share below 50 percent of the final price can be explained by increased outlays on development and taxes, the blame to some extent lies with the Crop Authorities themselves. (Bank of Tanzania, 1982: 103)

The marketing boards were equally inefficient in the provision of inputs such as fertilizers and pesticides. Rarely were these inputs distributed in time to make them effective. In addition, crops were hardly ever collected in time. Crops that could not be stored, such as green tea leaves, were either completely damaged after being plucked or left unharvested owing to a shortage of transport facilities for haulage.

Even when crops were collected, small farmers would receive promissory notes in lieu of actual payments. These pieces of paper had to be held until such time as both money and a cashier were available. Since it was not always clear when the money would be available, farmers would go to the payment stations every day with the hope of being paid. Sometimes the waiting period was more than a month. Thus, instead of the marketing boards giving agricultural credits as they were designed to do, they were actually borrowing from the farmers. Due to inflation, this delay in payment was also an indirect tax to farmers. As discussed in the previous section, farmers were also being implicitly taxed through overvalued domestic currencies (Mshomba, 1997).

Since inputs such as seeds, fertilizers, and pesticides were under the monopoly control of the government and inputs for other crops were rarely available, the potential for diversification was limited. Some policies directly reduced or prevented crop diversification, thus reinforcing, albeit unintentionally, the legacy of colonialism. (See Cases 1 and 2 at the end of this chapter.)

To some degree, the ill-advised agricultural policies are explained by the disparity in political and social power, as suggested above—urban versus rural, big farmers versus small farmers, public sector versus private sector, men versus women, one region versus another, and so on.[18] These policies are also explained, in part, by the conflicting objectives used to justify government intervention in the agricultural sector. Westlake (1994: 27) identified four fundamental objectives: "raising government revenue; accelerating economic growth; improving the distribution of income; [and] enhancing food security." Other objectives were to increase foreign exchange and reduce the monopoly power of private traders. As Westlake pointed out, "there are conflicts between them, especially in the short run," and "for each objective there may be conflicts between the short and long-run" (27).

Westlake noted, for example, that the objective to raise government revenue and/or increase equity through producer prices may dampen the incentive to produce and, thus, negatively affect future economic growth. To illustrate this point, consider that following the independence of Ghana, the United Ghana Farmers' Cooperative Council (UGFCC), a government-sponsored organization claiming to represent farmers, announced the following: "They [farmers] were prepared to accept a reduction in cocoa price from 72 shillings to 60 shillings per load as their 'voluntary contribution' to the development effort" (Stryker, 1991: 94). However, continued decreases in real producer prices, world prices notwithstanding, contributed to the decline of cocoa output. Another illustration is that uniform pricing devised to bring equity, as in the case of maize pricing in Zambia noted earlier, can also create a disincentive for some producers.

Another of Westlake's examples of conflicting objectives is that food security in the short run may be achieved at the expense of a misallocation of resources and, thus, may slow economic growth in the future; this situation can even reduce the potential to be food secure in the long run. On the other hand, emphasis on export (cash) crops, which is both a legacy of colonialism and an emphasis of policies of the World Bank and the International Monetary Fund (IMF), may have increased the disparity of incomes between men and women. African men tend unilaterally to control income generated from export crops.

Yet a comprehensive set of objectives for any sector will, inevitably, have apparent conflicts. The two real challenges are to have a clear understanding of those objectives and the opportunity costs associated with the policies formulated to achieve those objectives and to strike the right balance between those objectives. For example, does equity for farmers mean equal producer prices irrespective of different production and marketing costs, or does it mean adequate access to land, farm inputs, and buyers for all farmers? Does breaking the monopoly power of private traders mean increasing the number of private traders or replacing them with a government monopoly?

It has also been difficult to strike the right balance for these objectives because the implementation of policies, that is, the projects aimed at achieving the policies, is compartmentalized. Success is measured using very narrow and myopic parameters. Individuals charged with increasing production of a particular crop are praised for increasing its output, regardless of the opportunity cost involved. (See Case 1 at the end of this chapter.) Crop authorities charged with funneling revenue from farmers to the state are praised for an increase in revenue, regardless of whether such an achievement was due to a decrease in producer prices or to improved management of the institution.

Since the mid-1980s, many sub-Saharan African countries have reformed their agricultural sectors and reduced direct government control. Agricultural output is determined by many factors, some of which cannot be controlled by policies. It is important to note, however, that agricultural output increased in sub-Saharan Africa by an average annual rate of 4.6 percent for the 1990–1997 period compared to an average annual growth rate of 1.7 percent for the 1980–1990 period (World Bank, 1999).

Sub-Saharan African countries are highly dependent on international trade. Some of their major commodities, such as coffee and cocoa, are produced almost solely for export. These countries need the foreign currency obtained through exports so they can import essential inputs, machinery, and manufactured goods. Government intervention that diminishes agricultural production therefore threatens food security and compromises a country's ability to participate effectively in international markets and to garner the gains from trade that so many analysts believe to be key to economic development.

Trade Orientation and Openness

Trade orientation can be described as the extent to which a country is integrated into the world economy, as measured by trade ratios.

Trade ratios are a country's exports and imports as a percentage of GDP. These ratios are high for most sub-Saharan African countries, as they are in the three Asian countries shown in Table 2.4. This is not surprising given that some of their major commodities, such as coffee and cocoa, are produced primarily for export. At the same time, Africa depends on the rest of the world for inputs, machinery, and other manufactured goods. This dependence on trade by African countries is not atypical of other small economies, developed and developing alike.[19]

Although trade orientation can be viewed simply as a snapshot of the actual amount of trade in which a country is engaged, *openness* ("outward orientation") is the extent to which a country's trade policies allow free trade. These terms, *trade orientation* and *openness,* are not synonymous. A country with high trade ratios, for example, does not necessarily have more open trade policies. Conversely, a country with low trade ratios may actually have more open trade policies. Although trade orientation is determined in part by a country's trade policies, it also depends on such factors as a country's size, the trade policies of trading partners, world prices of a country's major export goods, and the level of domestic vertical integration of economic activities, that is, forward and backward linkages in production.[20]

Many studies have used trade ratios in a misguided way or have been constrained to use the ratios as a proxy for openness. However, recent studies have used better measures of openness, such as deviation of actual from predicted trade flows, direct measures of trade barriers, the parallel market premium, and direct price comparisons (Harrison 1996: 420–425). Nonetheless, as Harrison pointed out, "no independent measure of so-called 'openness' is free of methodological problems" (425).

Moreover, the challenge in measuring openness extends beyond Harrison's methodological concerns. Even if data were available to allow various measurements of openness and their aggregation, that would still provide only a quantitative, and not qualitative, measure of openness. A qualitative measure is one that would adjust the quantitative measures by taking into account reasons for trade policies, such as food and energy security, national security, revenue generation, protection of infant industries, equity, and preservation of culture. These qualitative considerations have been neglected in empirical studies, partly because there is no agreement on their relevance and partly because they are difficult, if not impossible, to quantify. Nonetheless, it is hoped that future studies will incorporate these qualitative considerations to the extent relevant and possible, especially in cross-sectional studies.

Table 2.4 Ratios of Exports and Imports to GDP, 1973–1992

Country	Exports/GDP			Imports/GDP		
	1973–1979	1980–1989	1990–1992	1973–1979	1980–1989	1990–1992
Botswana	47	61	51	70	62	67
Burkina Faso	6	6	5	21	23	21
Burundi	11	9	7	14	18	21
Cameroon	19	11	17	21	15	12
Central African Republic	14	11	7	14	15	10
Chad	11	14	15	21	26	22
Congo	26	44	39	24	29	20
Côte d'Ivoire	33	33	29	29	25	18
Gabon	48	48	42	24	21	15
Gambia	31	19	16	51	54	64
Ghana	28	18	14	27	19	20
Guinea-Bissau	6	9	6	39	39	32
Kenya	22	19	14	30	26	24
Lesotho	11	12	13	106	140	120
Madagascar	13	10	10	15	13	17
Malawi	23	22	22	34	28	34
Mali	11	13	14	23	27	18
Mauritania	31	40	42	36	31	57
Mauritius	38	40	44	49	51	58
Niger	12	17	12	13	20	15
Nigeria	23	20	36	16	13	21
Rwanda	10	7	5	17	18	16
Senegal	23	18	14	34	32	22
Seychelles	13	12	13	69	58	47
Sierra Leone	21	13	19	31	19	20
South Africa	15	15	16	19	20	16
Swaziland	60	61	59	70	85	77
Tanzania	15	8	15	26	21	46
Togo	23	22	18	37	39	30
Zambia	39	31	29	27	29	30
Zimbabwe	27	22	22	21	21	14
Indonesia	23	24	25	14	16	21
Malaysia	44	53	71	36	45	72
South Korea	25	31	25	32	32	28

Source: Calculated using data from World Bank (1995).

Caution about measurement of openness notwithstanding, the impact of openness on economic growth will now be considered. Many studies have attempted to estimate this impact.[21] In sum, these studies suggest a positive relationship between outward orientation and economic growth. A careful study by Harrison (1996) of developing countries that estimated the impact of seven different measures of openness on economic growth found that a "greater openness is associated with higher growth" (443).

Many studies that have compared and contrasted African countries with Asian countries have concluded that the apparent relative economic success of the latter is due to their relative outward orientation. Although this may prove to be correct and is increasingly accepted, it is important to remember that the studies to date have not conclusively settled the question of the causality between openness and economic growth. Many studies simply assume causality to be in one direction, from openness to economic growth; some recent studies suggest the causality between openness and economic growth runs in both directions. Some studies have shown no causal effects running from exports to economic growth.[22]

The conclusion that openness causes economic growth has often been reached on the basis of questionable assumptions. Consider, for example, Dollar's study (1992) of ninety-five developing countries for the period 1976–1985.[23] He used price data estimated by Summers and Heston (1988) that assumed that countries consume the same basket of goods and services. In addition, Dollar made several assumptions. (1) Except for the existence of trade barriers and goods that are not traded internationally (nontradeables), the absolute purchasing power parity (PPP) holds.[24] (2) The relative price levels of nontradeables are determined only by relative differences in endowments that cannot be measured and, therefore, assumption 3 is made. (3) GDP per capita is a proxy of relative per capita factor availability. (4) Relative price levels are only a function of GDP per capita and population density. (5) GDP growth is a function only of real exchange rate distortion and variability (estimated under assumptions 2 through 4), as well as investment. Based on these assumptions, Dollar estimated price distortion caused by trade policies, measured as a ratio of actual prices over some predicted prices. The higher the actual prices relative to predicted prices, the higher the distortion. African countries were found to distort prices the most.

There are significant problems with the assumptions made in Dollar's study. First, although the Penn World Tables estimated by Summers and Heston (1988) may cautiously be used for international comparisons, one must be sensitive to their pitfalls (Heston and Summers, 1996). For example, countries do not consume identical baskets of goods and services. In addition, some of the data used to construct the Penn World Tables are not reliable, particularly for low-income countries. Variables estimated using such data become even less reliable.[25]

The assumption about the PPP is critical to Dollar's study. Since he assumed that only the existence of trade barriers and nontradeables causes deviation in the PPP, he tried to isolate the deviation caused by the existence of nontradeables. Thus, he regarded whatever remained as a measure of price-distorting trade policies. However, deviations from the PPP may reflect other factors such as transportation and information costs, departures from free competition (in production), and different price elasticities of demand.

To the extent that PPP does not hold owing to various factors, the choice of the goods and services for the identical baskets may have an upward bias in prices for countries that are net importers of those goods and services. They import them because they are cheaper where they come from. The relatively large difference between actual prices and predicted prices for African countries may, therefore, also reflect the choice of goods and services—not just price distortion.

When one aggregates all the assumptions above, it may not be possible to determine the exact nature of a systematic bias that may exist in the study. The main problem with Dollar's study, however, is that given the bold assumptions, it is difficult to reach sound conclusions. Not surprisingly, Dollar found a number of anomalies and outliers. However, he considered the apparent anomalies to be outweighed by the advantage of applying his specification to a large number of countries.

It is interesting to note that Dollar, who started with 117 countries, omitted developed countries in his final empirical work. "The justification for focusing on developing countries only (and omitting 22 developed countries) is that the effect of openness on growth is likely to be substantially different for backward and advanced economies" (534). If the difference in economic development is so important, however, how could developing countries, with such a disparity in per capita incomes among them, be lumped together, dummy variables notwithstanding? According to the data used by Dollar, the per capita income disparity between two of the countries included in the study, Burundi and Hong Kong, for example, was 1 to 16. The per capita income disparity between Hong Kong and all the omitted developed countries, except Canada and the United States, was less than 1 to 2.

Although assumptions are a "necessary evil" in any empirical work, it is difficult to interpret results when a study is compounded with a series of unrealistic assumptions and inconsistencies.[26] Yet Dollar went so far as to conclude that:

> The results strongly imply that trade liberalization, devaluation of the real exchange rate, and maintenance of a stable real exchange rate could dramatically improve growth performance in many poor countries. The estimated gains of shifting to an Asian level of outward orientation and real exchange rate stability are increases of 1.5 percentage points in Latin America's per capita growth and 2.1 percentage points in Africa's. (540)

In another study of forty-one developing countries, the World Bank (1987) concluded that "the economic performance of the outward-oriented economies has been broadly superior to that of inward-looking economies in almost all respects" (83). Although this conclusion is likely to be correct, it must also be interpreted with caution, to the extent that it does not consider unique salient features of individual countries. An aspect of the World Bank study that is relevant to the discussion here is that it presented a trend of trade policies in sub-Saharan African countries.[27] The forty-one countries in the study included twelve sub-Saharan African countries (see Table 2.5). For the period 1963 to 1973, they were classified as follows: two moderately outward oriented, four moderately inward oriented, and six strongly inward oriented. For the period 1973 to 1983, the only two SSA countries that were moderately outward oriented were reclassified as moderately inward looking, and two of the four countries that were moderately inward looking were reclassified as strongly inward looking. Except for Chile and Uruguay, Central and Latin American countries showed the same general trend toward inward orientation in the 1970s. This World Bank study indicated that African countries became more inward looking in the 1970s and early 1980s. This change is not surprising given the earlier discussion on interest rate, exchange rate, and agricultural policies.

In addition to these policies that worked to hamper trade, other trade restraining policies were in effect in many sub-Saharan African countries in the 1970s and 1980s. They included tariffs and quantitative restrictions as well as other nontariff barriers such as price controls and state monopolies (UNCTAD, 1988a; DeRosa, 1991). These policies were implemented to complement other protective policies and/or to achieve certain desired goals.

The perpetual nature of protection can be seen where, for example, an overvaluation of the domestic currency led to a shortage of foreign currency. To deal with such shortages, governments im-

Table 2.5   Classification of Forty-One Developing Countries by Trade Orientation, 1963–1973 and 1973–1985

	Outward Oriented		Inward Oriented	
Period	Strongly Outward Oriented	Moderately Outward Oriented	Moderately Inward Oriented	Strongly Inward Oriented
1963–1973	Hong Kong Korea, Republic of Singapore	Brazil Cameroon Colombia Costa Rica Côte d'Ivoire Guatemala Indonesia Israel Malaysia Thailand	Bolivia El Salvador Honduras Kenya Madagascar Mexico Nicaragua Nigeria Philippines Senegal Tunisia Yugoslavia	Argentina Bangladesh Burundi Chile Dominican Republic Ethiopia Ghana India Pakistan Peru Sri Lanka Sudan Tanzania Turkey Uruguay Zambia
1973–1985	Hong Kong Korea, Republic of Singapore	Brazil Chile Israel Malaysia Thailand Tunisia Turkey Uruguay	Cameroon Colombia Costa Rica Côte d'Ivoire El Salvador Guatemala Honduras Indonesia Kenya Mexico Nicaragua Pakistan Philippines Senegal Sri Lanka Yugoslavia	Argentina Bangladesh Bolivia Burundi Dominican Republic Ethiopia Ghana India Madagascar Nigeria Peru Sudan Tanzania Zambia

Source: Table 5.1 in World Bank (1987: 83). Reprinted by permission.

posed strict licensing requirements and quantitative restrictions on imports. Reduced supplies of imports caused prices to increase as shortages of goods ensued. Governments tried to combat this problem with price controls, which caused even more shortages. This escalation of events led countries to believe the solution was for the government to participate directly in and, to varying degrees, even to monopolize the foreign exchange market, imports, production, and the distribution of goods. In this way, not only did the level of protection increase; government bureaucracy also expanded into a perplexing maze.

It would be cynical to describe trade policies in Africa simply as reactionary. Policies were also implemented with clearly perceived objectives such as food and energy security, the generation of government revenue, and import substitution. The focus here will be on the last two.

As is characteristic of developing countries, sub-Saharan African countries have limited sources of government revenue. A relatively large proportion of output in these countries does not enter commercial channels. In addition, most transactions are not recorded. Therefore, governments have not been able to rely much on income taxes. For this reason, tariffs may be used not primarily as a trade barrier, as they are in developed countries, but rather to generate revenue. As Table 2.6 demonstrates, the share of revenue generated by import duties and export duties was more than 20 percent for most countries in the early 1980s.

The simple average share of revenue generated by custom duties for developed countries in the 1990s was less than 1 percent (IMF, 1997). However, developed countries also depended heavily on tariff revenues in their early stages of economic development. For example, in the first quarter of the nineteenth century, custom duties accounted for an annual average of 86 percent of the total government revenue in the United States. Later, between 1890 and 1915, customs duties contributed an annual average of 46 percent to the total government revenue in the United States (U.S. Bureau of the Census, 1976: 1106). Shares of government revenue generated by international transactions do not necessarily reflect the degree of a country's openness. Several factors affect the amount of revenue generated by import and export duties. They include price elasticities of imports and exports, the magnitude of smuggling, efficiency in revenue collection and recording, and taxes on other revenue-generating activities. It appears, however, that the trend in many countries, noticeably Cameroon, Ethiopia, Gambia, Ghana, Mauritius, and Sierra Leone, is a reduction in the repression of the export sector.

Besides seeking government revenues, many sub-Saharan African countries have imposed trade restrictions in hopes of encouraging domestic production. A strategy known as import substitution uses trade barriers that insulate domestic industries from for-

Table 2.6   Import and Export Duties as Shares of Government Revenue, 1980–1982 and 1990–1992

Country	Duties	1980–1982	1990–1992
Botswana	Import duties	37	18
	Export duties	0	0
	Total	37	18
Burkina Faso	Import duties	38	NA
	Export duties	2	NA
	Total	40	NA
Cameroon	Import duties	25	14
	Export duties	8	1
	Total	33	15
Ethiopia	Import duties	15[a]	16
	Export duties	17[a]	1
	Total	32[a]	17
Gabon	Import duties	15	15[b]
	Export duties	2	1[b]
	Total	17	16[b]
Gambia	Import duties	60	43
	Export duties	5	0
	Total	65	43
Ghana	Import duties	13[a]	25
	Export duties	19[a]	9
	Total	32[a]	34
Kenya	Import duties	21	13
	Export duties	1	0
	Total	22	13
Lesotho	Import duties	58[c]	54
	Export duties	0[c]	0
	Total	58[c]	54
Liberia	Import duties	33	NA
	Export duties	1	NA
	Total	34	NA
Madagascar	Import duties	18	38
	Export duties	3	7
	Total	21	45
Malawi	Import duties	23	16[d]
	Export duties	0	0[d]
	Total	23	16[d]
Mali	Import duties	16	NA
	Export duties	3	NA
	Total	19	NA
Mauritius	Import duties	34	40
	Export duties	15	4
	Total	49	44

continues

Table 2.6   continued

Country	Duties	1980–1982	1990–1992
Senegal	Import duties	32	NA
	Export duties	1	NA
	Total	33	NA
Sierra Leone	Import duties	37	37
	Export duties	9	0
	Total	46	37
South Africa	Import duties	4	3
	Export duties	0	0
	Total	4	3
Swaziland	Import duties	57	NA
	Export duties	6	NA
	Total	63	NA
Tanzania	Import duties	10[a]	NA
	Export duties	4[a]	NA
	Total	14[a]	NA
Togo	Import duties	26	NA
	Export duties	2	NA
	Total	28	NA
Uganda	Import duties	16	NA
	Export duties	22	NA
	Total	38	NA
Zaire	Import duties	23	30
	Export duties	9	4
	Total	32	34
Zambia	Import duties	8	21
	Export duties	0	0
	Total	8	21
Zimbabwe	Import duties	8	18[b]
	Export duties	0	0[b]
	Total	8	18[b]

Source: Calculated using data from various issues of the International Monetary Fund's *Government Finance Statistics Yearbook.*
   a. 1980–1981.
   b. 1990–1991.
   c. 1982.
   d. 1990.

eign competition in order to reduce the reliance on imported manufactures and encourage domestic production. Such barriers include tariffs and quotas, import licenses, and an exchange rate system that reduces the price of imported inputs. An import substitution strategy is defended on a number of grounds, including the infant industry argument, the existence of externalities, export pessimism due to deteriorating terms of trade for primary products and trade barriers in developed countries, and the general apparent link between industrialization and economic development (Grabowski, 1994).

There is an emerging consensus that the outward orientation and economic success of Asian countries were preceded by an import substitution strategy (Alam, 1989; Helleiner, 1986, 1990; Edwards, 1993; Grabowski, 1994).

> Virtually all successful exporters of manufactures except Hong Kong began their industrialization with import substitution under significant protection. Protection in support of import substitution may be usefully thought of as a temporary, and obviously costly, device to assist in the restructuring and development of an infant economy. Its costs are unfortunately, in practice, more certain than its ultimate benefits. (Helleiner, 1990: 888)

Asian countries successfully used the import substitution strategy to cushion their economies against external shocks and provide a stepping-stone toward outward orientation. In addition, Asian countries did not totally replace their import substitution strategy with export expansion. Instead they "pursued a combined strategy of export promotion in some sectors and import substitution in others" (Schmitz, 1984: 14). Although the relevance of openness to economic growth should not be diminished, a relatively fuller picture of the model must be presented to African countries if they are to learn from the Asian model. Was Asia successful because it combined export expansion with import substitution? Would Asia have been less successful (or more successful) if it had abandoned import substitution altogether? Was the economic crisis in the late 1990s in Asian countries such as Indonesia, South Korea, and Thailand a result of excessive openness or too much government intervention and regulation? These are questions open for future careful, in-depth research. The answers might also be useful for sub-Saharan African countries.

For the purpose of this book, the immediate logical question is: Why were Asian countries successful with their import substitution strategy when African countries were not? The answer to this question has two parts that may seem to contradict each other. First, in African countries, trade barriers were too severe and too broad. Second, from an outcome perspective, import substitution did not actually take place in African countries. Riddell (1994) assessed the impact of import substitution strategy in SSA in terms of its two main objectives: (1) to promote domestic production of manufactured goods, particularly consumer good industries; (2) to increase the degree of interlinkage between the manufacturing sector and other sectors of the economy. Riddell concluded that the achievement has been minimal. In other words, African countries paid the cost of pursuing import substitution without reaping the benefits.

To elaborate—first, the severity and the broadness of protective policies in Africa can be seen clearly in the interest rate and exchange rate policies that, in essence, tried to subsidize all domestic investors and importers, respectively. Distortions by Asian countries, in pursuit of import substitution, were less severe and more targeted at specific industries such as textiles, industrial chemicals, iron, and steel.

Second, it would appear that African countries did not have a genuine agenda for import substitution. Many of these countries did not give the private sector an ample chance to develop industries so as to benefit from protection against imports. Some countries, especially those where the government took considerable direct control of the economy, had just as many barriers against the growth of their domestic private sector as they had barriers to international trade. The result was an increased monopoly by the government and its institutions.

Asian countries, instead, allowed domestic competition and prices to adjust to market forces, albeit within the limits of existing policies. In its 1994 report, UNCTAD showcased Japan, South Korea, and Taiwan as examples of countries in situations in which "government intervention can be extremely effective in advancing development" (UNCTAD, 1994: viii–ix). Commenting about the role of the government in South Korea's import substitution strategy, Alam (1989: 247) said:

> The power of government in [South] Korea, however, was not used to alienate the private sector. While the government took early measures to institutionalize its ascendancy over the private sector through its nationalization of commercial banks, the control over foreign loans, the screening of technology imports, and the like, there was never any doubt about the role of the private sector as the principle vehicle of growth.

It is also not clear that import substitution actually happened in Africa. The strategy did not reduce the need for imports. The irony of the implementation of the import substitution policy is that many factories that were built were highly dependent on imported inputs. Because of the shortage of foreign exchange, it was not possible to meet import demand. As documented by a number of studies in the 1970s and early 1980s, the industrial sector expanded too quickly relative to the growth of the foreign exchange–generating sectors. At the same time, the terms of trade moved against sub-Saharan Africa, particularly for the non-oil-producing countries (Helleiner, 1986). The foreign exchange crisis cut the flow of imports to a trickle. In the 1970s and 1980s many industries in Africa were underutilized because of the lack of imported inputs or spare parts.

Conclusion

Ill-advised policies and excessive government intervention in the areas of private investment, exchange rates, the agricultural sector, and overall trade restrictions in sub-Saharan African countries have reduced the extent to which these countries would have otherwise benefited from trade. Nonetheless, there exists significant potential for these countries to reap gains from trade.

It is important to note that this study does not assume perfect competition can exist in markets in Africa (or anywhere else, for that matter). Market imperfections such as externalities, monopoly elements, and information constraints are prevalent, especially in sub-Saharan Africa. Moreover, social and economic goals such as equity, alleviation of poverty, preservation of culture, and protection of infant industries call for cautious and guided government intervention.

Nevertheless, market forces cannot be ignored or assumed away, as policies of the 1970s and early 1980s in many sub-Saharan African countries tried to do. Policies that blatantly ignore market conditions (imperfect as they may be), whether in the pursuit of import substitution or export expansion, create inordinate rent-seeking opportunities and are not sustainable. In addition, government intervention does not necessarily require direct government involvement. For these reasons, the current structural adjustment programs implemented in sub-Saharan African countries, whether they are classified as outward oriented or, more generally, as market oriented, should be cautiously supported. Exchange rate unification is particularly important to achieve trade liberalization. A study by O'Connell (1997) elaborated how exchange rate unification may be even more important in liberalizing trade than the reduction of tariff rates.

Moving toward more market-oriented economies and allowing the private sector to play a larger role in the economy is good for

Africa. At the same time, Africa must try to avoid swinging to the other extreme of relying excessively on the market system and the private sector.[28] A critical analysis of structural adjustment programs is beyond the scope of this book. However, African countries must be extremely cautious about any structural adjustment programs that call for reduced government subsidies for education and health.

As important as appropriate domestic policies are, the impact of external policies and outside assistance should not be underestimated. The hailed export expansion policies of Asian countries did not succeed on their own. They were stimulated and supported by "easing of access to developed-country markets, greater availability of commercial loans, and growing importance of international subcontracting" (Alam, 1989: 235). Sub-Saharan African countries need even more of this kind of external support because, unlike the Asian countries with which they are often compared and contrasted, they are entering this new phase before completing the import substitution phase. Their export base is more narrow and more susceptible to external factors than that of Asian countries at the time of their transition to export expansion.

Not surprisingly, African leaders are, therefore, calling for economic partnerships with developed countries to assist them in this transition. The following appeal by President Yoweri Museveni of Uganda may represent what many other current African leaders seek. "Uganda needs just two things. We need infrastructure and we need foreign investment. That is what we need. The rest we shall do by ourselves" (Goldberg, 1997: 62). President Clinton's strategy for economic partnership with Africa, announced at the 1997 meeting of the Summit of the Eight in Denver, called for increased investment in Africa and increased openness in developed countries for African exports.[29] It could be a needed boost for the economies of sub-Saharan Africa, if implemented in a true spirit of partnership and good will.

Sub-Saharan African countries must continue to present their case to the international community and seek appropriate assistance, especially as they reform their economies. To maximize the impact of any assistance or preferential treatment, domestic policies must be congruent with the objectives of the assistance. At the same time, domestic policies, in general, must foster self-reliance, in order to reduce and eventually eliminate the need for external assistance.

Case 1: The Near Elimination of Pigeon Peas in Tanzania

In Babati District, Tanzania, maize and pigeon peas (*cajanus cajan*) are the two most important crops.[30] Pigeon peas, a drought-resistant crop, are produced mainly for sale. In the 1970s, Babati produced about 15,000 tons of pigeon peas a year, worth about $3.5 million (1998 prices) to farmers. Up until the early 1970s, private traders were allowed to market cereal crops and all types of beans and peas. Most of the traders for pigeon peas were local Asian traders who bought them from the farmers and exported them to India and other countries in Asia.

Two policies of the late 1970s and early 1980s, however, undermined the production of pigeon peas. The first was that the National Milling Corporation (NMC), a government corporation, became the sole legal buyer of food crops from farmers. The second was the establishment of the Maize Programme.

The NMC was established in 1974. Initially, its new status as sole legal buyer in itself did not create a problem for producers of pigeon peas. The problem arose when the NMC and the government exporting agency, General Agricultural Products Exports (GAPEX), did not know what to do with the peas they bought. They were not able to export them, either because they had insufficient knowledge of the foreign market for pigeon peas or, as some government officials claim, because the disgruntled private traders dissuaded their former trading partners from buying peas from the government. The outcome was that in 1980/1981, the NMC was left with two mountains of bags of peas in the Babati Stadium and in another field adjacent to their regional headquarters in Arusha. The peas ended up rotting and supplying a nurturing environment to rodents.

Following these losses, the government allowed private traders to buy pigeon peas, though the NMC remained the sole legal buyer of other food crops from farmers. Given fixed costs involved in the procurement of crops, however, buying pigeon peas alone was not attractive to many potential traders. It was not profitable to many traders to be in the agricultural marketing business if they could buy only pigeon peas. For that reason, farmers had difficulty finding buyers who would pay them reasonable prices. Production fell.

The Maize Programme was intended to increase maize production by using hybrid seeds and following good standards of crop husbandry. Under the Maize Programme, farmers were prohibited from intercropping maize with other crops. The argument was that monocropping would allow more efficient crop husbandry with maize, such as weeding and the use of pesticides, and even permit mechanization. The emphasis was on increasing the production of maize, as this was (and still is) the most important staple in Tanzania. However, the policy of monocropping did not take into account the opportunity cost to the farmer. Of course, the farmer is more concerned with total income per given unit of land than output of a particular crop.

In Babati, as in other parts of Tanzania, small farmers often intercrop maize with at least one other crop, one of which is pigeon peas. Perhaps the main reason for intercropping is the economies of scope involved. The term *economies of scope,* in this case, refers to a situation in which a farmer's average cost of production decreases by producing two or more crops jointly (i.e., intercropping) rather than separately. Surface irrigation (the only type of irrigation that may be available to small farmers), for example, takes just about the same amount of time whether a farmer has a single crop, maize (the main crop), or both maize and pigeon peas. Likewise, because these crops require different spacing and have different growth patterns, intercropping does not significantly reduce the amount of corn one would have produced under a single crop system on the same area of land. Also, some crops provide shade for others. Other advantages of intercropping are increasing the total output per unit area of land, better protection of soil from erosion, better utilization of nutrients and moisture, interrupting the spread of pests and diseases, and the addition of nutrients into the soil by some crops that can be used by other crops (Ngugi et al., 1990: 41–42).

A very important social factor is also associated with intercropping, having to do with income distribution between men and women. The secondary crops, such as bananas in a coffee farm or peas and beans in a maize farm, are usually the only crops on which women can rely for income; in many cases women do not own or share in the ownership of land. Although insistence on monocropping might, therefore, increase income generated from the single crop, it could significantly reduce income for women.

Producing more than one crop has other benefits that are not limited to intercropping. It reduces the risk to the farmer in case one crop fails.[31] In addition, even though crops may be planted at the same time, their harvesting periods may be different, thus spreading the stream of income to the farmer. For example, pigeon peas are harvested about three months after harvesting maize, even when they are planted at the same time. The remaining stalk from various crops can also have different uses. Corn stalk is good for feeding cattle, and the stalk of pigeon peas provides firewood.

The disadvantages associated with intercropping—the fact that it limits mechanization and the difficulty in efficiently spraying chemicals and applying fertilizers—are mainly important for big farmers. Of course, those using machines in agriculture do not need the government to tell them the merits of monocropping. Most small farmers, however, still rely on hand tools and rarely use chemicals and fertilizers for maize.

The two policies, one involving marketing and the other production, combined nearly to eliminate the production of pigeon peas in Tanzania. Babati's production in the early to mid-1980s dropped to about 3,000 tons a year, 20 percent of what it was in the 1970s. In fact, in the village in which the author grew up, Sinon, Arusha, Tanzania, the production of pigeon peas completely disappeared in the early 1980s. Government policies that were supposed to help farmers increase their income and increase diversification instead caused a near elimination of this drought-resistant crop.

The government's insistence on monocropping ended in the late 1980s and so did the monopsony power of the NMC. Babati's output of pigeon peas has climbed back since then to more than 17,000 tons in 1995/1996.

Case 2: From Coffee to Cut Flowers in Tanzania

Coffee has been the most important cash crop in Tanzania since the 1970s. [32] It is almost completely an export crop, with only 5 percent of the output consumed domestically. Coffee accounts for about 20 percent of Tanzania's total export revenue. Because of its importance as a source of foreign currency for the government and a source of income for about 15 percent of the population, the government has played an active role in the promotion of coffee. From 1976 to 1986, the Coffee Authority of Tanzania controlled the marketing of coffee and the distribution of inputs to coffee farmers. (The government also controlled other major crops: tea, cotton, cashew nuts, tobacco, and sisal.) A unique feature of the government control over coffee production was a law that prohibited farmers from uprooting coffee trees to switch to other crops. Although this law was ineffective among small farmers, it affected large farmers because their plantations were registered and more conspicuous.

In the late 1980s, some investors wanted to invest in cut flowers, also for export. The land areas suitable for cut flowers, in terms of basic soil and weather requirements and with quick access to an international airport, had coffee trees on them. Because of the law prohibiting uprooting coffee trees and because of other bureaucratic and licensing barriers, these investors were delayed in obtaining a permit to uproot coffee trees and start their flower businesses, even at a time when coffee prices were plummeting.

A change of policy in the late 1980s allowed diversification from coffee to cut flowers. This change has had significant results. In 1996 there were six cut-flower companies in Arusha (in northern Tanzania): AFROFLORA, Continental Flowers, HORTANZIA, KILIFLORA, Kombe Roses, and Tanzania Flowers. KILIFLORA started in 1992 with 6 hectares of land (1 hectare is about 2.5 acres), and by 1996 it had expanded to 30 hectares. In August 1996 it had about 500 full-time workers and about 300 part-time workers. A coffee farm of comparable size would potentially employ only about 75 to 100 people (McFarquhar and Evans, 1972: 27). An important feature is that employees receive benefits such as leave, medical services, and limited but important round-trip transportation to the farm. Also important is that 90 percent of the employees of KILIFLORA and the other cut-flower producers are women. This is significant because women in general, for a variety of reasons, have fewer job opportunities.

The harvesting and exporting of cut flowers is also relatively continuous throughout the year, whereas the harvesting of coffee is concentrated into two to three months. The flow of foreign currency is, therefore, relatively continuous with cut flowers, with a significant increase in the winter months in Europe when the demand for imported cut flowers increases.

Notes

1. The neoclassical growth model pioneered by Solow (1957) asserts that investment affects the economic growth rate only during the transition period as the economy spirals from one steady state to another. A *steady state* is a situation in which the capital-to-labor ratio is constant, so that, with a given technology, output per unit of labor is also constant. For a general discussion of the neoclassical growth model, see any standard intermediate macroeconomic textbook. For a review of studies that critique the model, see Schmidt-Hebbel et al. (1996).

2. This situation is only for illustration. One cedi is not sufficient to purchase anything.

3. When dealing with low inflation rates, real interest rates can be approximated by the Fisher equation: Real interest rate = nominal interest rate

minus the rate of inflation. The Fisher equation underestimates the real interest rate, especially when the inflation rate is high.

4. The eight countries were Cameroon, Mauritius, Morocco, and Tunisia (middle income) and Kenya, Malawi, Tanzania, and Zimbabwe (low income).

5. Note that in a situation in which interest rate ceilings apply only to depositors, and borrowers pay market-clearing interest rates, both depositors and borrowers are implicitly taxed. The equations for demand (line DD) and supply (line SS) in Figure 2.2 are, respectively, 200–5i and 5i, where *i* is the interest rate and cedis are in millions. Thus, at an interest rate ceiling of 10 percent, only 50 million cedis are available for lending. If this interest rate ceiling applies only to depositors, and borrowers pay the market clearing interest rate, such that 200–5i = 50, the lending interest rate would be 30 percent. In terms of Figure 2.2, this lending interest rate can be shown by projecting up the dotted line from the 50 million cedis mark to the DD line. The 30 percent rate is higher than the interest rate that would prevail in the absence of an interest rate ceiling on depositors (i.e., the equilibrium rate, 200–5i = 5i, where *i* would be 20).

6. Real interest rate $= \dfrac{1 + .1}{1 + .25} - 1 = -.12$

7. The real value of each payment is determined each month, and those values are then added together for the total real value of the payments.

8. The CFA countries are Benin, Burkina Faso, Cameroon, the Central African Republic, Chad, the Congo, Côte d'Ivoire, Equatorial Guinea, Gabon, Mali, Niger, Senegal, and Togo. These countries use the CFA franc, tied to the French franc, as their currency. From 1948, when the CFA franc was first established, until 1994, the exchange rate was fixed at CFA francs 50 for 1 French franc. The CFA franc was devalued in January 1994 to CFA francs 100 for 1 French franc (UNCTAD, 1995b: 134).

9. For a discussion of how government intervention helps to create clientelism and patronage politics, see Bates (1994).

10. *Seignorage* refers to the real output the government obtains by printing money and spending it. However, printing money increases the supply of money and leads to inflation (World Bank, 1988: 55–78). Such a result means that this way of financing government expenditure creates an inflation tax on holders of money.

11. In sub-Saharan Africa, the agricultural sector is the main source of export revenue.

12. Capacity underutilization is also attributed to external factors such as the deteriorating terms of trade and the oil price shocks.

13. The positive impact of capital inflows on capital flight may be due not only to the fear of future taxes but also to the fact that some of those funds are being misappropriated by corrupt individuals and transferred to safe havens abroad.

14. In fact, some countries subsidized producers of food crops. However, even in those countries, oftentimes indirect taxes emanating from trade and macroeconomic policies (e.g., exchange rate policy) outweighed the effect of subsidies (Krueger et al., 1988). Nonetheless, it is fair to say that the overall rate of taxation was lower for producers of import-competing food products than for producers of export goods.

15. Market prices even for homogeneous products may differ within a country owing to differing production costs, demand, and transportation costs.

16. For a comparison and a contrast of Kenyan and Tanzanian agricultural policies, see Lofchie (1994).

17. Calculated using data from Wilde (1984: 85, 97).

18. For a discussion on the role of politics in policy formation in Africa, see Bienen (1990). For a discussion on how policymakers attempt to maximize their private benefits in the policies they devise, see Landau (1990).

19. The situation for African countries is unique to the extent that their dependence is explained by what Ake (1991: 43) called "*disarticulation* or *incoherence*" of the colonial economy.

20. Lack of vertical integration in African countries is explained, in part, by the incoherence of the colonial economy (Ake, 1991, chapter 3; Boahen, 1987, chapter 4).

21. For a good review of some of those studies, see Edwards (1993).

22. See Jung and Marshall (1985), Darrat (1986), Esfahani (1991), and Harrison (1996).

23. The idea here is not to dismiss Dollar's study nor to suggest that his is an extreme case. Nonetheless, his study serves as an example of conclusions reached by some empirical studies based on questionable assumptions.

24. Absolute PPP implies that the equilibrium exchange rate between two or more countries is given by the price ratios in those countries. For example, if a basket of goods is $100 in the United States and 200,000 cedi in Ghana, the exchange rate should be 2,000 cedi per dollar. Another way of explaining PPP is that goods in different countries tend to have the same price when measured in a single currency.

25. In their assessment of the precision of the country estimates, Summers and Heston (1988) gave thirty-three out of forty-three African countries in the study the lowest grade, a D. The rest got a C grade. High-income countries got a grade of A.

26. A lack of appropriate data, especially for developing countries, has often been the justification for using any other data available.

27. Caution must still be exercised. Edwards (1993) warned about the World Bank's subjective classification, specifically of Chile and Korea. For example, he wondered why Korea was classified as "strongly outward oriented in both the 1963–73 *and* 1973–85 periods, even though it is well known that during the early years of the 1963–73 period the Korean trade regime was significantly more restrictive than the later period" (1387). Similar doubts were raised by Helleiner (1990: 883–884). Even more caution must be exercised with empirical studies like Alam's (1991), which was based on this classification.

28. For a discussion of the limits of trade policy reforms and the challenges of the private sector, see Rodrik (1992) and Richardson and Ahmed (1987), respectively.

29. This group, traditionally called the Group of Seven (G7), comprises Canada, France, Germany, Italy, Japan, the United Kingdom, and the United States. Russia was invited to attend the 1997 meetings.

30. Some of the information in this case was obtained by the author in Arusha, Tanzania, in 1996 and 1998 from officials of the Arusha Regional Agricultural Development Office, small farmers, and commodity merchants.

31. For details, see "Risk Avoidance," chapter 6 in Upton (1996).

32. Some of the information in this case was obtained by the author in Arusha, Tanzania, in 1996 from officials of the Arusha Regional Agricultural Development Office and officials of KILIFLORA, a company that produces cut flowers.

THREE

◆

The Generalized System of Preferences

The Generalized System of Preferences (GSP) is a program under which developed countries provide preferential reduction or removal of tariffs on products from designated developing countries. The program has been implemented under the auspices of the General Agreement on Tariffs and Trade (GATT) and its successor, the World Trade Organization (WTO).

The History of GATT and the WTO

At the end of World War II, nations made efforts to establish international institutions that would address political and economic issues in the world. The United Nations was founded in 1945 to promote peace and international cooperation. The International Bank for Reconstruction and Development (the World Bank) and the IMF were also established in 1945 to provide long-term and short-term loans, respectively. GATT was established in 1947 (and became operational in 1948) with the mission to liberalize world trade.

GATT was formed from parts of the International Trade Organization (ITO), a proposed specialized agency of the United Nations. GATT was established with minimal institutional arrangements, in order to expedite its approval; it was supposed to be temporary, and its functions were to be assumed by the ITO. The ITO never came into existence, however, because the U.S. Congress refused to ratify the ITO, claiming that to do so would undermine the national sovereignty of the United States in trade policy (Raghavan, 1990: 49).[1]

GATT membership rose from 23 countries, which signed the original treaty in 1947, to over 114 signatory members and 19 de facto members on December 31, 1993 (U.S. International Trade Commission, 1994: 41).[2] Although GATT was technically only a provisional treaty throughout its forty-eight years of existence, over time it actually amounted to an increasing number of complex agreements, administered and enforced by its operating body. These agreements were designed to reduce barriers to trade. There were eight rounds of multilateral trade negotiations under GATT. The first seven rounds of negotiations were launched in Geneva (1947); in Annecy, France (1949); in Torquay, England (1950–1951); and in Geneva (1955–1956, 1961–1962 [the Dillon Round], 1964–1967 [the Kennedy Round], and 1973–1979 [the Tokyo Round]) (Raj, 1990: 13, 242). The eighth round, launched in Punta del Este, Uruguay (1986–1993 [the Uruguay Round]), was the one from which the WTO was born. Each round of negotiations sought and accomplished, to varying degrees, a reduction of trade barriers among members.

It is estimated that the first six rounds of negotiations reduced average tariffs in developed countries from about 40 percent to about 8 percent (Laird and Yeats, 1990: 1). The Tokyo Round was relatively farther reaching in scope because it additionally reduced nontariff barriers. These included government procurement requirements, restrictive licensing procedures, and health and safety standards that created unnecessary obstacles to international trade. This achievement was important because as average tariff rates in industrial nations decreased, the propensity to use nontariff barriers increased. Under the Tokyo Round, industrial countries also reduced their tariffs by a weighted average of 36 percent over a period of eight years, bringing their average tariff to about 5 percent.

Like the rounds preceding it, however, the Tokyo Round of negotiations failed to integrate the two areas of textiles and apparel and of agriculture into GATT. Inclusion of these two was not to come until the Uruguay Round of multilateral trade negotiations under GATT. The Uruguay Round was concluded on December 15, 1993, with fifteen trade agreements. A new international organization, the WTO, was established through the Uruguay Round to replace GATT.

The WTO and the fifteen agreements went into effect on January 1, 1995. The WTO facilitates the implementation, administration, and operation of these agreements. It also brings all rules and agreements reached under GATT into a single body of operation. Under the WTO, member countries subscribe to all of its rules and agreements. This is an important departure from the old system under GATT whereby members could pick and choose the agreements to which they wanted to subscribe. "Whereas, in the past, countries could take an *à la carte* approach to the agreements, membership of the WTO implied membership of all its multilateral agreements" (Raby, 1994: 13).

Also worth noting is that under the WTO, the dispute settlement procedures have been streamlined and unified. The procedures restrain nations from taking unilateral action in addressing disputes.

> Article 23.1 requires members of the WTO to use the dispute settlement procedures whenever they "seek redress of a violation of obligations or other nullification or impairment." It also states that members shall "abide by the rules and procedures of this Understanding." Thus several instances where the United States in the 1980s took unilateral and independent action without proceeding through the GATT would be inconsistent with the new rules. (Jackson, 1994: 121)

As of March 1, 1999, there were 134 members of the WTO, including 38 sub-Saharan African countries. Over 90 percent of the world's trade is conducted among WTO members.

A basic principle of the WTO and its predecessor, GATT, is non-differentiated treatment, commonly called the *most favored nation* (MFN) principle. The term means that a member country must treat all other members equally in respect to tariff policy.[3] If a member country lowers the tariff rate on a commodity entering from another member country, for example, it must likewise lower the tariff rate on that commodity entering from all member countries. An exception to the MFN rule was made for already existing preferential tariff treatment, such as that which existed among Commonwealth countries (Langhammer and Sapir, 1987: 2). An exception was also made for free trade areas.

In 1971 agreement was reached under GATT to allow an additional, and broader, exception to the MFN principle. Under this exception, developed countries were not only permitted but encouraged to lower or remove tariffs on goods coming from developing countries. This was known as the Generalized System of Preferences.

The History and Operation of the GSP

The history of the GSP program parallels that of the United Nations Conference on Trade and Development (UNCTAD). Following World War II, when international trade grew very rapidly, it was apparent to developing countries that trade was mostly benefiting industrialized countries. Trade interests of developing countries were overlooked as industrialized countries strove to improve their own individual positions (Raj, 1990: 1–2). A committee established by GATT in the late 1950s to investigate complaints from developing countries arrived at the following conclusions:

i.   only few of the tariff concessions made by GATT rounds up to then had been on items considered at the time to be of export interest to the developing countries;

ii. tariffs on manufactured products of interest to the developing countries were generally higher than duties on items exported by the developed countries;

iii. tariffs in developed countries discriminated among the developing countries on the basis of origin as a result of such arrangements as Commonwealth preferences or preferences granted by the newly created European Economic Community to its African associates;

iv. the tariff structure in the developed countries discriminated against the development of processing industries in the developing countries;

v.   quantitative restrictions were at least as damaging as tariffs in terms of both their levels and their structure; and

vi. various other measures in the developed countries (such as internal taxes) also discriminated against exports of developing countries. (Langhammer and Sapir, 1987: 4–5)

An Argentine economist, Raul Prebisch, was also concerned about these problems and others facing developing countries; he argued forcefully in the 1950s for reforms in international trade. Later, in 1964, UNCTAD was established to represent the views of developing countries, and Prebisch was named its first general director.[4] Operating on the premise that there was a widening gap between the rich and the poor and that the terms of trade were adverse for developing countries, UNCTAD focused on: (1) international commodity agreements intended to support and stabilize prices, (2) financial aid from developed nations to compensate for decreases in export earnings, and (3) trading preferences for exports from developing countries to make markets in developed countries more accessible.

The idea of preferential tariffs was tirelessly pursued by UNCTAD and the principle of GSP was reached by the second plenary session of the entire membership of UNCTAD in New Delhi in 1968 (MacPhee, 1989: 3). UNCTAD established the following objectives for the GSP program in favor of developing countries: (1) to increase their export earnings, (2) to promote their industrialization, and (3) to accelerate their rate of growth (MacPhee, 1989: 1). However, the GSP program could not start immediately because the MFN principle under GATT prevented any member country from granting such preferential tariff treatment. It was not until 1971 that the MFN provision was waived to allow a legal basis for the GSP program to become operational.

At the conclusion of the Tokyo Round of GATT in 1979, a more permanent waiver of the MFN principle was reached with the agreement on the Enabling Clause, which allowed "developed countries to 'accord differential and more favourable treatment to developing countries, without according such treatment to other contracting parties'" (OECD, 1983: 15).

The GSP program included lower tariffs for exports from developing countries and nonreciprocity by developing countries in tariff reductions. Provisions were also made to favor the least developed among developing countries. Twenty-nine sub-Saharan African countries were designated as "least developed" under the U.S. GSP program as of March 1998.[5]

Although referred to collectively as "the GSP program," there are actually a number of individual GSP programs, introduced by developed countries between 1971 and 1976. The countries include Australia, Austria, Canada, those in the European Union, Finland, Japan, New Zealand, Norway, Sweden, Switzerland, and the United States (UNCTAD, 1995c).[6]

The agreement on the GSP program is a nonbinding commitment. It is, therefore, temporary in nature. A preference-giving country can suspend its own program in whole or in part, as it wishes. Likewise, the agreement does not prevent subsequent reduction of trade barriers on an MFN basis, whether unilaterally or following multilateral trade negotiations (Raj, 1990: 26). Because of the unilateral nature of the program, the implementation of the GSP varies from one country to another. Each country determines the goods to be covered by its GSP program, the preferential margin, and the developing countries to be accorded the preferential treatment.

A preference-giving country can add, remove, and/or redesignate a product or a country at its own discretion. For example, according to various notices from the president to the Speaker of the House of Representatives, the following sub-Saharan African countries were suspended from and/or added to the U.S. GSP program between 1985 and 1995:

1. Central African Republic was suspended in 1989 for failing to take "steps to afford internationally recognized worker rights." It was reinstated in 1991 after satisfying "the worker rights standard of the law."
2. Ethiopia was added in 1992 following the country's "initiation of economic reforms."
3. Liberia was suspended in 1990 for worker rights violations.
4. Mauritania and Mozambique were designated as least-developed countries in 1990. However, three years later, in 1993, Mauritania was suspended from the GSP program for worker rights violations.
5. Namibia was added in 1991 following its independence from South Africa in 1990.
6. South Africa was added in 1994 following the collapse of apartheid and its democratic elections in May of that year.
7. Sudan was suspended in 1991 for worker rights violations.

Setting aside isolated decisions by individual countries, the differences between the GSP schemes are explained mainly by import sensitivity of particular sectors in the preference-giving countries and historical ties between developed countries and developing countries (OECD, 1983: 18). For these reasons, each GSP program is in some way unique. However, the programs also share some basic elements, including rules of origin, value-added requirements, quantitative limits, and standards on country or product graduation.[7]

Under the rules of origin, preference-giving countries require products to be imported directly from the beneficiary country. Exceptions are made where products are transported through another country without entering commercial channels of that country while en route to the preference-giving country.

The value-added requirement extends the one on the rules of origin. It specifies that for a product to qualify for GSP treatment, a minimum proportion of it must be produced in the preference-receiving country. This minimum requirement is framed in terms of value. For example, the United States specifies a 35 percent minimum. "[For a product to meet the value-added requirement,] the sum of the cost or value of materials produced in the beneficiary country plus the direct costs of processing must equal at least 35 percent of the appraised value of the article at the time of entry into the United States" (U.S. International Trade Commission, 1991: vii).

Although this rule has the potential of reducing the number of products that receive preferential tariff treatment, preference-giving countries have provisions that increase the possibility of beneficiary countries qualifying for GSP. For example, some GSP programs count inputs imported from the preference-giving country as originating from the preference-receiving country. This is often referred to as the "donor country content" provision. Needless to say, this provision provides incentive for preference-receiving countries to use inputs from preference-giving countries.

Some GSP schemes have cumulative rules of origin. Under these rules, inputs from all developing countries or, more typically, from certain regional groupings of developing countries are counted as originating from the preference-receiving country (OECD, 1983: 26). This provision has the potential of stimulating trade among developing countries.

Sub-Saharan African countries enjoy the two provisions, the donor country content and the cumulative rules of origin, from the GSP scheme of the European Union (EU) under the Lomé Convention (OECD, 1983: 27, 73–74). Even without these provisions, however, it is unlikely that the value-added requirement would have a noticeable impact on sub-Saharan Africa, whose exports to developed countries are made up mainly of unprocessed and semiprocessed primary products. As Langhammer and Sapir (1987: 61) have pointed out, the value-added requirement affects mainly countries exporting highly processed products produced using imported intermediate goods.

Another common element of the GSP schemes is that of quantitative limits (quotas). The quantitative limits are intended to limit total imports and/or imports from individual countries. Limits are placed on total imports to protect domestic producers. The limits are determined mainly by the sensitivity of domestic producers to imports. For example, in the EU scheme, prior to the conclusion of the Uruguay Round of GATT, goods eligible for GSP were divided into three categories of "non-sensitive," "semi-sensitive," and "sensitive," depending on their impact on domestic production and employment in particular sectors in the member states' economies (Langhammer and Sapir, 1987: 22; OECD, 1983: 28–29). Following the conclusion of the Uruguay Round, the EU scheme removed quantitative limits on GSP imports. Instead it placed GSP imports into four categories and reduced tariffs on those imports, respectively, by 15 percent, 30 percent, 65 percent, or 100 percent (duty-free), according to the sensitivity of the products (UNCTAD, 1995c: 4). These reductions are on the most-favored-nation tariff. It is important to note that the sensitivity of domestic producers to imports is not determined by the intrinsic nature of the imported product but rather by the vulnerability of domestic producers to outside suppliers.

Individual country ceilings are intended to distribute the potential benefits of the GSP scheme among the beneficiary countries and/or to favor certain countries. For example, the United States has a "competitive need" limitation under which a country loses its GSP eligibility with respect to a product in the succeeding year if "during any calendar year U.S. imports from that country: (1) account for 50 percent or more of the value of total U.S. imports of that product; or (2) exceed a certain dollar value" (U.S. International Trade Commission, 1991: iv). Competitive need limits are waived for the GSP beneficiaries designated as least developed countries. Waivers can also be granted (1) to a country that provides easy access to U.S. goods and protects U.S. intellectual property rights, (2) for a product not produced in the United States, and (3) for a product for which total U.S. imports from all countries are small or "de minimis" (U.S. International Trade Commission, 1991: iv–v). Sub-Saharan African countries have not been affected by the competitive need limits under the GSP program.

Since the GSP program is intended for developing countries, GSP schemes include a graduation policy in their framework. Under this policy, a country is "graduated" from the list of beneficiary countries when it reaches a certain level of development, usually measured in terms of gross national product (GNP) per capita. The GNP per capita limit was set at $8,500 and is indexed to increases in U.S. GNP (U.S. International Trade Commission, 1991: vi). Hong Kong, Singapore, South Korea, and Taiwan were graduated from the U.S. GSP program in 1989 (United Nations, 1992: 1).

Although it is difficult to predict the life span of the GSP programs, Seychelles is the only country in sub-Saharan Africa that could possibly be graduated in the foreseeable future, based on the GNP per capita threshold. As was shown in Table 1.1, the GNP per capita for Seychelles in 1995 was $6,620. Given the very low GNP per capita of many other sub-Saharan African countries, though, their concern regarding the graduation element is that the GNP per capita criterion is set too high. They believe their exports would be enhanced with a more stringent criterion that would make upper- and middle-income countries ineligible for GSP benefits.

There are two main reasons why it is unlikely that the GNP per capita yardstick would be lowered. First, developed countries believe they have already accounted for the concerns of poor countries by including provisions that favor the least developed among developing countries. Second, middle-income countries that are threatened by their own success (concerned they will be graduated) are asking for more lenient criteria. Countries that have been graduated from

GSP programs have also not departed quietly. Some have even managed to be reinstated. For example, Bahrain was graduated from the U.S. GSP program in 1988. However, it was reinstated in 1990, based on the World Bank's revised statistics that indicated that Bahrain's GNP per capita did not exceed the GSP statutory limit.

The graduation policy is also applied to individual products (United Nations, 1992). For example, the U.S. program includes a discretionary product graduation principle under which products from certain countries permanently lose their beneficiary status, usually in response to petitions from domestic producers. Factors considered in discretionary product graduation actions are the country's general level of development; the country's competitiveness in the particular product; the country's practices relating to trade, investment, and worker rights; and the overall economic interests of the United States (U.S. International Trade Commission, 1991: vi).

It is important to note that, overall, the provisions for the GSP schemes are not primarily based on the needs of developing countries. Instead, they are mainly determined by the sensitivity of domestic producers to imports in preference-giving countries (DeVault, 1996a). This is reflected in the product coverage and the depths of preferential tariff reduction for different categories of products and the safeguard measures built into the system (OECD, 1983: 39–40).

The precedence of domestic concerns is certainly clear in the global quantitative limits of the GSP schemes. Even individual country ceilings are used to protect domestic producers. Assessing the U.S. GSP scheme, Langhammer and Sapir (1987: 61–62) concluded that individual country limits have worked mainly "to protect [U.S.] producers rather than redistribute the benefits of the GSP to the least developed countries." DeVault (1996b) and MacPhee and Rosenbaum (1989) reached the same conclusion, that the U.S. competitive need limits benefit the U.S. competing firms almost exclusively.

The donor country content provision and the cumulative rules of origin may be perceived as indicators of a genuine concern by developed countries for developing countries. Three points put such a perception into context. First, as noted earlier, the donor country content provision is an incentive for preference-receiving countries to use inputs from preference-giving countries, thereby increasing exports from developed countries.

Second, the donor country content provision is not unique to the GSP program. Many developed countries have in their tariff schemes offshore assembly provisions (OAPs) that are applied to a much wider range of goods and countries than those in the GSP program. Under OAPs, a country exempts from tariffs its domestically produced components contained in imports. For example, suppose the ad valorem tariff rate on imported bicycles in France is 10 percent, and Gabon assembles bicycles using components from France. Suppose further the free-trade price of a bicycle is 150 French francs, and the value of French-made components is 100 francs. Without an OAP, the tariff for each bicycle would be 15 francs (10 percent of 150 francs). However, with an OAP, the tariff for each bicycle would only be 5 francs (10 percent of Gabon's value added, 50 French francs).

Third, there are some calculated benefits to developed countries as a result of the cumulative rules of origin. This provision reduces the potential for a developed country to divert trade from a low-cost producing developing country to a high-cost producing developing country. Such trade diversion can cause a net welfare loss to the preference-giving country; the prevention of such diversion, therefore, benefits the country.[8] The following example illustrates how the "cumulative rules of origin" provision works to prevent trade diversion.

Suppose Kenya and Tanzania both produce leather luggage, and the United States imports these products. Tanzania produces luggage using domestically produced leather. Kenya uses leather imported from Tanzania. Leather constitutes 80 percent of the final value of luggage. Because of the differences in production efficiency, Kenya's luggage is sold for $200 per unit while Tanzania's luggage is sold for $215 per unit, under free trade. Suppose the United States has a uniform pre-GSP tariff rate of 20 percent on leather luggage. Therefore, the tariff-inclusive prices for Kenya's luggage and Tanzania's luggage are $240 and $258, respectively. U.S. consumers would buy leather luggage from Kenya since it is cheaper.

Now suppose the United States implements a GSP program that includes leather luggage in the product coverage and Kenya and Tanzania in the country coverage. Tariffs are eliminated on products under the U.S. GSP program if they satisfy the minimum value-added requirement of 35 percent. Under a strict application of this value-added requirement, Kenya's luggage would not qualify for GSP benefits since its added value is only 20 percent of the value of the final product. Therefore, the United States would import Tanzania's luggage at $215 per unit, even though Kenya is a lower-cost producer. However, with a provision that allows inputs from other developing countries, in this case Tanzania, to be counted as originating from Kenya, Kenya's luggage would qualify for GSP benefits. Trade diversion would therefore be prevented, thus avoiding the possibility of a net welfare loss for the developed country.

The Potential Impact of the GSP Program

The potential impact of the GSP program can be divided into two parts, static and dynamic. The *static impact* refers to the change in equilibrium of the market price and quantity before and after the implementation of the GSP program. The *dynamic impact* refers to other changes in the economy, such as investment and industrialization, that are associated with the implementation of the GSP program. Theoretically, the potential static effects of the GSP program on preference-receiving countries can be analyzed in terms of trade creation and trade diversion.

Trade creation takes place when the GSP program leads a product source to shift from high-cost producers in a preference-giving country to low-cost producers in a preference-receiving country whose exports were constrained by tariffs. *Trade diversion* occurs when the GSP program causes a product source for a preference-giving country to shift from a low-cost non-preference-receiving country to a high-cost preference-receiving country. Trade creation and trade diversion are determined by several factors. Trade creation depends on policies in each country that inhibit or foster trade, in addition to the following four factors.

First, the magnitude of the tariff reduction (the margin of preference) is important. The greater the reduction in a tariff, the greater the difference between the pre-GSP price of an import good and its post-GSP price and, thus, the greater the potential for trade creation.

Second, trade creation depends on the price elasticities of demand (i.e., consumers' responsiveness to changes in price) in the preference-giving and preference-receiving countries. The higher the price elasticity of demand in each country, the greater the size of trade creation. This is because a tariff reduction increases the quantity demanded in the importing country and decreases the quantity demanded in the exporting country. The latter phenomenon occurs because the tariff reduction in the importing country tends to increase the price of that product in the exporting country.[9] Therefore, if demand in the exporting country is very elastic, there would be a sharp decrease in quantity demanded, making more of the good available for exports.

Third, the price elasticities of supply (i.e., producers' responsiveness to changes in price) in the preference-giving and preference-receiving countries are also important. Higher price elasticities of supply are conducive to trade creation. If the quantity supplied is very responsive to prices, the reduction of tariffs would lead to a large decrease in production in the preference-giving country and a large increase in production in the preference-receiving country.

Fourth, trade creation could also occur as the income effect of the removal of tariffs causes greater consumption of the product and increases imports from the preference-receiving country.[10] The higher the income elasticity of demand (i.e., the sensitivity of demand to changes in income) in the preference-giving country, the greater the potential for trade creation.

In addition to trade creation, the other potential static effect of the GSP program is to divert trade from non-preference-receiving countries to preference-receiving countries. Such trade diversion depends mainly on two factors: the margin of preference and the cross-elasticities of demand between beneficiary countries' goods and their substitutes in nonbeneficiary countries (i.e., the substitutability of the goods of a preference-receiving country for the goods of a non-preference-receiving country). The greater the margin of preference (measured by the difference between the MFN tariff and the GSP tariff), the greater the trade diversion. The margin of preference erodes every time MFN tariffs are lowered for goods covered by the GSP program. In addition, the higher the cross-elasticity of demand, the greater the trade diversion.

As with the static impact of the GSP program, the dynamic impact is determined by domestic policies in the beneficiary countries. The potential dynamic impact of the GSP program is also in many ways similar to that of international trade in general. Reduced tariffs increase exports from and employment in the beneficiary countries. These new opportunities attract investment and stimulate industrialization and production of new products in those countries; this change diversifies their economic bases and, thus, diversifies their exports. It should be noted that diversification of exports could also be shown through the analysis of the static impact of the GSP program. This is because a reduction or removal of a tariff could make exportable a product that was previously, because of the tariff, not exported. However, it is mainly through the potential dynamic impact that the GSP program is expected to achieve its objectives.

It is important to note that the static gains and the dynamic impact of the GSP program may be undermined when quotas are in effect. If there is a quota on a product, then a greater tariff preference may simply mean greater quota rents. To whom the rents actually accrue—exporting firms, importing firms, the government of the preference-giving country, and/or the government of the preference-receiving country—depends mainly on how the rights to import and export the product are allocated. If, for example, the preference-receiving country allocates the quota to existing firms, there is a bias against new firms and maybe against new technology in the industry.

Empirical Estimates of the Impact of the GSP Program

Empirical studies of the GSP program can be divided into two main categories, *ex ante* studies and *ex post* studies. *Ex ante* studies, the type considered here, use estimated elasticities to forecast the change in exports as a result of the preferential tariffs. *Ex post* studies attempt to isolate the impact of preferential tariffs on the actual flows of trade (Langhammer and Sapir, 1987: 29–32; MacPhee and Oguledo, 1991).

One of the early and very prominent *ex ante* studies is the one by Baldwin and Murray (1977) that focused on the GSP programs of the European Economic Community (EEC), Japan, and the United States. Their study compared the benefits to beneficiary countries, as a group, of MFN tariff cuts to losses associated with the erosion of the margin of preference. The study made three assumptions. One was that imports from beneficiary countries and nonbeneficiary countries into a benefit-giving country are imperfect substitutes. The justification of the assumption was that beneficiary countries are developing countries, whereas nonbeneficiary countries are other developed countries. Therefore, there are differences in quality, delivery time, and credit arrangements (Baldwin and Murray, 1977: 31). Another assumption was that cross-elasticities between beneficiaries and preference-giving countries and between beneficiaries and nonbeneficiaries are equal. Finally, they assumed that MFN tariff cuts cover a broader array of goods and, unlike the GSP programs, do not have stringent trade-limiting provisions, such as quantitative and value limits. They concluded that "our calculations of the static effects, based on a differential product model, indicate that the developing countries stand to gain more from MFN tariff cuts than they will lose from the simultaneous erosion of their GSP preferential tariff margins" (44). Baldwin and Murray contended that the broader product and country coverage of an MFN tariff would generate benefits for developing countries that would exceed the loss of GSP benefits.

Pomfret (1986a, 1986b) vigorously challenged this conclusion. First, he argued that Baldwin and Murray underestimated the cross-elasticity of demand between beneficiary goods and nonbeneficiary goods and that, hence, they underestimated trade diversion generated by the GSP program. "At the margin preferred and non-preferred country manufactured goods seem highly substitutable (e.g., South Korea and Taiwanese exports to the EEC, Israeli and Spanish exports to the USA, or Singapore and Hong Kong exports to Japan)" (1986a, 535, N5).

Second, he pointed out that Baldwin and Murray compared actual GSP programs with hypothetical, broader MFN cuts that have no quantitative or value limits.

> In such a comparison the MFN tariffs are obviously superior, which provides a case for more liberalisation rather than less, but it is not a fair test of preferential versus non-preferential tariff reductions. As a political matter the developing countries may gain more by throwing their weight in support of wide-ranging MFN tariff cuts, but then again the developed countries may not respond to such an appeal; by *assuming* a positive response, [Baldwin and Murray's] calculations cannot shed light on this issue. (1986A: 535–536)

A rebuttal from Baldwin and Murray (1986) emphasized the significant difference between economic structures of beneficiary countries and nonbeneficiary countries. They dismissed Pomfret's example of the countries whose goods are at the margin by claiming that the sample is too small to make a generalization. They also pointed to a study by Sapir and Lundberg (1984) that also found the trade diversion impact of the GSP program to be very small—less than one-third of the gross trade expansion. Regarding their policy recommendation, they argued that many of the beneficiary countries' goods that were denied GSP benefits because of quantitative or value limits qualified for MFN tariff reductions at the conclusion of the Tokyo Round.

In their studies, Baldwin and Murray have emphasized that their conclusion of the net benefits of MFN tariff reductions is in reference to beneficiary (developing) countries as a group. Individual countries that are affected by quantitative limits have even higher potential for a net benefit from MFN tariff reductions. However, the higher potential to which they refer might not be as high as they suggest. The reason is that those are also the countries whose goods are most likely to be at the margin (as described by Pomfret), that is, whose goods are most likely to be highly substitutable for goods from nonbeneficiary countries. Thus, for them the trade diversion impact of the GSP program is very high.

In fact, those countries may not experience a net benefit at all from MFN tariff reductions, even if the reductions apply to a wider range of products.[11] Most of the exports that benefit from the GSP program come from high-income countries whose goods are highly substitutable for goods from nonbeneficiary countries. About 75 percent of U.S. imports eligible for GSP treatment in 1993 came from only ten countries—high-income, developing countries (U.S. International Trade Commission, 1994: 131).

The least developed countries, like most in sub-Saharan Africa, are not affected by quantitative limits. Therefore, they stand to lose from MFN tariff reductions. This is the case unless the trade diversion impact of the GSP program for them is zero and/or the MFN tariff reductions include exports from those countries that were not covered under the GSP program.

It is unlikely that the debate over the net static impact of MFN tariff cuts and a simultaneous erosion of GSP preferential tariff margins for beneficiary countries as a group will ever be settled. The studies like those of Baldwin and Murray and of Pomfret help to explain, in part, why developing countries may have differing views about MFN tariff cuts. Within the range of preference-receiving countries, one can expect the two groups of countries mentioned above—(1) countries with goods that are highly substitutable for those in non-preference-receiving countries and (2) the least developed countries—to be against tariff cuts that erode the margin of preference.

Although the discussion above suggests that the least developed countries favor GSP programs over MFN tariff cuts, a more fundamental inquiry is to consider to what extent the GSP itself really has been useful to sub-Saharan African countries. It is important at this point to revisit the determinants of trade creation and trade diversion: (1) the margin of preference, (2) the price elasticities of demand in the preference-giving country and in the beneficiary country, (3) the price elasticities of supply in the preference-giving country and in the beneficiary country, (4) the income elasticity of demand in the preference-giving country, (5) domestic policies in both beneficiary countries and preference-giving countries, and (6) the cross-elasticity of demand for goods from beneficiary countries and goods from nonbeneficiary countries.

1. *The margin of preference.* Three main observations are important here. One is that since some of the major exports of sub-Saharan Africa such as unprocessed coffee, cocoa, and minerals were already exempted from tariffs or faced very low tariffs, the GSP program has had very minimal effect on them, if any.

A second observation is that in developed countries, domestic industries that were traditionally protected by high tariffs and other stringent policy tools were also, typically, excluded from the GSP treatment. Of course, it is not by coincidence that most of those industries, such as various textiles, footwear articles, and various agricultural products, are also the ones in which developing countries have the most comparative advantage. These are the industries in which producers in developed countries are most vulnerable to outside competition.

By way of background for the third observation, African countries tend to use the Yaoundé Convention and its successor more than GSP arrangements for goods they export to Europe. The Yaoundé Convention, which was signed in 1963, covered eighteen African countries that were independent at that time. Under this convention, most dutiable imports from those countries entered the EEC duty free. The GSP program of the European Community (EC) was established in 1971. Since the first Lomé Convention, which was signed in 1975 and succeeded the Yaoundé Convention, over 95 percent of all dutiable imports from the African, Caribbean, and Pacific (ACP) states enter the EC duty free (Davenport, 1992: 233; OECD, 1983: 73–74). Because the preferential treatment under the Lomé Convention is more extensive than that under the GSP program, ACP countries tend to use the former arrangement more than the latter. The current (fourth) Lomé Convention expires in the year 2000, and it is unlikely that it will be renewed in its current form of nonreciprocity.

The third observation, then, is that the GSP programs may have actually reduced the margin of preference for sub-Saharan African exports to the EC. Since the Yaoundé Convention (which was established before the GSP program) and its successor, the Lomé Convention, extend preference only to a subgroup of developing countries, the GSP program with its wider country coverage reduces the margin of preference enjoyed by the ACP countries on their exports to what is now known as the European Union. This is a notable reduction because of a high cross-price elasticity of goods among developing countries. Although it is also true that there are more preference-giving countries under the GSP than under the Lomé Convention, about 70 percent of sub-Saharan African exports are destined to the EU.

2. *Price elasticities of demand.* The major exports of most sub-Saharan African countries are primary products. (See Table 1.3.) The price elasticities of demand for primary products are very small, thus

making the potential for the GSP program to create trade for those products also very small.

3. *Price elasticities of supply.* The price elasticities of supply for primary products are also not very helpful for trade creation. These price elasticities are small as well. Therefore, a decrease in price in the preference-giving country does not cause a significant decrease in quantity supplied. Likewise, an increase in price in the beneficiary country does not cause a substantial increase in quantity supplied. Explanations for the low elasticity of supply include the perennial nature of some primary commodities; limited substitution in agricultural production due to different requirements of different crops for weather and soil conditions; large fixed costs of expanding production, for example, in mining; and uncertainty about the long-term nature of the change in price. For sub-Saharan Africa, the price elasticity of supply is also limited by the relatively small research and development budgets and limited credit availability. As discussed in Chapter 2, credit availability was especially a problem in the 1970s (when the GSP programs were established) and in the early 1980s.

4. *Income elasticities of demand.* This fourth determinant of trade creation, income elasticities of demand for primary products, is also very small. Thus, if one considers the potential of the income effect of price decreases in preference-giving countries to create trade in sub-Saharan Africa, it can only be expected to be negligible, at best.

The discussion of the low elasticities is not meant to suggest that the reduction of trade barriers in developed countries is of no relevance to sub-Saharan Africa. Such reductions are important. Given the degree of free trade that already exists, however, margins of preference that are small and mostly just involve primary products will have only a marginal impact on trade creation.

5. *Domestic policies.* Trade creation also depends on policies in beneficiary countries and in preference-giving countries. For example, excessive taxation of domestic producers of export goods through price controls and/or overvalued domestic currencies, as discussed in Chapter 2, limits trade creation. In the same manner, production and export subsidies and nontariff barriers in preference-giving countries reduce the trade creation potential of the GSP programs.

6. *Cross-elasticity of demand.* The trade diversion impact of the GSP program thus depends mainly on the cross-elasticity of demand for goods from beneficiary countries and goods from nonbeneficiary countries, that is, the substitutability of such goods. Casual observation of sub-Saharan African exports and the product coverage of the

GSP programs suggests that trade diversion in favor of exports from Sub-Saharan Africa would be minimal.

◆   ◆   ◆

All the above factors notwithstanding, the impact of the GSP program ultimately depends on the degree to which SSA exports are eligible for GSP treatment and the degree to which the GSP schemes are utilized. The empirical evidence is not encouraging. In 1993 only about 18 percent of total imports by OECD countries with GSP schemes received the GSP treatment (UNCTAD, 1995c: 20–23). As shown in Table 3.1, in 1994 only about 5.4 percent of total imports by the United States from thirty-four sub-Saharan African countries received duty-free access under the GSP program.[12] South Asian countries seem to have been able to take better advantage of the U.S. GSP program, as indicated by the figures in Table 3.1 for Malaysia and Thailand.

For only four countries—Mozambique, Swaziland, Zimbabwe, and Namibia—did more than 20 percent of their exports to the United States in 1994 receive duty-free access. The high percentage of GSP exports from Mozambique is explained by the fact that cane sugar, which is covered by the U.S. GSP, dominates exports from Mozambique to the United States. In absolute terms, among SSA countries, South Africa is the leading beneficiary of the U.S. GSP program. It accounted for about 60 percent of the total SSA exports to the United States that benefited from the GSP program in 1994.

There are two main reasons why such a small percentage of SSA exports receive GSP duty-free access. First, not all products are covered by GSP schemes. For example, in 1993, only about 30 percent of total imports (or about 50 percent of the MFN dutiable imports) from the least developed countries by OECD countries with GSP schemes were eligible for GSP treatment. Nontariff barriers, quantitative restrictions, rules of origin, and administrative rules pertaining to GSP schemes also limit the amount of imports that receive GSP benefits.

Second, exporting countries are often unable to take advantage of GSP schemes, as limited as they may be. From 1976 to 1994, the utilization ratio—that is, imports that receive the GSP treatment divided by imports eligible for the GSP treatment for OECD imports from the least developed countries—fluctuated around 50 percent. The main reasons for the low utilization ratio for sub-Saharan African countries (and least developed countries in general) are human resources and institutional constraints. Many lack national focal points responsible for using GSP schemes.

Table 3.1   GSP Duty-Free Exports to the United States and Total Exports to the United States in 1994 (U.S.$1,000)

(1)	(2)	(3)	(4)
Country	GSP Duty-Free Exports	Total Exports	(2)/(3)
Mozambique	11,634	15,328	.759
Swaziland	19,393	37,576	.516
Zimbabwe	40,195	102,402	.393
Namibia	6,470	27,843	.232
Burkina Faso	72	445	.164
Madagascar	7,767	56,983	.136
Senegal	1,376	11,432	.120
Sierra Leone	5,970	51,230	.116
South Africa	190,315	2,030,223	.094
Kenya	9,112	108,674	.084
Mali	334	4,106	.081
Mauritius	15,683	217,131	.072
Equatorial Guinea	23	326	.071
Malawi	3,951	56,506	.070
Tanzania	1,038	14,928	.070
Côte d'Ivoire	10,693	185,354	.058
Botswana	480	13,655	.035
Togo	126	4,088	.031
Cameroon	1,400	55,189	.025
Ghana	2,869	198,486	.014
Zaire	2,419	187,725	.013
Central African Republic	2	249	.008
Uganda	275	34,858	.008
Niger	16	2,385	.007
Benin	52	10,074	.005
Ethiopia	147	34,100	.004
Gambia	8	2,368	.003
Mauritania	11	3,517	.003
Zambia	168	63,477	.003
Burundi	7	7,687	.001
Lesotho	51	63,008	.001
Guinea	36	92,055	.000
Congo	11	403,030	.000
Angola	5	2,061,227	.000
Total	332,110	6,157,665	.054
Total (excluding South Africa)	141,795	4,127,442	.034
Malaysia	5,020,715	13,977,161	.359
Thailand	2,486,305	10,307,201	.241

Source: U.S. Department of Commerce.

For example, as of 1995, Chad, Guinea, Guinea-Bissau, and Sierra Leone had not notified Japan of the names of their certifying authorities. Likewise, Benin, Central African Republic, Comoros, Djibouti, Equatorial Guinea, Gambia, Guinea, Madagascar, Mali, Mauritania, Niger, Rwanda, São Tomé and Principe, Sierra Leone, Somalia, Togo, and Uganda had not notified Sweden of the names of their certifying authorities. This notification is a prerequisite for the utilization of some GSP schemes, including Japan's and Sweden's (UNCTAD, 1995b: 133, 142). According to the Ghana Chamber of Commerce, which is a certifying authority, some exporters simply do not care to go through the process necessary for their products to be certified.

It is important to note that the numbers in column (2) in Table 3.1 do not measure the increase in exports associated with the GSP program. They simply represent the value of exports that received the GSP treatment. Extrapolating from Davenport's study (1992) of the preferential treatment accorded African products by the EU, the increase in exports associated with the GSP program can only be a fraction of the numbers in that column. Considering the small percentage of SSA goods that receive the GSP treatment to begin with, one can only speculate that the benefits associated with the GSP program are very small.

Of course, the dynamic effects of the GSP program must also be considered. These are almost impossible to quantify, especially for SSA, which suffers from a scarcity of reliable data. Only the most daring have ventured into this area of empirical work on Africa.

Truett and Truett (1992) examined the impact of the U.S. GSP program on nonprimary exports from four sub-Saharan African countries: Kenya, Mauritius, Tanzania, and Zambia. They found that the U.S. GSP program had a positive effect only on Tanzania and Zambia and a negative impact on nonprimary exports from Kenya and Mauritius. Perhaps because of data constraints, they only used a simple regression model in which the dependent variable is the quantity of exports of nonprimary goods from these countries to the United States. The explanatory variables are a relative price index, real GNP in the United States, average propensity to consume in the beneficiary countries, and GSP as a dummy variable with the value of zero before 1976 (that is, before the U.S. GSP program was in existence) and the value of one thereafter. The sample period was 1967 to 1987.

In constructing the relative price index, they used wholesale price indices or consumer price indices. This in itself is a problem because prices of nontraditional exports (a small sector of the economies of the beneficiary countries) may not have moved in congruence with overall prices. Also, government-set prices in Tanzania, for example, in the 1970s and early 1980s (from which the consumer price index was constructed) may not have reflected changes in actual prices.

More important, however, the study neglected key policy variables in the beneficiary countries such as public-sector investment, export taxes and/or subsidies, and foreign exchange policies. In Tanzania and Zambia, for example, in the late 1970s and early 1980s, because of foreign currency considerations, the government required certain amounts of products to be exported even when there was a shortage of those products in the domestic market. This may explain why Truett and Truett obtained the results they did. The increase in the exports of nonprimary products from Tanzania and Zambia may have had nothing to do with the GSP program. Moreover, at the introduction of the U.S. GSP program, the manufacturing bases in Tanzania and Zambia were relatively very low compared to those in Kenya and Mauritius and, thus, had a higher propensity for growth, with or without the GSP program.[13]

The dynamic impact of the GSP program is certainly an area deserving more rigorous investigation in the future. As explained earlier, one of the objectives of the GSP program was to stimulate industrialization in developing countries. Given how the program has been implemented, however, it has had the potential of hindering industrialization (and thus, diversification) in sub-Saharan Africa, rather than enhancing it. Most GSP programs discriminate against processed primary products and labor intensive goods, such as textiles, from developing countries. Africa's main exports are primary products. The GSP programs tend to reduce trade barriers more on unprocessed primary products than on processed ones. As a result, the effective rate of protection tends to increase for companies in developed countries that process primary products, as illustrated by the discussion that follows.

The effective rate of protection measures actual protection on the domestic value added. The formula for calculating the effective rate of protection is given by:

$$g = \frac{t - \Sigma a_i t_i}{1 - \Sigma a_i},$$

where
g is the effective rate of protection of the final product;
t is the nominal tariff rate on the final product;
a_i is the ratio of the cost of input i to the price of the

final product, at free trade prices; and
t_i is the nominal tariff on input i.

Here is a numerical illustration. Suppose this is the situation before the GSP program was implemented.

t is 30 percent—the nominal tariff rate on chocolate;
a_i is 50 percent—the ratio of the cost of cocoa beans to the price of chocolate; and
t_i is 10 percent—the nominal tariff on cocoa beans.

The effective rate of protection on chocolate would be:

$$g = \frac{.3 - (.5)(.1)}{1 - .5} = 50\%$$

Now suppose the GSP program removes the tariff on cocoa beans but not on chocolate. The effective rate of protection on chocolate would now be:

$$g = \frac{.3 - (.5)(0)}{1 - .5} = 60\%$$

In this case, the effective protection for chocolate producers (i.e., those who process cocoa beans into chocolate) in the preference-giving country would increase as a result of the GSP. They would obtain their inputs at a relatively lower cost. This would allow them to produce more chocolate and, thus, limit imports of chocolate from Côte d'Ivoire or Ghana, for example.

Many studies have shown that developed countries have escalated tariff structures where the nominal tariffs on processed products are higher than nominal rates for raw materials. For a long time developing countries, including sub-Saharan African countries, have been complaining about this tariff structure that discriminates against their efforts to industrialize. Ironically, the GSP program may have exacerbated the very discriminatory practice that it was created, in part, to correct.

Not everyone agrees that sub-Saharan African exports face escalating tariffs worth complaining about. A study by the World Bank staff, which has been disseminated in four slightly varied papers, questioned the validity of complaints from sub-Saharan African countries (Amjadi and Yeats, 1995; Amjadi et al., 1996; Ng and Yeats, 1996; and Yeats et al., 1997). Focusing on the EU's tariffs on sub-Saharan exports of wood, rubber, leather, jute, cotton, flax, wool, iron, manganese, copper, nickel, lead, zinc, tin, groundnuts, copra, palm nuts, soya bean, and cotton seed, they concluded that

> for these important commodities not only do tariffs *not* escalate against Africa (a zero duty is applied to all stages of the chain), but Africa receives preferences that should improve its ability to compete internationally and enhance its attraction as a location for commodity processing. (Amjadi et al., 1996: 21)

The conclusion of the study by the World Bank gives one pause to reconsider the extent to which trade barriers are applied against exports from sub-Saharan Africa. It is true that for political convenience and sentimental reasons, African leaders and advocate groups have sometimes exaggerated the impact of external factors in explaining the slow economic growth in sub-Saharan Africa. Exaggeration, whether it is intentional in order to draw attention or simply a result of benign ignorance, is often safe (that is, politically correct) because it has the appearance of being very sympathetic to Africans' economic conditions. The possible danger, of course, is that unduly blaming others may diminish the validity of genuine complaints and the likelihood of Africa's finding real solutions for its problems. This is especially true when policymakers fail to recognize the significant impact domestic policies have on the economy.

Of course, World Bank studies are not necessarily free of biases or political agendas either. A critical analysis of the World Bank study reveals that it significantly underestimated the range and extent of actual overall trade barriers in developed countries on African goods, as shown in these three observations.

First, the World Bank study examined the question of trade barriers against African goods by focusing on the EU. It is well understood that the EU is, relatively, the least protectionist region as far as goods from sub-Saharan Africa are concerned, because of the Lomé Convention. It is also true that the EU is the single most important destination of sub-Saharan Africa's exports. From 1992 to 1995 an annual average of about 55 percent of sub-Saharan exports was destined to the EU. However, it is important to remember that about 25 percent of SSA's exports were destined to other developed regions that are, relatively, more protectionist.[14]

Second, conspicuously missing from the list of goods considered in the World Bank study are coffee, cocoa, and sugar, which alone account for about 50 percent of sub-Saharan Africa's agricultural export earnings (World Bank, 1994a: 221). These commodities face escalating tariffs even in the EU, not to mention other developed countries.

Third, the escalating structure of trade barriers in developed countries is higher when nontariff barriers are taken into account. In other words, the incidence of nontariff barriers increases with each stage of processing. The study by the World Bank minimized the role of external barriers in the marginalization of sub-Saharan Africa in world trade.

The GSP and Nontariff Barriers

The GSP program is supposed to give preferential treatment to products from developing countries by reducing tariffs on those products. As already discussed, the preferential treatment is limited by (1) a number of conditions, such as rules of origin, the value-added requirement, quantitative limits, and administrative rules; (2) erosion of the margin of preference; and (3) uncertainty about both the margin of preference and the rules. The margin of preference for products from developing countries is even less when nontariff barriers in developed countries are taken into account.

Even without taking the GSP program into account, tariffs have, over time, become a less important tool of trade protection in developed countries. In the 1950s, the average tariff rate in OECD countries was about 40 percent. In the early 1990s, it was only 5 percent. This does not necessarily mean, however, that developed countries are considerably more open today than they were in the past. Although the tariff walls have been falling, nontariff barriers have been on the rise.

Clark and Zarrilli (1992) identified major beneficiaries under various GSP schemes and how they were affected by nontariff barriers in 1991. They found 100 percent of GSP-covered imports from Gambia and Mauritania into Japan were affected by nontariff barriers, as were 89 percent of GSP-covered imports from Niger into Canada and 76 percent from Kenya into Norway.

Nontariff barriers come in many forms. These include quotas, "voluntary" export restraints, variable import levies,[15] health and safety standards, packaging and labeling requirements, domestic content requirements (i.e., that the finished product must contain a certain proportion of domestic output), government procurement policies, seasonal import restrictions, and shipping regulations (Hillman, 1991: 39–61; Laird and Yeats, 1990: 244–251). Production subsidies (and export subsidies) also limit imports since they increase domestic production. Perhaps the World Bank staff who prepared the four papers previously mentioned did not factor in the nontariff barriers in their discussion about tariff escalation because they contended that the nontariff barriers that Africa faced were minimal.

> As was the case with tariffs, non-tariff barriers do not provide an important general explanation for Africa's poor trade performance although these restrictions were important for some specific types of agricultural products like beef and sugar. (Amjadi et al., 1996: 79)

> What caused Africa's marginalization in world trade? There is little evidence that it was government-imposed restrictions in OECD markets. The share of African exports subject to nontariff barriers is far lower than that of other developing countries that launched successful and sustained export-oriented industrialization drives. (Yeats et al., 1997: 24)

Again, these World Bank studies considerably underestimated the range and extent of actual nontariff barriers on sub-Saharan Africa's exports.[16] Although most of the underestimation is a result of data limitations, the authors did not provide sufficient warning about these limitations in drawing their conclusions.

They used the following formula to calculate the share of African exports covered by nontariff barriers (Laird and Yeats, 1990: 21):

$$C_j = \frac{\Sigma \, (D_i \times V_i)}{\Sigma \, V_i},$$

where:
C_j is coverage ratio;
j is importing country (or region);
D_i is dummy variable on product i; it takes the value of 1 if one or more nontariff barriers is applied to the product or zero otherwise; and
V_i is the value of imports of product i.

Suppose, for example, the following table (in which NTBs stands for nontariff barriers) represents total imports into the EU from Uganda.

Product	Value of Imports	NTBs	$D_i \times V_i$
green coffee	$1,500	no	0
roasted coffee	$100	yes	$100
raw cotton	$600	no	0
beef	$300	yes	$300

In this example:

$$\Sigma\ (D_i \times V_i)\ = 400;\ \Sigma\ V_i = 2500;\ \therefore\ C_j = 400/2500 = .16$$
(16 percent).

For sub-Saharan African countries, most of which have a very high degree of specialization in only a few commodities, the coverage ratio can be misleading. A large percentage of SSA's exports is unprocessed primary products that do not face nontariff barriers. As Amjadi and Yeats noted (1995: 6 [n6]), the four products—crude petroleum, pearls and precious metal, unprocessed cocoa, and unprocessed coffee—that account for about 65 percent of African exports to OECD countries do not encounter nontariff barriers in the EU and the United States. This situation suggests that nontariff barriers are concentrated on processed products and nonprimary exports—precisely the industries that SSA countries would want to develop.

Another problem with the coverage ratio measure is that it is downward-biased (Laird and Yeats, 1990: 263; Clark and Zarrilli, 1992: 286–287). Trade barriers in developed countries cause SSA's volume of exports to decrease. At the same time, since developed countries can influence world prices, their protectionist policies cause prices of their imports to decrease.[17] Therefore, products facing extensive and intensive nontariff barriers would have minimal aggregate values and, thus, bias the nontariff barrier coverage ratio downward. Note that if, for example, an existing nontariff barrier became so intensive as to eliminate imports of that product altogether from some country, the coverage ratio for that country would actually decrease, suggesting, incorrectly, that the nontariff barriers have been reduced. Using our earlier hypothetical numerical example, if additional nontariff barriers cause imports of beef to be zero, the coverage ratio would drop from 16 percent to only about 4.5 percent.

The downward bias of the nontariff barrier coverage ratio and the higher degree of specialization in SSA call for a very cautious comparison of nontariff barrier coverage ratios for OECD imports from SSA and those from other developing countries. A low nontariff barrier coverage ratio may imply more intensive nontariff barrers. In addition, even if two countries faced identical nontariff barriers against a particular product, the relative importance of that product to each country and the experience (maturity) level in production could be different enough to render comparison meaningless.

Another observation regarding the nontariff barrier coverage ratio is that it does not incorporate production and export subsidies in

OECD countries. These subsidies are discussed at length in Chapter 4. Production and export subsidies act, indirectly, as nontariff barriers as they distort prices, increase domestic production, and reduce imports. Such subsidies, especially export subsidies, are pervasive in developed countries and have a severe impact on SSA.

All food items and agricultural raw materials account for more than 50 percent of export revenue in about two-thirds of all sub-Saharan African countries.[18] The agricultural sector is also the most protected and subsidized sector in OECD countries, which must have a significant impact on sub-Saharan Africa's agricultural sector, particularly on production, exports, and imports of temperate-zone products. In 1994, the monetary transfers to producers (i.e., the producer subsidy equivalent) of wheat, maize, and rice in OECD countries resulting from agricultural policies was about U.S.$50 billion (OECD, 1997: 34). That amount of transfers was five times the total export revenue generated from exports of all foods items from sub-Saharan Africa in 1994. It was almost three times the value of the net foreign aid flows to all of sub-Saharan Africa in 1994 (Lancaster, 1999: 70). Note that the amount of transfers reported does not even include subsidies for food processing (OECD, 1997: 21).

In view of the agricultural subsidies alone in OECD countries, particularly in the EU, it is not clear how one can reach the conclusion that nontariff barriers "do not provide an important general explanation for Africa's poor trade performance" (Amjadi et al., 1996: 79). It is apparent that the objective of the World Bank studies was to show that domestic policies in SSA are the ones responsible for the marginalization of Africa in world trade. One need not diminish the role of external factors to argue that domestic policies have also been an impediment to trade. In order to determine whether external factors or domestic policies are more responsible, more objective and comprehensive studies are needed than those by the World Bank cited above. In summary, the gradual bulging of direct and indirect nontariff barriers in OECD countries, especially agricultural subsidies, has eroded the margin of preference accorded by the GSP program to SSA.

The Benefits to Preference-Giving Countries

Thus far, only the potential benefits of the GSP program to preference-receiving countries have been discussed. Now we address some of the benefits of the program to preference-giving countries. From the perspective of preference-giving countries, the GSP program has tangible and intangible advantages. These countries gain from the benefits of reducing tariffs and, at the same time, are viewed as being benevolent, that is, "donor" countries (U.S. International Trade Commission, 1991: iii; OECD, 1983: 27; Baldwin and Murray, 1977).

It is misleading, however, to characterize preference-giving countries under the GSP as "donor" countries. (To some extent, even the term *benefit-giving* countries is misleading.) The term *donor* suggests a net transfer of wealth from developed to developing countries. On the contrary, it is widely agreed that reducing tariffs and other trade barriers increases a country's welfare by allowing a more efficient allocation of resources and increasing the purchasing power of consumers' incomes. Even selective reductions of tariffs in developed countries, therefore, benefit those countries as well.

Testifying before the House Ways and Means Subcommittee on Trade in 1995, Robin Lanier of the International Mass Retail Association elaborated on those benefits. She argued that the GSP program helps U.S. companies keep production costs down by importing raw materials under the GSP program. She added:

> Most important, [it] gives consumers a break at the checkout. ... For example, if the GSP trade program expires, certain products would see significant price increases at retail—as much as an 8 percent increase on Christmas tree lights, 9.2 percent for fishing rods, 4.7 percent for ceiling fans, and 10 percent on ceramic tiles. All of these products are currently being imported at zero duty under the GSP. (quoted in Roach, 1995: 16)

As discussed earlier in "The Potential Impact of the GSP Program" section, the static effects of the GSP program are trade creation and trade diversion. Consider Figures 3.1 and 3.2, which illustrate those effects in a preference-giving country. Suppose the United States is the preference-giving country, Botswana the preference-receiving country, and Italy the non-preference-receiving country. Figure 3.1 presents a trade creation case. *DD* and *SS* represent demand for and supply of cattle leather in the United States. *Pbo* is the price of leather in Botswana. Before the GSP program, the price of leather in the United States is *Pus*, that is, *Pbo* plus the MFN tariff rate, t.[19] The volume of imports is Q2Q3. Following the GSP program, the price of leather in the United States falls to *Pbo*, and the volume of imports increases to Q1Q4. As a result, consumer surplus increases by areas *A+B+C+D*, producer surplus decreases by area *A*, and tariff revenue decreases by area *C*. There is a net welfare gain to the U.S. economy of areas *B* (associated with production) and *D* (associated with consumption).

Figure 3.1   Trade Creation Impact of GSP

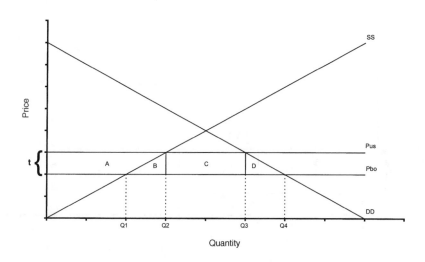

Figure 3.2 presents a trade diversion case. *DD* and *SS* here represent demand for and supply of glassware in the United States. *Pbo* is the price of glassware in Botswana. *Pit* is the price of glassware in Italy. Before the GSP program, both Italy and Botswana face a uniform MFN tariff rate. The United States imports glassware from Italy, where it is produced at a lower cost than in Botswana. The pre-GSP price of glassware in the United States is *Pus*, that is, *Pit* plus the MFN tariff rate. The volume of imports is *Q2Q3*. Following the GSP program, the United States shifts from Italy to Botswana as a source of glassware. The preferential tariff reduction makes glassware from Botswana cheaper for U.S. consumers, even though Italy is the lower-cost producer. The price in the United States falls to *Pbo*, and the volume of imports increases to *Q1Q4*. Consumer surplus increases by areas *A+B+C+D*, producer surplus decreases by area *A*, and tariff revenue decreases by area *C+E*. If areas *B+D* exceed area *E*, there will be a net welfare gain to the U.S. economy. If area *E* exceeds areas *B+D*, however, there will be a net loss. Even though there are gains associated with production (area *B*) and consumption (area *D*), there is a possibility of a net welfare loss because the terms of trade for the United States deteriorate as it switches its source of glassware from Italy to Botswana.

Most of the empirical studies that have tried to estimate the trade creation and trade diversion impact of the GSP program have

Figure 3.2   Trade Diversion Impact of GSP

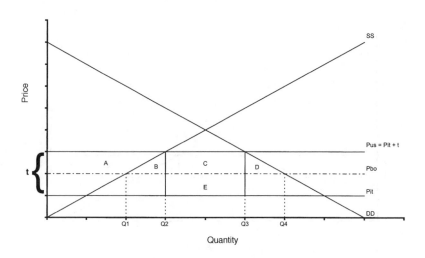

found trade creation to be considerably greater than trade diversion (MacPhee and Oguledo, 1991; MacPhee, 1989). This evidence suggests a net welfare gain for preference-giving countries. Note that even if trade diversion were prevalent, that would not necessarily mean that there would be a net welfare loss. For there to be an overall net welfare loss in the economy, area *E* in Figure 3.2 must exceed the sum of areas *B+D* in Figures 3.1 and 3.2. Therefore, the possibility of an overall net loss to a preference-giving country is very remote. In fact, when the dynamic effects of the GSP program such as the repercussions of increased income in developing countries are taken into consideration, a net welfare gain to the preference-giving country is almost certain.[20]

Thus, there is no donation or aid (i.e., net transfer of wealth) from preference-giving countries to preference-receiving countries. The term *benefit-giving* is also misleading to the extent that it suggests that the only countries benefiting are the preference-receiving countries. Preference-giving countries benefit as well.[21]

The GSP program has another potential benefit to developed countries: It can be used as a political tool. If a preference-giving country is not pleased with a preference-receiving country, the latter can unilaterally be removed from the GSP program. This possibility makes the GSP program a convenient foreign policy tool. For one thing, the fact that some action has been taken can please any group or groups that have lodged complaints against the preference-receiving country. In addition, the GSP program has minimal economic impact on many of the poorer preference-receiving countries anyway, so its removal may not necessarily severely damage the relations between the two countries. (Of course, this depends on the publicity involved and the preference-receiving country's premium on its image in the world.) The GSP program can, therefore, be used strategically, especially if what the preference-giving country wants to accomplish is only to appear to be doing something.

For example, Central African Republic, Liberia, Mauritania, and Sudan have been suspended from the U.S. GSP program following complaints about worker rights violations in those countries. (Central African Republic was reinstated in 1991.) Mauritania was accused of allowing slavery in its country.[22] Apart from the possible external costs of having their names tarnished, fairly or otherwise, the actual U.S. GSP program is useless to these countries. The share of each of these countries' exports to the United States is less than 2 percent. The share of *those* exports that received duty-free access under the U.S. GSP program is less than 1 percent for each one of the four countries. Being removed from the U.S. GSP program, therefore, has virtually no real direct impact on these countries. Yet, it gives the United States the appearance of being firm, for example, on the Mauritanian government's failure to eliminate slavery.

Considering themselves "donor" countries, preference-giving countries engage in laborious, heated debates every so often to decide whether or not to continue this "donation" to developing countries, that is, to renew the GSP program. Believing the GSP program is a form of aid, African countries (and other developing countries) campaign for the program to continue. People accept as conventional wisdom the rhetoric that the GSP program amounts to transferring wealth from rich nations to poor nations, when that is not the case. This is especially true in SSA where, owing to a lack of adequate resources and data (and sometimes complacency), very few studies are done to assess fully the impact of any particular program.

Conclusion

The idea of the GSP program arose from a genuine concern of UNCTAD for the widening income gap between the rich and poor nations and the understanding that trade can enhance economic growth. The institution of preferential treatment has merit, especially considering that some of the factors responsible for the growing income gap between rich and poor countries are built into world trade patterns. For example, food products (and primary products in general), which are the main exports of many sub-Saharan African countries, have relatively low income elasticities of demand, meaning that an increase in incomes worldwide would decrease the percentage of income spent on food. Over time, as income increases, the relative prices of food decrease, thus causing the terms of trade for SSA to deteriorate.

Likewise, changes in technology and tastes reduce the demand for natural raw products as producers switch to cheaper synthetic materials and as technological changes minimize the use of inputs. This also works to accelerate the deterioration of the terms of trade. According to the World Bank, from 1963 to 1986 world industrial production increased by an annual average of about 4 percent while the consumption of raw materials only increased by an average of 1.5 percent (World Bank 1994b: 39–40).

Although the idea of preferential treatment has merit in theory, in practice the structure of the GSP program has depended mainly on the good will of the rich countries. On the one hand, the presence of the GSP program suggests concern and good will toward developing countries. On the other hand, the limitations within the GSP program reveal that the primary determining factor of the structure of the program is the political power of interest groups in developed countries and not the income gap that the program is supposed to bridge. The impact of domestic political power is revealed especially in product coverage and nontariff barriers. When imports from developing countries of products listed under the program threaten domestic production of a politically powerful industry, safeguard measures are quickly applied. As a result, the benefits of the GSP program to developing countries have been almost coincidental.

In summary, it appears that the benefits of the GSP program to SSA have been minuscule. This is partly the result of such factors as the inability of SSA to utilize the GSP schemes, domestic policies in SSA that depressed investment and production of export products, limitations within the GSP program, nontariff barriers in developed countries, and declining MFN tariffs. Yet African countries and other developing countries, through UNCTAD, have been calling for the continuation of GSP. Why? Perhaps because something is better than nothing. Other things being equal, the GSP program has some marginal benefits. In fact, high-income, preference-receiving countries, which produce goods that are close substitutes for those produced in non-preference-receiving countries, may gain considerable benefits through trade diversion. In addition, some governments in SSA, like those in Ghana, Kenya, Mauritius, and Zimbabwe, try to work with the private sector to devise strategies to take full advantage of the program.[23]

Having the GSP program also helps to keep alive the discussion about the role of trade in economic development. It acknowledges the income disparity between nations. It serves as a testimony, symbolic as it may be, that rich nations have an obligation—economic, social, moral, or otherwise—to help poor nations. The GSP program is, therefore, seen as one means of bridging the income gap. Some have described it as a form of aid more acceptable to developing countries than direct aid (Raj, 1990: 43–44).

This discussion has identified domestic policies in SSA, limited product coverage, and nontariff barriers in developed countries as some of the factors that have limited the benefits of the GSP program to SSA. These factors are currently changing in the direction that would increase the potential benefits of the program, the reduction in the margin of preference notwithstanding.

Most sub-Saharan African countries are implementing structural adjustment programs that encourage private investment and expansion of the export sector. In 1997, the United States expanded product coverage for least developed countries by about two thousand products. They include products of interest to SSA, such as live animals, meat, vegetables, fruits, peanuts (unprocessed), cottonseed oil, and tobacco. The Uruguay Round of GATT reached an agreement in 1993 to reduce direct and indirect nontariff barriers in the textile industry and agricultural sector in developed countries. It would be ironic if developed countries were to decide not to renew the GSP program, given these changes.

Sub-Saharan African countries must, however, be realistic about both the potential impact and the duration of the GSP program. The potential benefits of the GSP program, both static and dynamic, are still small even if they are fully achieved. The program must be seen for what it is, a temporary arrangement that can boost policies and strategies that are key in bringing economic growth. The GSP program, for example, cannot be expected to be an important factor in attracting foreign direct investment to SSA. Fundamental factors of development such as education, health services, macroeconomic stability, infrastructure, and laws and procedures governing investment are much more important in determining domestic and foreign private investment in sub-Saharan Africa. Therefore, although the potential for the GSP program to benefit SSA seems to have increased, SSA must focus on the fundamentals of development.

SSA countries must also be aware of the intangible costs of the GSP program. There are costs to clinging to any program that has a perceived "donor-donee" relationship. Doing so reduces the bargaining power of SSA (and other developing countries) and can even obscure judgment as to which programs or agreements to bargain for in bilateral or multilateral negotiations.[24] Countries must be careful not to be automatically against everything that appears to reduce the "donation," without careful consideration of its full impact.

Notes

1. The United States raised similar concerns in 1994 with respect to the World Trade Organization. However, the U.S. Congress voted in favor of the WTO.

2. Some countries followed the GATT rules on a de facto basis and were extended the benefits of membership.

3. Frequent debates in the United States about extending MFN status to the People's Republic of China (the PRC) can be confusing to those not familiar with the MFN principle. In fact, the PRC is not yet a member of the WTO; the question is whether the United States should treat it as if it were, thus allowing it to benefit from the same treatment that all WTO members receive from the United States. The United States and China reached a trade pact in November 1999, however, which increases the latter's likelihood of being accepted into the WTO.

4. A permanent secretariat of UNCTAD is headquartered in Geneva.

5. This information was obtained from the U.S. Department of Commerce. The countries were Angola, Benin, Burkina Faso, Burundi, Cape Verde, Central African Republic, Chad, Comoros, Democratic Republic of Congo, Djibouti, Equatorial Guinea, Ethiopia, Gambia, Guinea, Guinea-Bissau, Lesotho, Madagascar, Malawi, Mali, Mozambique, Niger, Rwanda, São Tomé and Principe, Sierra Leone, Somalia, Tanzania, Togo, Uganda, and Zambia.

6. Austria, Finland, and Sweden discontinued their GSP programs in 1995 following accession into the European Union. They have since been applying the EU scheme. Some former communist countries established GSP schemes after the collapse of the Soviet Union.

7. For details, see OECD (1983).

8. The occurrence of trade diversion and its impact on the economic welfare of a country are discussed and illustrated in a later section, "The Benefits to Preference-Giving Countries."

9. This would be the case if the preference-giving country is a large importer of that commodity and, thus, can influence the world price of that product. For a small importer, the price in the beneficiary country would not change.

10. *Income effect* refers to the situation in which a reduction in the price of a commodity increases consumers' income real purchasing power.

11. Countries that are scheduled to be graduated would, however, benefit from an MFN tariff reduction. In 1988, a year before they were graduated from the U.S. GSP scheme, Hong Kong, South Korea, Singapore, and Tai-

wan accounted for 55 percent of all preferential exports to the United States (United Nations, 1992: 2).

12. The U.S. GSP program is used here mainly because the data were comprehensive and readily available. Although GSP data for the EU might also have been useful because of the EU's importance to SSA's exports, it is important to remember that African countries tend to use the Lomé Convention arrangement instead for their exports to the EU.

13. Even though the study (Truett and Truett, 1992) was on the impact of the U.S. GSP program on nonprimary (manufactured) products, it only described changes in exports of primary products such as sugar, coffee, and copper.

14. The percentages were calculated using data from UNCTAD (1997a: Annex A.1).

15. A *variable import levy* is a tax on imports that is adjusted frequently (in some cases, on a daily basis) to achieve a targeted domestic price (Hillman, 1991: 43).

16. Attention is paid here to the studies by the World Bank (Amjadi and Yeats, 1995; Amjadi et al., 1996; Ng and Yeats, 1996; Yeats et al., 1997) because, for better or worse, policymakers pay attention to what the World Bank publishes. While conducting research for this book, the author discussed trade policy issues with some officials at the U.S. Department of Commerce. In a telephone discussion with one official, the author was advised that the problem for Africa was not U.S. trade policies. Backing his position, the official cited "some careful studies by the World Bank." The reference was to the four papers mentioned above.

17. Since the developed country is importing less of the product, the amount of the product demanded in the world market decreases. As a result, the world price of the product likewise decreases.

18. All food items include food and live animals (SITC 0), beverages and tobacco (SITC 1), oil-seeds (SITC 22), and animal and vegetable oils and fats (SITC 4). (SITC refers to Standard International Trade Classification.) Agricultural raw materials include hides and skins, rubber, forestry products, cotton, jute, vegetable textile fibers, and crude vegetable and animal materials (SITC 2–22–27–28) (UNCTAD, 1997a).

19. In this simple illustration, factors such as nontariff barriers and transportation costs are held constant, at zero.

20. Brown (1987, 1989) showed that even nonbeneficiary countries can gain from the GSP program in spite of trade diversion if the respending of foreign exchange by beneficiary countries is concentrated on goods from the nonbeneficiaries.

21. A reviewer of this manuscript observed that the right first approximation of the impact of preference giving might, in some cases, still be that transfers are generated. One such case would be when a preference-giving country provides preferences to a receiving country that is too small to affect the equilibrium price in the preference-giving country. This case would be like a terms-of-trade gain for the preference-receiving country.

To use the reviewer's example, consider giving a preference to a small exporter already exporting $50 million worth of a product. There will be a transfer of tariff revenues to the recipient country, on the original $50 million volume of exports, plus an additional loss of tariff revenue on any trade diversion as the preference-receiving country moves up its supply curve to export goods that would be noncompetitive without the preference. This case would be an example of a transfer because the preference-receiving country benefits while the preference-giving country does not gain anything.

This is a valid observation, especially since preference-giving countries would tend to give preferences that are inframarginal, that is, that hardly undercut the effective rate of protection that domestic producers experience. Nonetheless, it is unlikely that the domestic price would not be affected at all when most of the preferences under the GSP program (as opposed to bilateral agreements) are given not to one but to many developing countries. This is because these countries, in aggregate, can influence prices. A decrease in price in the preference-giving country, as a result of the GSP program, will reduce production and consumption distortions in the country and, thus, benefit that country as well.

22. The existence of slavery in Mauritania was also reported by *The Economist* ("Master and Slave," 1996), Hecht (1997), and Burkett (1997).

23. The author learned this during his meetings with commercial attachés and ambassadors at African embassies in the United States and with government and business leaders in Ghana and Kenya.

24. Raj (1990: 44) also argued that the GSP program could have the reverse effect of that for which it is intended. It gives an opportunity to producers in developed countries to lobby for restrictive safeguards, something that would be more difficult to obtain under a nondiscriminatory tariff policy.

◆

FOUR

Two GATT Agreements: Agriculture, Textiles and Clothing

The Uruguay Round of GATT, launched in 1986, was successfully concluded on December 15, 1993. Its fifteen trade-related agreements took effect January 1, 1995. GATT's successor, the WTO, facilitates the implementation, administration, and operation of those agreements. The focus in this chapter is on two of those agreements: the Agreement on Agriculture and the Agreement on Textiles and Clothing.

Reactions to the Conclusion of the Uruguay Round

Immediately following the conclusion of the Uruguay Round of GATT, the media reported a wide range of views about the impact of the agreements on trade. Although their impact on developing countries was not discussed much in industrialized countries, the agreements certainly generated a great deal of interest, and concern, over how developing countries would benefit or lose.

For example, saluting the victory of the GATT negotiations, GATT director general Peter Sutherland remarked in December 1993:

> The most significant feature of this negotiation has been the large number of developing countries taking part, and taking part actively. Their contribution to the round has been a vital one, reflecting the importance of the multilateral trading system in creating and maintaining opportunities for sustainable development. (Voice of America press release, December 16, 1993)

A staff reporter for the *Wall Street Journal* came to a different conclusion:

> For weeks, they [developing nations] have been on the outside looking in. While the U.S. and the Europeans have been arguing over who gets what piece of the world-trade pie, developing countries have wondered what's in it for them. Now, for some, the answer is clear: the crumbs. (Ingrassia, 1993: A6)

A reporter for *New African* magazine wrote:

> Perhaps one of the most perplexing and profoundly-debilitating things about the signing last December [1993] of the Uruguay Round accord of the General Agreement on Tariffs and Trade (GATT) was the fact that, even though they [African negotiators] were well aware that they had nothing to gain from it, African governments—like sheep being led to the slaughter—nevertheless went along and rubber-stamped the deal. (Samboma, 1994: 25)

What is one to make of these views? What roles and positions did sub-Saharan African countries play and take, respectively, particularly on the two agreements that are the focus of this chapter? What is the impact of these agreements on trade in sub-Saharan Africa?

Sub-Saharan Africa's Agricultural Sector in the World Market

Agriculture is the most important sector for most sub-Saharan African countries. The agricultural sector accounts for about 40 percent of the nonservice component of the GDP in sub-Saharan Africa, and it contributes about 25 percent of export revenue to sub-Saharan Africa. Nonetheless, in aggregate, SSA contributes only about 2.8 percent of world exports of agricultural products (all food items and raw agricultural materials).[1] Its imports of these products are about 3.2 percent of world imports (UNCTAD, 1997a). Because of their small shares in the world market, sub-Saharan African countries cannot influence world prices, and, therefore, they are price-takers for almost all commodities. The only clear exceptions are Côte d'Ivoire and Ghana for cocoa.[2]

The key SSA exports of agricultural products are coffee, cocoa, tea, cotton, sugar, and tobacco. Other SSA agricultural exports include wood, natural rubber, nuts, maize, vegetables and fruits, hides and skin, fish, and meat. Major imports include wheat, rice, and other cereals.

Agricultural Policies in OECD Countries

Domestically, agriculture is not nearly as important to OECD countries, as a source of employment and foreign currency, as it is to many sub-Saharan African countries. From 1992 to 1994, in OECD countries, the annual average percentage of agriculture in the GDP was about 1.8, the percentage of agricultural employment within total civilian employment was 8.8, the percentage of agricultural exports within total exports was 9.3, and the percentage of agricultural imports within total imports was 9.4 (OECD, 1997: 53).

These domestic export and import percentages translate into much more significant proportions in the world market. For example, in 1994, for all food items, 66 percent of world imports originated in OECD countries, and 70 percent of world exports were destined to OECD countries (UNCTAD, 1997a: 50–51, 70–71). Changes in demand and supply in OECD countries, therefore, influence world prices. As a result, agricultural policies in OECD countries are of great interest to the rest of the world.

Those policies are of even greater interest to sub-Saharan Africa. OECD countries are important consumers and suppliers of sub-Saharan African exports and imports, respectively, of agricultural products. About 75 percent of sub-Saharan Africa's exports of agricultural products are destined to OECD countries, and about 68 percent of imports of agricultural products originate in OECD countries.[3]

The agricultural sector in OECD countries reflects a long history of protection and domestic support. It has been protected by quotas, tariffs, voluntary export restraints, seasonal prohibitions of imports, and so on. The sector has also been supported by a variety of instruments, such as price floors, subsidized credit, payments for not growing, and payments to supplement market prices when those prices are below certain target levels ("deficiency payments"). In addition, the agricultural sector has been supported with export subsidies, which in many countries were a consequence of domestic supports.

Domestic supports led to an accumulation of large stocks of commodities. In addition, as Sanderson (1990: 3) explained, the accumulation was reinforced by the "*ratchet effect*—price guarantees are increased during boom periods but are slow in coming down when markets weaken." Consequently, agricultural export subsidies have been widely used in OECD countries, especially in the EU, to encourage the sale of surpluses in the world market.

The EU, which by the dictates of comparative advantage would be a net importer of many agricultural products, has been the second largest exporter (after the United States) of these products because of its Common Agricultural Program (CAP). CAP consists of common farm policies and price support programs for agriculture within the EU. The United States, a net exporter of many agricultural products even without government support, has been increasing its world market share by subsidizing production and exports. There has existed an undeclared competition in the provision of subsidies by industrialized nations, notably among the United States, the EU, and Japan.

Domestic support and export subsidies in OECD countries (large producers) have a spiral effect. For export commodities, subsidies in a large country increase the volume of exports in the world market and depress world prices of agricultural products, thus causing a need for still additional subsidies to cushion farmers' income. For import commodities, protection and domestic subsidies in a large country decrease the volume of imports, causing a decrease in demand in the world market and, thus, a decrease in world prices; this decrease, in turn, exerts pressure for additional protection and support. This spiral is even stronger across countries, as the United States, for example, protects its farmers against the effect of EU subsidies.

Table 4.1 provides some measures of the impact of agricultural policies in the OECD countries. The producer subsidy equivalent (PSE) is an indicator of the value of the monetary transfers to producers resulting from agricultural policies. They include transfers from consumers of agricultural products and transfers from taxpayers. The values are in nominal terms. The percentage PSE is the total value of PSE as a percentage of the total value of production valued at domestic prices. This is a good measure of the trend of the relative assistance to farmers provided by agricultural policies.

Commodity world prices were at a trough (the low point of the price cycle, so to speak) in 1986–1988. Protection and subsidies are usually used to increase prices for domestic farmers, so those two means of support were, relatively, at the highest level in that period, as shown by the percentage PSE. The nominal assistance coefficient (NAC) also reveals the increase in assistance in the 1986–1988 period. The NAC is the ratio of the world price plus the unit PSE to the world price (OECD, 1997: 21–23).

Table 4.1   The Average Annual Impact of Protection and Support on Agriculture in OECD Countries

	1979–1986	1986–1988	1989–1991	1993–1995
PSE in U.S.$ (billions)	99	159	160	174
Percentage PSE	34	45	40	41
NAC	1.47	1.78	NA	1.66
PSE per farmer in U.S.$ (thousands)	NA	11	NA	14
CSE in U.S.$ (billions)	−66	−119	−119	−122
Percentage CSE	−26	−37	−33	−31

Sources: OECD (1994, 1995a, 1997).

Notes: Consumer subsidy equivalent (CSE); nominal assistance coefficient (NAC); producer subsidy equivalent (PSE).

$$NAC = \frac{PW + PSE_u}{PW},$$

where

PW is world price at the border, and

PSE_u is PSE divided by domestic volume of production.

The NAC is a rough indicator of the disparity between the world price and the domestic price.

For example, in the 1986–1988 period, the NAC was 1.78, which means the domestic price level of agricultural products in OECD countries, on average, was about 78 percent higher than the world price. There is a very wide range of NACs among OECD countries. In the 1986–1988 period, it ranged from 1.12 for Australia to 4.75 for Norway. The United States, the EU, and Japan had the following NACs, respectively: 1.39, 1.95, and 3.26 (OECD, 1997: 38). Agricultural policies in OECD countries constitute a transfer of income from domestic consumers of agricultural products. As such, consumer subsidy equivalents (CSE), net transfers from consumers resulting from agricultural policies, are entered with a negative sign. Note in Table 4.1 how the percentage CSE (the total value of transfers as a percentage of total consumption valued at producer prices) also peaks in the 1986–1988 period.

The impact of agricultural policies in OECD countries on consumers and producers in the rest of the world is the opposite of the impact of those policies on domestic consumers and producers. Since these policies depress world prices, they act as subsidies to consumers and taxes to producers in the rest of the world. Thus, within each country in the rest of the world, individuals will be in favor of or against OECD policies depending on whether they are net buyers or net sellers of agricultural products. The overall opinion of each country depends much on whether a country is a net importer or is (or has the potential of being) a net exporter of agricultural products. Thus, during the Uruguay Round, a group of low-cost producing countries, the Cairns Group, pressured OECD countries to liberalize the agricultural sector.[4] On the other side, net importers of food, led by Egypt, Jamaica, Mexico, Morocco, and Peru and supported by African countries, were concerned with changes that would cause food prices to increase (Hopkins, 1993: 149; UNCTAD, 1994: 133).

It is apparent that African countries were more concerned with the short-run impact of liberalization in OECD countries (an increase in the import bill) than with its long-run impact (an increase in their own exports). The agricultural policies of industrialized nations, coupled with high taxes by African governments on their farmers, reduced the export potential of the agricultural sector in Africa. The Agreement on Agriculture is important to sub-Saharan Africa countries, therefore, because it may eventually lead to more open markets for their agricultural products.

The Agreement on Agriculture

Following the inception of GATT, industrialized nations, led by the United States, protected the agricultural sector from the jurisdiction of GATT. This sector was treated as exceptional. Domestic policy objectives took precedence over trade policy.

The degree of protection increased over time, a trend that could not continue indefinitely. The cost of agricultural policies on government budgets became onerous. Disagreement among OECD countries ensued. For example, the United States (the original staunch supporter of domestic policies in agriculture) felt that the EU and Japan had gone too far with their mercantilist agricultural policies. Furthermore, agricultural policies in OECD countries failed to achieve some of their goals, such as aiding disadvantaged rural areas and supporting small producers (OECD, 1997: 9–14; Sanderson, 1990: 3–4). These concerns led OECD ministers to recommend policy reforms in 1987 that would lower assistance to farmers, reduce price distortions, and reduce domestic market imbalances. Subsequent OECD ministerial-level meetings reaffirmed the need to grad-ually liberalize the agricultural sector.

Although the objectives of policy reforms were clearly stated, the implementation of reforms necessary to achieve them was a different matter. With the exception of Australia and New Zealand, which had the lowest degree of agricultural support in OECD countries to be-gin with, the implementation level in general was modest (Vietta and Cahill, 1991). Nevertheless, the 1987 recommendation propelled further discussions in subsequent OECD ministerial meetings. These discussions and concerted pressure from low-cost producing coun-tries, particularly those in the Cairns Group, led to an agreement, at the conclusion of the Uruguay Round of GATT, to liberalize the agri-cultural sector.

The Agreement on Agriculture set the agricultural sector en route to trade liberalization, albeit slowly. It also provided a frame-work for future negotiations "aimed at more meaningful liberaliza-tion" (UNCTAD, 1994: 133). The agreement had three main ele-ments: market access, domestic support, and export subsidies (see the summary in Table 4.2).

Market Access

Market access involves tariffication, that is, converting all nontariff barriers that limit imports into tariffs that would provide domestic producers approximately the same level of initial protection. In addi-tion to the nontariff barriers listed in Chapter 3 and earlier in this chapter, license requirements and outright import prohibition have also been common, particularly in developing countries. Over time, tariffs are less restrictive compared to most nontariff barriers, and they are also more transparent.

The agreement requires countries to bind all resulting and exist-ing tariffs and reduce them by an average of 36 percent in developed countries over a period of six years and by an average of 24 percent in developing countries over a period of ten years. (To *bind* tariffs means to establish tariff ceilings.) Countries are also required to re-duce each individual tariff by at least 15 percent in developed coun-tries and by 10 percent in developing countries. Although the re-quirement for the minimum tariff reduction was intended to ensure that protection in all markets was reduced, a closer look at this ele-ment of the agreement shows that countries are left with a great deal of leeway. The focus here is on three factors that can effectively cause protection to be maintained at the pre–Uruguay Round level or even

Table 4.2   Summary of the Agreement on Agriculture

Subject	Rules	Base Period	Liberalization		Implementation Period
Market access	1. Tariffication of NTMs 2. Bind overall tariffs 3. No new NTMs	1986–1988	DCs: LDCs: LLDCs:	Reduce tariff by 36% Reduce tariff by 24% Tariff binding; no reduction	1995–2000 1995–2004
Domestic support	Specification of trade-distoring support policies	1986–1988	DCs: LDCs: LLDCs:	Reduce support by 20% Reduce support by 13.3% Support binding; no reduction	1995–2000 1995–2004
Export subsidies	1. Commodity specific categorization of assistance 2. No new subsidies for other commodities	1986–1990	DCs: LDCs: LLDCs:	Reduce 36% in terms of value and 21% in terms of volume Reduce 24% in terms of value and 14% in terms of volume Support binding; no reduction	1995–2000 1995–2004

Sources: GATT Secretariat (1994: 6–8); OECD (1995a: 15–18); UNCTAD (1994: 132–134); Tangermann (1994, 1996).
Notes: Non-tariff measures (NTMs); developed countries (DCs); less developed countries (LDCs); least developed countries (LLDCs).

Table 4.3   Estimated Actual Rate of Protection for Wheat and Sugar, 1979–1993 and 1986–1988 (percentage)

Country or Region	Wheat		Sugar	
	1979–1993	1986–1988	1979–1993	1986–1988
EU	57	106	150	234
United States	20	20	126	131
Japan	308	651	126	184
Brazil	56	98	NA	NA
Mexico	27	–1	–42	–58
Other Latin American countries	–25	–17	35	41
Nigeria	190	249	29	32
South Africa	7	10	50	98
Sub-Saharan Africa	–1	10	16	44

Source: Ingco (1996: 437).

raised to a higher level: the base period, "dirty" tariffication, and the method of calculating averages of tariff reductions.[5]

During the base period, 1986–1988, commodity world prices were in a trough. Since trade barriers are usually used to increase prices to domestic farmers, protection was relatively higher during that period. (The percentage PSE in Table 4.1 provides anecdotal evidence of higher relative support during 1986–1988 in OECD countries.) As a result, tariff equivalents based on that period are higher than tariff equivalents based on a more inclusive base period. Ingco's study (1996) suggested that ad valorem tariff equivalents estimated using 1979–1993 as the base period are significantly lower than those estimated using 1986–1988 as the base period, as shown in Table 4.3.[6] The negative rates of protection shown in Table 4.3 suggest that producers were taxed instead of supported, a phenomenon common in developing countries.

A number of studies (Ingco, 1996; OECD, 1995b; Tangermann, 1996) have shown that countries not only decided to use an "outlier" period as a reference point but also declared tariffs (for the purpose of implementing the Uruguay Round) that were higher than the protection that prevailed in 1986–1988. This situation is what is referred to as "dirty" tariffication. Although an accurate estimation of "dirty" tariffication is limited by data constraints, Ingco's study (1996) gave some suggestive evidence of its prevalence. The degree of "dirty" tariffication varied widely among countries and commodities, appearing mainly in sensitive commodities, as suggested by the numbers in

Table 4.4   Estimated Ad Valorem Tariff Equivalent and Tariffs Declared in Country Schedules for Wheat and Sugar, 1986–1988

Country or Region	Wheat		Sugar	
	Estimated	Declared	Estimated	Declared
EU	103	156	234	297
United States	20	6	131	197
Japan	651	240	184	126
Mexico	−1	74	−58	173
South Africa	10	75	98	124
Morocco	14	224	585	221

Source: Ingco (1996: 434). (Ingco's study contains estimates for additional commodities and additional countries.)

Table 4.4. For example, sugar and wheat, sensitive commodities in the United States and the EU, respectively, exhibit "dirty" tariffication. Although Japan could have bound its tariffs higher, note that its protection level in 1986–1988 was very high, especially for wheat.

A third important shortcoming of the market access element is that the overall tariff reductions are calculated on a simple average. Except for the constraint that each tariff be reduced by at least 15 percent in developed countries and 10 percent in developing countries, governments can eliminate low tariffs on less sensitive products and maintain high tariffs on others and still meet the rules of the agreement. It is possible, for example, as Tangermann (1994: 146) pointed out, for a country to meet the overall 36 percent simple average reduction by reducing tariffs on three items with very high tariff rates by 15 percent each and eliminating (that is, reducing by 100 per cent) a fourth item that had a very low tariff rate to begin with.

That appears to be what countries did. In implementing the market access element of the Agreement on Agriculture,

> The EU has exhibited a tendency to reduce low tariffs more than high tariffs. Japan and the USA have behaved in a similar way. As a consequence of this behaviour, even though the *average rate of reduction* was 36 percent in all countries, *average tariff levels* in all three countries were reduced by less than 36 per cent, and after tariff reductions the coefficient of variation of tariffs rate is, in all three countries, larger than before reductions. (Tangermann, 1996: 319)

Considering the base period that was used, "dirty" tariffication, and tariff reductions based on a simple average, it is possible for tariff equivalents to be more protective than the nontariff barriers they replace. Some estimates suggest that for sensitive commodities such as sugar and dairy products in the United States, if tariff ceilings were applied, they would provide more protection than that provided by nontariff barriers prior to the Uruguay Round, even at the end of the implementation period (Ingco, 1996: 436–438; Tangermann, 1996: 322–323).

Some tariffs have been bound at prohibitive levels, that is, at levels that would, in effect, prohibit imports.[7] This situation is true in developing countries as well. For example, sub-Saharan African countries that were allowed to set tariff bindings almost arbitrarily also bound their tariffs at very high levels. The following countries bound their tariffs (simple averages) at 100 percent or more: Burkina Faso, Burundi, Gambia, Kenya, Lesotho, Malawi, Mauritius, Mozambique, Nigeria, Tanzania, Zambia, and Zimbabwe (Sorsa, 1996: 289). Although all countries under the agreement had to bind their tariffs, most sub-Saharan African countries, being least developed, are not obligated to reduce their tariffs.

Domestic Support

Developed countries are required to reduce domestic production subsidies by 20 percent over a period of six years. Developing countries are required to reduce those subsidies by 13.3 percent over a period of ten years. These reductions are applied on the aggregate measure of support (AMS) rather than on individual commodities. AMS is the total value of support to all agricultural commodities in a given country. Countries, therefore, have broad discretion to reduce support from some commodities and even increase it on others (sensitive commodities).

In addition, given the biased nature of the base period (domestic support was highest in 1986–1988), the AMS commitments by OECD countries are actually redundant. AMS had already been reduced in the early 1990s to the levels below the final bound levels scheduled to be achieved by the year 2000. In other words, many OECD countries had actually already fulfilled their AMS commitments even before the implementation of the Agreement on Agriculture began (Tangermann, 1996: 324–325; OECD, 1995b: 39–42).

The so-called commitment by the United States would likewise be amusing, if one were to consider it lightheartedly.

The commitment entered into by the United States requires it to reduce its total AMS from the base period level of US$23.9 billion to a final bound level at the end of the implementation period of US$19.1 billion. Deficiency payments accounted for almost US$10 billion during the base period and have been included in the base and final bound commitments. However, they are excluded from current annual total AMS calculations. The result is a drop in current total AMS of such magnitude that the US need not contemplate any further change in policy in order to meet its AMS commitment. There are, therefore, likely to be virtually no policy changes required in response to AMS commitments in the US during the implementation period of the Agreement. (OECD, 1995b: 40)

What this means is that when the United States calculates its AMS to verify commitment fulfillment, it does not include deficiency payments as part of the AMS. (*Deficiency payments* are payments made to farmers to supplement market prices when those prices are below certain target levels.) However, when it calculates its AMS bound level commitment, deficiency payments are included!

The effectiveness of the AMS commitments will develop over time, since they were set in nominal terms. Inflation will slowly (very slowly, in developed countries where inflation rates are low) erode their real value.

With the exception of South Africa, sub-Saharan Africa did not make any AMS or export subsidy commitment (Sorsa, 1996). This is not surprising given that the net impact of macroeconomic and agricultural policies in most sub-Saharan African countries has been to tax farmers instead of subsidizing them. This is especially the case for export commodities.

Export Subsidies

Developed countries are required to reduce export subsidies by 36 percent in terms of value and by 21 percent in terms of quantities benefiting from such subsidies over a period of six years. The corresponding figures for developing countries are 24 percent and 14 percent, over a period of ten years. Export subsidies subject to reduction commitments include, inter alia, direct subsidies contingent on export performance, subsidies to reduce marketing costs of exports, and internal transport subsidies for exports (OECD, 1995b: 51).

Two main factors make this commitment more effective than the first two. The most important is that in many OECD countries, there was an increase in export subsidies after the base period (1986–1990).[8] As a result, just bringing export subsidies to the levels of the base period would be an accomplishment, especially presuming that subsidies would have continued to increase had the Agreement on Agriculture not been reached. The other main factor is that commitment levels were set on individual groups of commodities and not on aggregate, unlike the AMS reductions. This disaggregation of commodities, although partial, constrains countries to juggle export subsidies only within commodity groups.

The Impact of the Agreement on Agriculture on Sub-Saharan Africa

It is important to emphasize that since the Agreement on Agriculture left countries with a wide range of policy options, predicting its impact is difficult at this point. For example, countries can use different tariff rates within the tariff ceiling to achieve a target domestic price. In effect, this practice would work similarly to a variable import levy, which is not allowed under the Agreement on Agriculture (Ingco, 1996: 427).

In addition, health and safety standards, especially for products from developing countries, can be used to limit the actual liberalization in agriculture. Although the Agreement on Sanitary and Phytosanitary Measures reached by the Uruguay Round of GATT was supposed to standardize health and safety measures, unilateral trade restrictions are still common. For example, in December 1997, the EU banned Mozambican fish, claiming that cholera could be transmitted to European consumers through fish products. Japan, the largest importer of Mozambican fish, did not impose such trade restrictions. More important, in its January 1998 message to the EU's ministries of health, the World Health Organization testified that the fish import restrictions were not justified ("UN Agency," 1998).

The liberalization potential of the agreement is constrained further by a special safeguard clause. Countries are allowed to impose additional tariffs if imports of a particular product exceed a "trigger level" in terms of percentage of domestic consumption or if import prices fall below a "trigger price" based on the 1986–1988 price level (UNCTAD, 1994: 134). Thus, similar to the GSP program, the impact of the agreement will depend mainly on the spirit in which each country or region implements it.

All the limitations notwithstanding, the impact on sub-Saharan Africa of agricultural policy reforms in the OECD countries can be assessed by considering their potential impact on market accessibility and prices. Of course, since it is difficult to predict how much liberalization will actually occur, any assessment of the impact of the Agreement on Agriculture at this point must, to some degree, be speculative.

A safe prediction is that there will be only modest liberalization during the implementation period. In fact, it is possible that protection for some commodities, such as sugar, beef, and dairy products, will increase. Levels of OECD protection for nontraditional exports from sub-Saharan Africa, such as cut flowers, fruits, and vegetables, are difficult to predict at this point. Given varying possible outcomes, it is difficult to estimate what the impact of the Agreement on Agriculture will be on the volume and the diversification of export commodities from sub-Saharan Africa.

Regarding processed agricultural commodities, studies show that the market access commitments have somewhat reduced tariff escalation in the OECD countries on product chains that are important to developing countries, such as cocoa, coffee, vegetables, fruits, and nuts (UNCTAD, 1997b: 55–56). Such reduction of the difference between the nominal tariffs on processed products and the nominal rates on raw materials will tend to reduce the effective rate of protection on processed products in OECD countries. However, this potential increase in market openness for processed products may be countered by an increase in export subsidies for processed products.

Although commitments for export subsidy reductions are made on a disaggregated basis, each commodity group is still broad enough to allow decreases and increases of export subsidies within the group. One impact of an export subsidy is the increase in the domestic price of the product being subsidized. If this is a raw product, domestic producers who use it as an input will also demand an export subsidy, at least for the exported part of their output. Thus, export subsidies tend to escalate with value added. Given the commitment to reduce export subsidies and the constraint to reduce them within commodity groups, countries will most likely shift export subsidies to products with greater value added, for example, from wheat to wheat flour (Hathaway and Ingco, 1996: 50).

This possibility, however, should not concern sub-Saharan Africa too much. Export subsidy escalation will not be nearly as important as tariff escalation might be in deterring processing in sub-Saharan Africa. This conclusion is mainly based on the fact that the processing of tropical commodities such as coffee, cocoa, and tea (the major exports of sub-Saharan Africa) in OECD countries does not receive export subsidies. Most likely, the reduction in tariff escalation would outweigh any increase in export subsidy escalation that might occur. Overall, therefore, the Uruguay Round may increase access of SSA processed products into OECD countries.

The impact of OECD policy reforms on world prices is also expected to be modest. Perhaps the main source of price changes will be reductions in export subsidies, currently the most binding commitment. Liberalization in OECD countries would tend to increase world prices of agricultural commodities because of the OECD's countries' large share of world trade in those commodities. Reducing their import barriers will decrease domestic prices, reduce domestic production, and, thus, increase imports of commodities by the OECD countries. Consequently, world prices of agricultural commodities will increase. Likewise, reducing domestic support and export subsidies will reduce domestic production, further increasing demand for imports and decreasing exports into the world market, thus causing world prices to increase. The upward pressure on prices will be counterbalanced by an increase in production in some countries and a decrease of imports in others, as producers and consumers respond to changes in prices.

Projections by the Food and Agriculture Organization (FAO) suggest that the Uruguay Round will cause world prices of food commodities to increase by varying percentages, ranging from 0 to 10 percent (Greenfield et al., 1996: 367). The magnitude of the price increases is probably exaggerated by the fact that the base period used by the FAO is 1987–1989, a period during which world prices for food commodities were relatively low. Nonetheless, the potential increase in food prices is not welcome news to net importers of foodstuffs, as many sub-Saharan African countries are at present.

Indeed, a concern of many sub-Saharan African countries during the Uruguay Round negotiations was that policy reforms in the OECD countries would increase their food import bill. As a result, many of them lent their support to Egypt, Jamaica, Mexico, Morocco, and Peru, countries that cosponsored a proposal requesting compensation for increases in import bills (Hopkins, 1993: 149; UNCTAD, 1994: 133).

It is an understatement to say that African countries need assistance to foster their economic development. Many of them have an annual per capita income of less than $500. However, tying requests for assistance to liberalization in agriculture fails to recognize sub-Saharan Africa's long-term potential in agriculture. Needless to say, the proposal weakened sub-Saharan Africa's already minimal leverage in bargaining. How could sub-Saharan African countries "pressure" developed countries to open markets for their agricultural products while at the same time asking to be compensated for such policy reform?

Agriculture is sub-Saharan Africa's major economic sector, and its current level of performance is far below its potential. Although the projections to the year 2000 by the FAO raise some concern about the food situation in Africa, the culprit is not the Uruguay Round but rather, according to the study, the population increase. The FAO projections suggest the following for Africa: The Uruguay

Round effect on agricultural exports will be an increase of about U.S.$1.1 billion (about 27 percent of the total projected increase), and its effect on agricultural imports will be an increase of about U.S.$1 billion (about 15 percent of the total projected increase) (Greenfield et al., 1996: 372).

The same forecast by the FAO projects the Uruguay Round to have a negligible impact on aggregate food production. However, it suggests that there will be a shift of production from "developed countries of those commodities which have been subject to a high degree of protection in the past" to "low-cost producing countries, including on the whole the developing countries" (Greenfield et al., 1996: 366–368).

An earlier study by Valdés and Zietz (1980) suggested that a 50 percent reduction in agricultural trade barriers in OECD countries would cause a net welfare gain of about U.S.$90 million (1977 prices) for the nineteen sub-Saharan countries included in the study. Table 4.5 shows potential changes in export revenues and import expenditures associated with such trade liberalization. Although a 50 percent liberalization is unlikely in the immediate future, sub-Saharan African countries can, under more open conditions, increase their agricultural exports and reduce their import expenditure, that is, their dependence on imports.

Moreover, the projections in Table 4.5 focused only on direct trade barriers. Results would have been more robust if the removal of domestic support and export subsidies in OECD countries (which, indirectly, also act as trade barriers) had been incorporated into the study. Direct trade barriers such as tariffs and quotas on imports from sub-Saharan African countries clearly reduce economic welfare in the region. However, indirect barriers in OECD countries, such as production and export subsidies, also reduce welfare to sub-Saharan African countries that are net exporters of the subsidized commodities.

Figures 4.1 and 4.2 illustrate the impact of trade liberalization in OECD countries on a price-taking developing country for a homogeneous product.[9] These figures refer to the situation in a developing country that is a net importer. For a net exporting developing country, trade liberalization in OECD countries will certainly increase its economic welfare.

The DD line represents the demand line for the product. The SS line represents the supply line for the product. The preliberalization price of the product is Pw0, which is the world price. At that price, the volume of imports is the horizontal distance, ab. Liberalization in OECD countries causes the world price to increase. In Figure 4.1, if the world price increases to Pw1, the volume of imports decreases

Table 4.5 Potential Trade Effects on Sub-Saharan African Countries of a 50 Percent Reduction in Agricultural Trade Barriers in OECD Countries

Country	Change in Agricultural Export Revenue		Change in Agricultural Import Expenditure (U.S.$1,000)	Major Affected Export Commodity in Absolute Terms
	U.S.$1,000	Percent		
Angola	11,623	3.9	−2,452	Coffee
[Burkina Faso]	195	2.1	−387	Pulses
Cameroon	21,391	4.8	−552	Cocoa
[Côte d'Ivoire]	49,581	4.2	−2,101	Cocoa
[Democratic Republic of Congo]	9,879	4.3	−4,802	Coffee
Ghana	31,152	4.4	−1,945	Cocoa
Guinea	245	2.7	−102	Coffee
Kenya	18,415	5.9	−5,884	Beef
Madagascar	16,925	8.4	−1,185	Sugar
Malawi	9,686	6.3	−220	Beverages/tobacco
Mali	2,955	10.0	142	Vegetable oils
Mozambique	12,251	17.1	−1,219	Sugar
Niger	1,045	7.7	311	Vegetable oils
Nigeria	19,840	3.9	829	Cocoa
Rwanda	1,597	2.9	59	Coffee
Senegal	20,500	7.1	649	Vegetable oils
Tanzania	11,653	5.8	−4,371	Beef
Uganda	13,369	3.1	−64	Coffee
Zambia	943	8.2	−449	Beverages/tobacco

Source: Valdés and Zietz (1980: 33). Calculations by Valdés and Zietz used the base period of 1975–1977.

**Figure 4.1   The Static Impact of Trade Liberalization in OECD
Countries on a Small Importing Country**

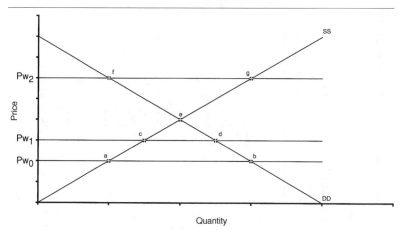

to cd. Consumer surplus decreases by area $Pw0bdPw1$ and producer
surplus increases by area $Pw0acPw1$. Thus, there is a net loss of area
abdc. However, if the world price increases to $Pw2$, the country becomes an exporter, the volume of exports being *fg*. Consumer surplus decreases by area $Pw0bfPw2$ and producer surplus increases by
area $Pw0agPw2$. If area *egf* is greater (less) than area *abe*, the country
will experience a net gain (loss).

**Figure 4.2   The Dynamic Impact of Trade Liberalization in OECD
Countries on a Small Importing Country**

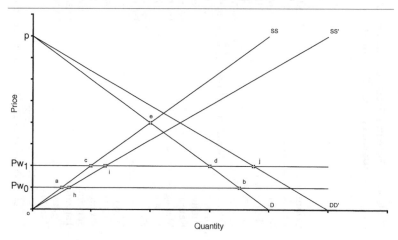

Figure 4.2 extends the analysis for possible shifts in the supply and demand lines. These shifts do not reflect changes in domestic policy. The increase in the world price and the stability of that price as a result of policy reforms in OECD countries and the establishment of new markets may induce more investment in the production of this product and, thus, increase supply to SS' (Valdés and Zietz, 1980: 16; Anderson and Tyers, 1990: 42–44). Likewise, the increase in the world price causes incomes of producers of this product to increase and, in turn, an increase in demand to DD'.[10] In this illustration, the volume of imports changes from ab to *ij*. The net change in consumer surplus is area *djp* minus area *Pw0bdPw1*. Producer surplus increases by the sum of areas *oha* and *Pw0hiPw1*. Even though the country continues to import this product, it will experience a net welfare gain if the sum of areas *djp* and *oha* exceeds area hbdi.

Becoming a net exporter, therefore, is not a prerequisite in order for sub-Saharan African countries to register net gains from the liberalization in OECD countries. Still, many sub-Saharan African countries do have the potential of being net exporters of food. The partial equilibrium analysis illustrated in Figures 4.1 and 4.2 and the empirical study by Valdés and Zietz (1980) did not adjust for liberalization of the agricultural sector in sub-Saharan Africa. However, as Sorsa (1996: 304) pointed out, it has been demonstrated that most gains from the Uruguay Round would come from countries' own liberalization efforts (Anderson and Tyers, 1990; Runge, 1993).

Yet, except for South Africa, sub-Saharan Africa did not commit to any significant liberalization in agriculture in the Uruguay Round. Although tariffication may have increased the transparency of trade barriers, tariffs have been bound very high. One could argue that at least now sub-Saharan African countries have bound their tariffs. Prior to the conclusion of the Uruguay Round of GATT, they had no tariff ceilings. However, these high tariff bindings, together with other duties and charges, allow countries effectively to have the same barriers on imports as they had before the Uruguay Round. More important, since production and export taxes are not covered by the WTO, the Uruguay Round has left most sub-Saharan policy options intact.

Sub-Saharan African Perspectives on the Agreement on Agriculture

The preceding discussion of the Agreement on Agriculture, which established that SSA countries could gain from liberalization in the OECD countries and their own liberalization, raises two questions.

Why did the SSA countries take a position (asking to be compensated) that may have contributed to the modesty of the policy reform package for developed countries? Why did they not commit to liberalizing their own agricultural sectors?

There are several possible explanations: the "too poor to compete" syndrome, uncertainty about their own potential, uncertainty about the impact of the agreements, a lack of clear trade objectives, income distribution and domestic politics, strategy, and the marginalization factor.

The "Too Poor to Compete" Syndrome

Since sub-Saharan Africa is economically poor, the first inclination is to think of it as a region that cannot compete in the world market. Ruling out the ability of sub-Saharan Africa to compete has often become a way of showing how sensitive one is to the region's economic situation. Thus, when negotiations to reduce export subsidies in developed countries began, the initial reaction from sub-Saharan African countries was to request compensation for increases in import bills, forgetting that many of them have the potential to be net exporters of food.

Instead of requesting compensation (connected to liberalization), African countries should have tried to organize themselves (1) to "pressure" developed countries to open their markets for nontraditional agricultural commodities and processed agricultural products and (2) to request concrete technical and financial assistance to produce nontraditional products and to develop the necessary processing capabilities. This is the kind of attitude that African leaders need, to give sub-Saharan Africa a chance to capitalize on its comparative advantage. To the extent that competition improves the allocation of resources, sub-Saharan Africa cannot afford not to compete. The poorer a country is, the more carefully it must consider current and future opportunity costs in the allocation of its resources.

Uncertainty About Their Own Potential

Perhaps the apparent fear of competition is a reflection of a more fundamental problem, uncertainty about one's own potential. Yet the high potential for increased agricultural output for most SSA countries has been documented in many studies. For example, as shown in Table 4.5, the removal of trade barriers in industrialized countries on agricultural products could increase exports from various sub-Saharan African countries by 2 to 17 percent. Moreover, the competitiveness encouraged by trade helps to reveal a country's potential and at the same time expand that potential.

Uncertainty About the Impact of the Agreements

The Uruguay Round consisted of many complex agreements. The agreements themselves, let alone their likely long-term impact, were not always clear to all participants. This is particularly the case for SSA, which had relatively very limited technical (and diplomatic) representation in the negotiations. Whereas developed countries had specialists for each specific area of negotiation, the SSA countries that participated in the negotiations were represented by generalists. For example, in the final negotiations of the Uruguay Round in 1993, Japan had more than 100 representatives, Tanzania had two, Ghana had one, and Angola had none.

Competent as those few sub-Saharan African representatives may have been, they were too few in number and their resources too limited to fathom all the intricacies of economics, law, science, strategy, and politics involved. It should be noted that UNCTAD did provide valuable technical assistance to developing countries. In addition, developing countries, for their part, used a group system to share information and formulate strategies together, where they could identify common interests. Even though these initiatives, especially the UNCTAD technical assistance, helped to bridge the information disparity between developed and developing countries, there was still significant uncertainty. Accordingly, SSA countries wanted to retain their policy options wherever possible. They signed off on the agreements because they knew it would be difficult to join the WTO later; they subsequently requested and attended workshops by the WTO to help them understand the agreements better.

A Lack of Clear Trade Objectives

The intricacies of negotiations notwithstanding, SSA countries seem to lack clear trade objectives or, perhaps, trade priorities. This problem is exemplified by their position, or lack of a clear position, on agricultural food production and food security. On the one hand, they wanted to be compensated for the increase in world prices resulting from the implementation of the agreement by developed countries. On the other hand, they bound tariffs at a very high rate that, if used, would increase domestic prices; this was done presumably to protect domestic producers and, thus, reduce these countries' dependence on food imports.

For a variety of reasons, countries usually want to achieve some minimum self-sufficiency in food. There is an argument that promoting food production in developing countries, which are largely rural, helps to reduce food insecurity because "most of those people who are food-insecure live in rural areas, earn a substantial share of their income from agriculture, and obtain some of their nutritional requirements directly from their own food production" (UNCTAD, 1997b: 63). If the objective of using tariffs, however, is to increase domestic prices and, thus, domestic production, the need to use and/or increase tariffs should be reduced by the overall increase in world prices of food resulting from the agreement.

Instead of considering this impact of the agreement on domestic production, SSA focused on its impact on net buyers of food. The concern here was food security for the urban population that buys most of its food. Of course, governments must be concerned with the welfare of their entire population. Yet the objective of promoting self-sufficiency in food production is inextricably linked with higher domestic prices, whereas the interests of urban residents are to keep food prices low. High tariffs on food products and compensation for high prices of food, to some extent, reflect a lack of clear objectives and/or clear programs to achieve objectives. Domestic policies in many sub-Saharan African countries that continue to tax farmers add to the obscurity of the objectives.

Income Distribution and Domestic Politics

Politics play an important role in determining government trade policies. In developed countries, although farmers are few in number, they are a strong political constituency and, thus, are supported at the expense of consumers. In sub-Saharan Africa, countries tend to support consumers at the expense of farmers, particularly producers of export crops, which have been taxed.[11] The interests of sub-Saharan African farmers were hardly represented in the Uruguay Round. For example, in Tanzania the Tanganyika Farmers Association, whose members are from all over the Tanzanian mainland, was not consulted for its views at any point during the eight years of negotiations.

Since urban residents (30 percent of the population) in sub-Saharan Africa are a powerful political constituency, governments tend to worry about them first. Sharp price increases, especially for staple foods such as maize, wheat, and rice, can cause civil and/or political unrest. For example, a 21 percent increase in the price of maize in Zimbabwe in January 1998 caused violent riots and looting in the capital city, Harare ("Zimbabwe," 1998).

Nonetheless, it is important to support policies that increase incomes for small farmers. Rural workers in the agricultural sector (70 percent of the labor force in SSA) are, on average, poorer than those working in urban areas in the manufacturing or service sectors. In Zimbabwe, for example, in the period between 1984 and 1993 (inclusive), the average wage for an agricultural worker was about one-fourth the average wage for a worker in manufacturing (World Bank, 1997c: 293, 297). Thus, policy changes that would benefit the rural labor force would reduce real income inequality.

Strategy

Another possible explanation for the agreement reached by SSA countries in the Uruguay Round—not to commit to trade liberalization—is that it was a strategic decision. Since the late 1980s, many SSA countries have been liberalizing their economies, typically under the guidance, "arm-twisting," and threats of the IMF and World Bank. The IMF and World Bank often exercise direct influence on countries' domestic policies, trade related or otherwise, and their budgets. Liberalization is an ongoing process that is often aided and/or rewarded with loans from those institutions. If SSA countries had committed to trade liberalization in the Uruguay Round, they could have lost leverage they might have had and could have been pushed even further in their negotiations for loans from the IMF and World Bank. That is, strategically, the WTO is not as important to SSA as are the IMF and World Bank.

The Marginalization Factor

It is important to note that since SSA countries are marginal players in world trade, their commitments were, to some extent, seen as a token. Some SSA countries were simply asked to "just give us a number" at which they wanted to bind their tariffs. Giving countries such flexibility may reflect a concern for the least developed countries, but it also reflects just how marginalized the commitments of SSA are.

◆ ◆ ◆

Whatever the reason(s) might be for a lack of real commitment to liberalize the agricultural sector, SSA must give the dictates of current and potential comparative advantage a chance, especially in agriculture. Unfortunately, the OECD countries have set a very bad example with their protective measures on the agricultural sector—both direct (e.g., tariffs, quotas, and voluntary export restraints) and indirect (e.g., domestic and export subsidies). These practices may cause some SSA countries to be skeptical about liberalizing their own agricultural sectors. However, inefficient policies in one country do not justify inefficiency in another. Retaliation (hardly the motive behind domestic policies in sub-Saharan Africa), which is often cited by politicians as an argument for restricting trade, does not make sense from an economic point of view. (Some case could be made for retaliation or threats of retaliation, though, if that might lead to a lowering of trade barriers by other countries.)

In addition, OECD countries did not get wealthy because of their protectionist agricultural policies. In fact, agricultural protection has cost these countries tremendous deadweight losses. For example, according to a study by Hufbauer and Elliott (1994: 4–5, 8–9, 12–13), U.S. protection of the sugar industry caused it a *net* welfare loss of about $580 million in 1990. This was about $257,000 of *net* welfare loss for each job created by protection.

One could almost say OECD countries have behaved like "spoiled" rich people, "wasting food" because they could afford to do so. Of course, as the Agreement on Agriculture suggests, even the "spoiled" OECD countries have come to the realization that they could not afford such costly protectionist policies indefinitely.

SSA cannot afford measures, such as export taxes or high tariffs, that breed an inefficient allocation of resources. Thus, for SSA, even policies or programs aimed at achieving export diversification or some minimum self-sufficiency in food must have clear and achievable objectives; be the least costly, given the objectives; and be implemented within the limits dictated by opportunity costs and other economic constraints.

The Textile and Clothing Industry in Sub-Saharan Africa

The overall exports of textile fabrics and apparel (clothing) from sub-Saharan Africa as a share of this region's total value of merchandise exports are small, only about 2 percent. However, the contribution of this sector to the total value of merchandise exports varies considerably among sub-Saharan countries, ranging from almost 0 percent in a few countries to over 50 percent in Mauritius (UNCTAD, 1997a: 112–133).

In addition, the percentages do not reveal the importance of the textiles and clothing industry in sub-Saharan African countries as a possible stepping-stone to industrialization. The textiles industry has served as a gateway to industrialization for many countries for many years, from the eighteenth century for the United Kingdom to the 1970s and 1980s for Mauritius.

Although producing the needed raw materials is neither a necessary nor sufficient condition for a country to develop a textiles industry, it is still perplexing that overall sub-Saharan Africa, with its large production of cotton, has not been able to develop this industry. Sub-Saharan Africa's share of cotton exports in the world market is about 10 percent. Currently cotton contributes more than 15 percent of the merchandise export revenue in the following countries: Benin, Burkina Faso, Mali, Sudan, Tanzania, and Togo. These and many other sub-Saharan African countries, therefore, have one important ingredient for developing and/or expanding the textiles industry.

It would seem that processing cotton would help sub-Saharan Africa in at least three ways. First, it would create vertical integration, lacking in many sectors in sub-Saharan Africa. Cotton is spun into yarn, and yarn is woven into fabric. Fabric is cut and sewn into garments, home furnishings (such as linens and draperies), luggage, and sewn toys. Second, processing cotton would generate more export revenue and/or reduce imports of textile fabrics and clothes. Third, the process would increase employment and incomes in sub-Saharan Africa.

The textiles and clothing industry, particularly clothing, is a relatively labor-intensive industry. The standardized work in the industry, that is, the operation of textile and sewing machines, does not require much technical knowledge. Workers rarely get formal training except for on-the-job training (Singleton, 1997: 26–33). Since the 1970s, there has been increased mechanization, automation, and large-scale production in textiles in developed countries. However, small- to medium-sized firms that continue to be labor intensive continue to thrive in the industry. In addition, small, labor-intensive operations are still the norm in apparel (Cline, 1990: 83–88).

The textiles and apparel industry, owing to its intensity in unskilled and semiskilled labor—resources that are relatively abundant in developing countries—has opened the door to industrialization for many countries. It did just that for Mauritius in the 1970s and 1980s. The textiles and apparel industry is also growing in a few other countries in sub-Saharan Africa, such as Kenya, Lesotho, Madagascar, South Africa, and Zimbabwe. Overall, however, the textile and apparel industry in SSA is underdeveloped.

If raw materials are available and relatively cheap labor is abundant in sub-Saharan Africa, what is holding (has held) back the textile and apparel industry in sub-Saharan Africa? There are several factors, including the colonial legacy, domestic policies, the lack of financial capital, poor infrastructure, a relatively limited supply of skilled labor and competent managers, and protection in developed countries.

The Colonial Legacy

The trade development initiatives by colonialists promoted production of raw materials primarily to supply industries in Europe. The transportation system—roads, railway, and ports—was developed with the main objective of shipping raw materials out of Africa. Colonial economic policies on investment, agriculture (e.g., what was to be produced and by whom), and trade were all geared toward assigning African colonies the role of producing primary products and limiting them to that role. Only in a few countries, such as Kenya and Zimbabwe, where colonialists dreamed they would stay for the longer term, did some meaningful industrialization take place. The exportation of cotton by African countries to developed countries accordingly is not unique to this commodity. Large proportions of all commodities produced in sub-Saharan Africa have been exported unprocessed.

Many sub-Saharan African countries have been independent since the 1960s. Almost forty years later, it is tempting to discount the impact of colonialism. The residual impact of colonialism—exploitation, an incoherent infrastructure, and constraining mentalities in the colonizing countries and Africa—is not, however, easy to correct and erase. There are still people within and outside sub-Saharan Africa who carry the colonial and prejudiced attitudes that Africans are not capable of producing manufactured goods. Thus, they believe Africans should continue to produce and export raw materials and import processed goods from those raw materials. Many African countries do have a natural comparative advantage in many raw materials. However, there are no natural barriers holding African countries back from developing a comparative advantage in other areas, such as the processing of those raw materials.

The negative impact of colonialism is more conspicuous where it left political instability behind. The political instability and/or dictatorships that ensued after independence, attributed to colonialism and perpetuated by the Cold War, destroyed resources and discouraged investment in many sub-Saharan African countries.

Domestic Policies

As discussed in Chapter 2, interest rate policies in the 1970s and 1980s in many countries inadvertently limited capital and, thus, limited investment opportunities. At the same time, exchange rate policies and cumbersome and ever-changing procedures for acquiring investment permits discouraged both domestic investment and foreign direct investment in the textile industry and other industries. In some countries, the government directly controlled the textiles industry.

In Tanzania, for example, most of the textiles industry was directly under the state's control. Although trade barriers and subsidies helped the state-owned factories grow, several factors—a shortage of working capital and skilled labor, inefficiency, inadequate maintenance (common in state monopolies), and a lack of imported raw materials—caused the capacity utilization in these factories to decline from about 60 percent in the 1970s to less than 20 percent (less than 5 percent in some factories) in the early 1990s (Mbelle and Sterner, 1991; Hastings and Msimangira, 1992; "How Africa Should Industrialize," 1995a).

Domestic policies on employment, such as minimum wage legislation and rules governing layoffs, may also have reduced sub-Saharan African competitiveness in the textiles and clothing industry. A study by Lindauer and Velenchik (1994) showed that wages in the manufacturing sector were higher in Africa than they were in Asia in the 1980s. It is important to note that the wages were measured relative to productivity and in a common currency; the lack of competitiveness was found whether the authors used official exchange rates or parallel market exchange rates. Although absolute manufacturing wages are relatively very low in Africa, the results from Lindauer and Velenchik are not surprising given that productivity in manufacturing in sub-Saharan Africa was also extremely low for the reasons discussed earlier. Moreover, in most of the 1980s, many sub-Saharan African countries still had significant direct control over production in the manufacturing sector. A study by Biggs et al. (1996), using data from 1994 and focusing on garment production, suggested that sub-Saharan Africa can compete on the basis of low relative wages.

The Lack of Financial Capital

Domestic policies on interest rates explain only part of the capital problem. Even with better domestic policies, financial institutions in sub-Saharan Africa are still underdeveloped and savings are very low. In such a situation, financial capital needed for buildings, machinery, and working capital is scarce.

Poor Infrastructure

Development of the textiles industry, and industrialization in general, requires a reliable and broad economic infrastructure for transportation (roads and railway), communication (telephones), production (electricity and water), and waste disposal (sewerage systems). The infrastructure in many sub-Saharan African countries is very poor both in absolute terms and relative to Asian countries with which they compete now and will in the future (World Bank, 1994c: 244–245). This situation makes it difficult to attract foreign direct investment.

A Limited Supply of Skilled Labor and Competent Managers

The textiles and apparel industry overall is labor intensive. Most of the labor required is unskilled and semiskilled labor, both types of which are readily available in sub-Saharan African countries. Some key jobs, however, require individuals who are highly skilled—for instance, technicians who service or repair machines, pattern designers, and managers who can effectively run production units and understand the intricacies of the textiles and apparel market. Sub-Saharan Africa, on average, lags behind developing Asian countries in the supply of such labor.

Protection in Developed Countries

This factor is mentioned with caution. The Multi-Fiber Arrangement (MFA), under which developed countries set quotas for textiles and apparels imported from developing countries, did not have much negative impact overall on sub-Saharan Africa. In fact, the MFA (and the Lomé Convention for the EU market) helped sub-Saharan Africa by insulating its exports from fierce competition with Asian producers who, under free market conditions, could have easily been exporting beyond their quotas. However, the MFA quotas set by the United States have limited imports of textiles from Mauritius and Kenya.

Mauritius became subject to the U.S. quota system in 1985. Although the quota did not reduce the volume of exports of textiles from Mauritius to the United States at the time, it discouraged potential investors who had their eyes on the U.S. market. Nonetheless, the Mauritius textile industry was able to grow, mainly because of its good domestic policies and access to the EU market.

Kenya's pillowcases and men's and boys' woven shirts became subject to U.S. quotas in 1994 when Kenya was already dependent on the U.S. market. The quota caused Kenya's exports of textiles to the United States to drop by almost 40 percent. The direct result was that about 10,000 jobs (out of about 15,000) were lost, and about thirty companies (out of about forty) exited the industry (Phillips, 1996; Jacobs, 1997: 88–89). (See the case at the end of this chapter.)

Protection of the Textile and Clothing Industry in OECD Countries

Perhaps in no area have OECD countries failed to practice what they preach about free trade as much as they have in the textiles and clothing industry. In the 1950s and 1960s, when GATT was negotiating reductions of tariff barriers, the United States and the EEC were actively increasing protection of their textile and clothing industries. The market-determined price differential (i.e., not attributable to dumping or subsidies) between imports and comparable domestic goods was used "as a basis for determining the need for protection," instead of using it as the basis for trade (Cline, 1990: 147).

This protection scheme was typical of many barriers. It worked as follows: (1) The scheme initially targeted products only from Japan and later covered products from emerging low-cost producing countries such as Taiwan, Hong Kong, South Korea, and even least developed countries such as Bangladesh (World Bank, 1987: 160) and Sri Lanka (Yoffie and Austin, 1983: 6). (2) The scheme initially covered only cotton products and then expanded to include wool and synthetic fibers and later all vegetable fibers and silk blends (UNCTAD, 1994: 129). (3) The scheme was envisioned to be temporary, then moved from one-year restrictions under the Short Term Arrangement (STA) to four-year restrictions under the Long Term Arrangement (LTA) and, later, the MFA. The MFA was established in 1974 under the auspices of GATT.

UNCTAD has characterized the MFA as "a major contradiction to the basic principles of GATT" (UNCTAD, 1994: 129). Cline (1990: 151) described the contradiction:

> Despite the dominant but arguable policy view at the time that the establishment of the MFA was on balance liberalizing compared to

the realistic alternatives, the arrangement was an embarrassing breach of GATT principles, not unlike the earlier glaring exception to these principles in GATT's dispensations granted to agricultural trade. The MFA violated the most-favored-nation principle by permitting discriminatory treatment among supplier countries. It broke the general GATT mandate of applying tariff rather than quota protection. It undermined the principle of assured market access through tariff binding by making access contingent. Importantly, the MFA also established a precedent of imposing quantitative restrictions against developing countries (and in this case Japan as well) but not against industrial countries.

The MFA has allowed industrialized countries to set import quotas. The U.S. MFA has set quotas even for the least developed countries such as Bangladesh and Haiti (U.S. International Trade Commission, 1994: 136). As noted earlier, two sub-Saharan African countries that have been affected by the U.S. textiles and apparel quotas are Mauritius and Kenya.

One of the achievements of the Uruguay Round, therefore, was to reach an agreement that lays the foundation for incorporating textiles and apparel into GATT, thereby phasing out the MFA. Developing countries had protested the protection of the textiles and clothing industry for decades. It became their main issue in the Uruguay Round (UNCTAD, 1994: 129). Unlike the previous rounds of negotiations, developing countries had some leverage in the Uruguay Round—the developed countries' demand to extend GATT discipline to the areas of intellectual property rights and services. It is very unlikely that the agreements on intellectual property and trade in services (areas in which industrialized countries have comparative advantage) could have been achieved without an agreement that promised to integrate the textiles and clothing industry into GATT.

The Agreement on Textiles and Clothing

The Agreement on Textiles and Clothing partly extends the MFA while gradually phasing it out over a period of ten years (January 1995 to December 2004). The two main components of the phasing-out process are summarized in Table 4.6. One is gradually to integrate into the WTO the textile and apparel products listed in October 1994 in the Annex to the Agreement. The other is gradually to increase quotas of the remaining products, over a period of ten years. The products listed in the Annex, that is, the product cover-

Table 4.6   Summary of the Agreement on Textiles and Clothing

Growth Stage	Period	Share of Imports to Be Integrated on the First Day of the Period (percent)	Increase in the Quota Rate (percent)
1	1/1/1995–12/31/1997	16	16
2	1/1/1998–12/31/2001	17	25
3	1/1/2002–12/31/2004	18	27
4	1/1/2005	49	no more quotas

age, are determined by importing countries. It is significant to note that countries may include products that initially were not even under the MFA.

Product integration. The product integration process will be carried out progressively in four stages. On January 1, 1995, products listed in the Annex, accounting for not less than 16 percent of the total volume of imports of all products in the list, were integrated into the WTO and, thus, were to be governed by its general rules. The volume of imports in 1990 was used as the base. On January 1, 1998, products accounting for not less than an additional 17 percent of the 1990 volume of imports were integrated. On January 1, 2002, products accounting for not less than an additional 18 percent of the 1990 volume of imports are to be integrated. All remaining products are to be integrated immediately following the end of the transition period, that is, on January 1, 2005 (GATT Secretariat, 1994: 8–9).

The agreement stipulated that the integration of products into the WTO must include products from each of the four groups: tops and yarns, fabrics, made-up textiles, and clothing. In addition, once a product has been integrated, it cannot be removed from the normal rules of the WTO.

Increase of quotas. During the transition period, quotas for the products yet unintegrated into the WTO are to be increased annually, as shown in Table 4.6. On January 1, 1995, former MFA quota growth rates were increased by 16 percent. On January 1, 1998, the growth rates were increased by 25 percent, and on January 1, 2002, they are to be increased by 27 percent.[12] On January 1, 2005, there should be no more quotas, as all the products will be covered by WTO rules.

◆ ◆ ◆

During the phase-out period, importing countries can use the "transitional safeguard mechanism" provision to impose restrictions on imports of textiles and clothing if they determine imports cause "serious damage" to their domestic industries. These new barriers can only be applied to products not yet integrated into the WTO. As already noted, however, this can apply to products that were not protected under the MFA and/or to countries that did not participate in the MFA.

Like many other multilateral agreements, the trade-liberating impact of this agreement during the phasing-out period will depend largely on the spirit with which countries implement it. Forty-nine percent of the products covered by the MFA are exempt from the WTO until the end of the ten-year period. Importing countries can, therefore, easily delay the integration of their sensitive products until the very last day of the transition period and still meet the obligations of the agreement.[13] The agreement stipulates that integration of products into the WTO must include products from each of the four groups. However, the selection of products to be integrated within those groups is completely at the discretion of importing countries.

Since countries can include products that were not initially under the MFA, they could first integrate those products, effectively resulting in zero liberalization. Even if integrating products that were under the MFA, countries could start with the products for which the quotas were not filled, that is, products for which quotas were redundant. Likewise, since the integration takes place on the basis of volume alone, "it is possible to integrate a high volume share, corresponding to a relatively low value, thus meeting the obligations of the Agreement, but deferring the economic impact" (Smeets, 1995: 99). In fact, protection of the products deemed to be sensitive could be increased during the transitional period with the application of the transitional safeguard mechanism.

As important as the Agreement on Textiles and Clothing might be, available evidence suggests that there will be no meaningful liberalization until the end of the transition period. Approximately 50 percent of the products listed in the Annex to the Agreement by the EU were not under restrictions under the MFA quota system. In the United States, the products integrated into the WTO on January 1, 1995, included no products that were subject to MFA quotas. The United States is expected to delay integration of up to 80 percent of the products that were subject to MFA quotas until the very last day of the phase-out period.

Other Related U.S. Trade Actions

After the Agreement on Textiles and Clothing was reached, the United States also changed its definition of the "rules of origin" to shift the "origin" of certain U.S. imports to targeted countries—China, India, and Pakistan. The changes became effective on July 1, 1996. For apparel products, "in most instances, the new rules will make the country in which assembly occurs the origin country [as opposed to where the parts were cut, under the old rule]" (Jacobs, 1995: 16). This change specifically targeted China, a non-WTO member that assembles parts cut in Hong Kong and Taiwan and is the largest source of textile and apparel imports into the United States. With more of those imports now considered Chinese, the United States can continue to shield its domestic producers even after the transitional period, so long as China is not a member of the WTO.[14]

For nonapparel products, such as bed linens, the countries of origin generally changed from those in which the fabric was cut and sewn to those in which the fabric was produced (Jacobs, 1995: 17). This change apparently targeted India and Pakistan. Their quotas under the MFA now include bed linens and other nonapparel products sewn in other countries using their linen. This causes their quotas to be reached more quickly, allowing the United States to keep more of their goods out.

Although this rule change was not intended to hurt sub-Saharan African countries, it has caused Kenya to suffer significant loss. Kenya's bed sheet production used fabric imported from Pakistan. With the rule change, the bed sheets were considered Pakistani and, thus, subject to U.S. quotas under the MFA. Since the United States was the most important market for "Kenya's" bed sheets, subjecting them to quotas forced many Kenyan sheet manufacturing facilities out of business (Jacobs, 1997: 89).

H.R. 1432, the African Growth and Opportunity Act, was introduced in the U.S. House of Representatives in 1998. The bill could have reversed the fate Kenya suffered under the MFA quotas and the change in the "rules of origin." Although the bill ultimately did not pass, it received a great deal of attention, in part owing to the unprecedented trip to Africa by President Clinton in 1998. Since components of this trade bill are still considered to be attractive to some, and it could be resurrected in some form in the future, it merits discussion.[15]

The bill combined some modest economic assistance with an important political statement. It called for the United States and sub-Saharan African countries to promote investment in sub-Saharan

Africa and to liberalize trade between the United States and sub-Saharan Africa. The bill had the support of the governments of many sub-Saharan African countries, and it represented a significant change in attitude on both sides of the Atlantic, shifting the emphasis from "aid" to "trade."

It should be noted, however, that the bill to some degree reflected underlying mercantilist attitudes, especially regarding the liberalization of trade in textiles and apparel. The January 13, 1997, letter from the House Ways and Means Committee to the U.S. International Trade Commission requesting the latter to conduct a study on the likely impact of the proposed legislation suggested that freer trade liberalization is good and would continue, so long as sub-Saharan Africa did not become too successful.

> Sub-Saharan Africa supplied less than one percent, or about $400 million, of U.S. imports of textiles and apparel in 1995. The bill provides that, until imports of these articles from Sub-Saharan Africa reach a much higher level, the transitional safeguards provided in Article 6 of the Uruguay Round Agreement on Textiles and Clothing should not apply. (U.S. International Trade Commission, 1997: A-2)

A partial equilibrium study by the U.S. International Trade Commission estimated that employment in the textiles and apparel industry would decrease, at most, by only 676 full-time equivalent jobs as a result of the removed quotas and duties on U.S. textiles and apparel imports from sub-Saharan Africa (U.S. International Trade Commission, 1997: 3-11–3-12). Almost the entire impact would have been on the apparel sector. The projected reduction in employment represented about 0.1 percent of employment in the apparel sector, that is, one job out of one thousand. These findings by the U.S. International Trade Commission were welcome by the proponents of the bill since they projected only a minor negative impact on employment in the U.S. textiles and apparel industry.

The proposition for trade liberalization on textiles and apparel in the bill hinged on projections that production of textiles and apparel would not grow much in sub-Saharan Africa, rather than on the intrinsic advantages of freer trade. The lack of competitiveness of sub-Saharan Africa was given a prominent place in the bill—it was the top-listed "finding."

> The lack of competitiveness of sub-Saharan Africa in the global market, especially in the manufacturing sector, make[s] it a limited threat to market disruption and no threat to United States jobs. An-

nual textile and apparel exports to the United States from sub-Saharan Africa represent less than 1 percent of all textile and apparel exports to the United States, which totaled $45,932,000,000 in 1996. Sub-Saharan Africa has limited textile manufacturing capacity. During 1998 and the succeeding 4 years, this limited capacity to manufacture textiles and apparel is projected to grow at a modest rate. Given this limited capacity to export textiles and apparel, it will be very difficult for these exports from sub-Saharan Africa, during 1998 and the succeeding 9 years, to exceed 3 percent annually of total imports of textile and apparel to the United States. [It was about 1 percent in 1997.] If these exports from sub-Saharan Africa remain around 3 percent of total imports, they will not represent a threat to United States workers, consumers, or manufacturers. (U.S. House of Representatives, 1998: 19, lines 15–25; 20, lines 1–11)

It is not clear how even a larger volume of imports would have represented a threat to consumers. Eliminating quotas and tariffs on U.S. imports of textiles and apparel from sub-Saharan Africa would increase consumer surplus. The study by the U.S. International Trade Commission (1997: 3–12) suggested that the *net* welfare gain to the United States, that is, the gain in consumer surplus minus losses in producer surplus and tariff revenue, would be somewhere between $47 million and $97 million a year. This is a relatively large gain considering that the trade barriers on sub-Saharan African exports of textiles protect only about 676 jobs. In other words, the *net* welfare gain in the United States from removing these trade barriers for each full-time equivalent job being protected by quotas and tariffs in the textiles and apparel industry is about $70,000 to $143,000.

It is well known that the textiles and apparel manufacturers are a powerful political constituency in the United States. Thus, one could argue it was only realistic (in an attempt to see the bill passed) to have taken this position that safeguard measures would be applied if imports from sub-Saharan Africa reached a "higher level" and to emphasize the lack of competitiveness of sub-Saharan Africa in the global market. Nonetheless, this position seemed to be hypocritical.

If sub-Saharan African countries were to use the same criteria for industries in which they lack comparative advantage, that is, if they were only to allow free trade for given products so long as their producers were not affected, they would not meet eligibility requirements of the U.S. bill. To be eligible to participate in programs and projects under the bill, sub-Saharan African countries would have been required, among other things, to "promote free movement of goods and services between the United States and sub-Saharan

Africa and among countries in sub-Saharan Africa"[16] (U.S. House of Representatives, 1998: 4, lines 6–8).

Although Sub-Saharan African countries (Kenya and Mauritius, in particular) would benefit from a more open textiles and apparel market in the United States, they must be careful not to become too dependent on the U.S. market. The resistance to freer trade by the U.S. textiles and apparel manufacturers and their political power leave a measure of uncertainty as to the future of U.S. trade requirements in this sector.

The Impact of the Agreement on Textiles and Clothing on Sub-Saharan Africa

Apart from the negative impact on Kenya of the related change in the "rules of origin" by the United States, the overall impact of the agreement itself during the implementation period will be minimal, if any.[17] The reason is that there will be only modest liberalization during the implementation period. Moreover, only two sub-Saharan African countries (Kenya and Mauritius) were subject to (U.S.) quotas to begin with, at the start of the implementation of the agreement.

The concern of sub-Saharan African countries is that when the textiles and clothing industry is fully integrated into the WTO in 2005, they will be fully exposed to competition with Asian producers who have a competitive advantage. That is, sub-Saharan African countries will lose the trade that had been diverted to their products by the margin of preference created by quotas on Asian products. A study by Biggs et al. (1996: 80) showed that the quota scheme adds to the cost of men's casual shirts imported into Europe from India and China by about 14 percent and 24 percent, respectively. Needless to say, investment decisions depend on the prospects for future demand, including exports, and in that sense the removal of the MFA may make the environment worse, not better, for African textile firms.

The African Growth and Opportunity Act was described by its proponents and supported by many African countries as a means of giving sub-Saharan Africa some lead time to prepare the region for such competition. It is possible that the act would have helped a few countries by serving as a catalyst and ushering U.S. investors to sub-Saharan Africa. The actual economic assistance stipulated in the act, however, was too modest to make any significant direct impact.[18]

Conclusion

The textiles and clothing industry and especially the agricultural sector represent two areas that have been most subsidized and protected in developed countries. Subsidies and protection in the EU made the region a net exporter of many agricultural products, in spite of its comparative disadvantage. Protection of the textiles and clothing industry in developed countries has grown at the same rate as these countries have been losing comparative advantage in this industry.

Bringing these two industries under WTO rules is certainly to be commended. However, the length of time it took for the agreements to be reached and the "nonimplementation" during the implementation period reveal how imbedded the mercantilist attitudes are, even in those countries most vocal about the merits of free trade.

The damage done by the agricultural policies in the OECD countries will have lasting negative effects on low-cost producing countries. For example, the price support program for sugar in the United States caused a growing use of high-fructose corn syrup (HFCS) as a sugar substitute. According to Gardner (1990: 47), HFCS accounted for less than 2 percent of U.S. caloric sweetener consumption in 1973. By 1987, it accounted for 36 percent. If the sugar industry in the United States were to be liberalized, the consumption of HFCS would decrease. However, the consumption of HFCS would still be higher than it would have been had the price support for sugar not been in place. In other words, the world demand for sugar is not going to be the same as it would have been without the protection.

The food security concerns raised by food-importing countries should not be used to delay liberalization in the OECD countries. Many sub-Saharan African countries can increase their food production. They should seek technical assistance to increase their agricultural output potential. However, it is important to note that simply increasing food production is neither a sufficient nor necessary condition for food security. Increasing food production does not necessarily mean everyone can afford food; similarly, if everyone can afford to buy their food, food security can be achieved through imports.

Although sub-Saharan African countries have a legitimate concern that the end of the MFA quotas would expose them to fierce competition and even lead to a reduction of investment in the textile sector, that concern should be considered within limits. It has been expressed even by some SSA countries whose policies had discouraged private domestic investment and foreign direct investment in this industry.

It is important not to exaggerate the importance of preferential treatment accorded during the MFA era to most of the textiles and apparel produced in sub-Saharan Africa. In fact, there has been a growing demand for apparel in sub-Saharan African countries themselves. Garments are not like coffee or cocoa, which are produced by sub-Saharan African countries almost solely for export to developed countries. In other words, the demand for textiles and apparels has not been the most critical issue for many sub-Saharan African countries. The slow growth of the textiles and clothing industry in these countries is explained more by factors associated with production (supply) than those associated with demand.

Another point should be made regarding the concern of sub-Saharan African countries about having to compete on equal terms with Asian producers. The competitiveness of a country's product can be derived from receiving preferential access to a market and/or from being a low-cost producer. For an industry in which different sizes of firms can coexist and prosper and in which products are highly differentiated, it is not clear why African countries cannot compete with other producers. Asian countries will continue to dominate this industry in the near future. However, with appropriate policies, improved infrastructure to reduce costs, and appropriate incentives for investment (such as reduced tax and tariff rates for enterprises in export-processing zones in Mauritius), sub-Saharan African countries will also become competitive producers of textiles and apparel.

Moreover, over the last twenty-five years, the economic growth and increased real wages in Asian countries have slowly been decreasing their competitive advantage in textiles and apparel. Although that trend has been somewhat stalled in the late 1990s by the economic crises in many Asian countries, labor costs are still higher in Asia than in sub-Saharan Africa. Asian countries, like the dominant producers of textiles and apparel before them, cannot maintain a competitive advantage in this industry indefinitely. Even Mauritius, a relative newcomer to the textiles and apparel industry, is starting to lose its competitive edge as factories move to Madagascar because of increased labor costs (Marriott, 1995).[19]

Many sub-Saharan African countries have cheap labor in their favor. According to Biggs et al. (1996: 78), the average monthly salary for a factory worker producing men's casual shirts in the export processing zone in China in 1994 was $120. On average, each worker produced $2,974 worth of shirts. Thus, the unit labor cost index (i.e., $120 ÷ $2,974) was 0.04. This was higher than the unit labor cost indices of 0.034 for Zimbabwe, 0.026 for Kenya, and 0.022 for Ghana. Sub-Saharan African countries also have the advantage of domestically produced raw materials (for example, cotton and wool).

However, these two factors alone—cheap labor and domestically produced raw materials—are not sufficient to develop a viable and competitive textiles and apparel industry. To develop such an industry also takes political and macroeconomic stabilities, good infrastructure, skilled labor and management, and policies that encourage and protect investment. These have been identified to be the key elements that have contributed to the Mauritian success (Craig, 1992; Perlez, 1990). The gradual development of the textiles and apparel industry in other countries, such as Kenya, Lesotho, Madagascar, South Africa, Swaziland, and Zimbabwe, is likewise explained largely by favorable production conditions. Tanzania, for its part, has shown how it is impossible to develop and *sustain* a textiles and apparel industry, even where demand is high, when supply-side constraints—lack of spare parts, poor infrastructure, and inefficient management—are prevalent.[20]

There is reason, however, to be cautiously optimistic about the future of the agricultural sector and the textiles and apparel industry in sub-Saharan Africa. New leaders in many countries are implementing political and economic reforms that are (1) introducing some measure of stability and accountability, (2) encouraging the growth of the private sector, (3) encouraging foreign direct investment, and (4) making their economies more open to trade (notwithstanding the actual commitments made in the Uruguay Round of GATT). They are positioning themselves to be able to take better advantage of international trade, a liberalized agricultural sector in OECD countries, and the preferential treatment they receive in the trade of textiles and apparel (and other commodities).

These initiatives coupled with investment in human capital and infrastructure, which may be possible with guided fiscal programming and debt relief, will give the textiles and apparel industry (and other industries) much of what it needs to take root and develop. In addition, they will reduce the reason for concern about competing on equal terms with Asian producers and, at the same time, make more legitimate the sub-Saharan African countries' request for assistance in the face of that concern.

Economic reforms, however, are known to cause short-run instability, such as increased unemployment and inflation. These potential consequences and the overall uncertainty associated with reforms can be reduced with external assistance in the form of debt relief and temporary, but genuine, preferential treatment in trade. Therefore, some form of preferential treatment in textiles and clothing should be extended for at least five years beyond 2004 for sub-Saharan African countries (and other countries in their situation). This is important, especially for those economies capable of using the textiles and apparel industry to develop an industrial base.

Case: Kenya's Investment Policies, Its Textiles and Clothing Industry, and U.S. Trade Policies

Like many other sub-Saharan African countries, Kenya, under pressure and guidance from the World Bank and the IMF, has been implementing economic reforms since the late 1980s. Under these reforms, emphasis has been placed on the importance of the private sector, particularly to those who generate export revenue.

In 1990, Kenya inaugurated the Export Processing Zones (EPZ) program, designed to give incentives for export-oriented production. Incentives include a ten-year corporate tax holiday (with a 25 percent corporate tax thereafter), a ten-year withholding tax holiday on remittance of dividends, a duty and value-added tax exemption on all inputs except vehicles, and exemption from a number of bureaucratic procedures and regulations. One important requirement of EPZ enterprises is that they must export 80 percent of their output. EPZ sales in the domestic market are "liable for payment of import duties and taxes and are treated as normal imports into Kenya" (Export Processing Zones Authority, 1998: 3). A similar program likewise designed to encourage manufacturing for exports, called Manufacturing Under Bond, is administered by Kenya's Investment Promotion Centre.

These initiatives (and those overseen by Kenya's Export Promotion Council) are meant to shift the means for developing the manufacturing sector from an import substitution policy to an outward-oriented policy. Among the industries in the manufacturing sector that were expected to benefit quickly from the incentives to invest was the textiles and apparel industry. Kenya has an experienced, productive, and inexpensive labor force in this industry and, therefore, could easily be very competitive, given the tax breaks mentioned above. In addition, machines used in this industry, particularly in clothing, are relatively mobile and can easily be moved from one country to another in response to new (even if temporary) incentives.

Table 4.7 Exports of Kenya's Textiles and Clothing to the United States and the World (U.S.$ millions)

	1991	1992	1993	1994	1995
(1) United States	5	8	23	37	36
(2) World	19	19	28	60	55
(3) (1)/(2) × 100	26	42	82	62	65

Source: U.S. International Trade Commission (1997: 1–5, 2–16, F-12, F-13).

In 1994, the manufacturing sector in Kenya contributed about 14 percent of the GDP (Republic of Kenya, 1998: 28). Although the textiles and clothing industry contributed only 9 percent of the manufacturing share of GDP, its share of the *manufacturing* share of *exports* was almost 30 percent. As indicated in Table 4.7, the United States is a very important market for Kenya's textiles.

Kenya's total value of exports of textiles and clothing rose to about U.S.$60 million in 1994, from an annual average of about U.S.$24 million from 1990 to 1993 (U.S. International Trade Commission, 1997: 2–25). This increase was caused mainly by a sharp increase in the volume of exports of shirts and pillowcases to the United States. Trade liberalization and export promotion seemed to bear fruit for Kenya's textiles and clothing industry.

Instead of receiving support for its outward-oriented policies, Kenya was warned by the United States in 1994 that its increased exports of shirts and pillowcases were causing damage to the U.S. domestic industry. The United States wanted the two countries to negotiate a quota system that would limit the growth of such exports.

Kenya, dumbfounded by the U.S. demands, was not sure how to respond. There was disagreement between and among individuals in the Ministry of Commerce and Industry and groups representing producers, such as the Kenyan Association of Manufacturers, the Export Promotion Centre, and the Export Processing Zones Authority.[21]

Some officials in Kenya were of the opinion that they should not negotiate with the United States. Their strategy was to delay formal discussions, hoping time would be on their side, as the implementation of the Agreement on Textiles and Clothing (which prevented the imposition of new quotas after December 31, 1994) was about to begin. This group of officials was also willing to let the United States impose the quota unilaterally, if the United States so desired. Kenya would then bring the case to GATT-WTO to challenge the United States to prove damage to its domestic industry.

It must be noted that U.S. imports of shirts and pillowcases from Kenya were a very small percentage of its total imports. For example, U.S. imports of men's shirts from Kenya for the twelve months ending July 1993 was about 0.14 percent of its total imports of men's shirts (Biggs et al., 1994: 46). With such relatively small imports, it was argued, the United States would not be able to prove domestic damage and might, therefore, not reach a unilateral decision to impose quotas.

Another group of Kenyan leaders thought that it would be better to negotiate. They were concerned that a unilateral decision by the United States would be more harmful to Kenya. They also hoped to persuade the United States not to impose quotas or at least to negotiate a large quota.

The power structure of these domestic deliberations supported those who favored negotiations. Moreover, it was even easier to make the decision to negotiate given that the United States was footing most of the bill to bring Kenyans to London (a so-called "neutral" location) and that the per diem was always attractive in a place like London. The outcome was the establishment of quotas, in 1994, on U.S. imports of cotton and synthetic-fiber shirts and cotton pillowcases from Kenya. Ironically, these quotas were established after the signing ceremony in Morocco, in April 1994, to establish the WTO. Thus, Kenya was subjected to quotas only a few months before the Agreement on Textiles and Clothing came into force on January 1, 1995 (from which time on, new quotas could not be imposed).

Kenyan representatives came back from the meetings even more divided. Those who were against negotiating with the United States felt betrayed. They contended that the objective of the meetings was to dissuade the United States from establishing quotas and not to negotiate the size of the quota. Those who were in favor of the negotiations congratulated themselves, pointing out that they were able to secure larger quotas than those proposed by the United States. The only thing every Kenyan familiar with this issue seems to agree on is that the U.S. representatives were far more prepared than the Kenyans. Reflecting on the gap in preparation and presentation between the Kenyan and U.S representatives, four years later, a Kenyan official at the Ministry of Trade remarked that "we were ambushed by the Americans." An official at the Kenyan Association of Manufacturers believes that "the outcome would have been different and more favorable to us if we had consulted with our supporters in the U.S." (Both interviews took place on July 10, 1998, in Nairobi, Kenya.)

Because of the disagreement among Kenyan officials and/or the lack of a clear understanding of the impact of a quota system, a decision could not be reached on whether to allocate quota rights, let alone on

Table 4.8   U.S. Imports of Cotton Shirts and Cotton Pillowcases from Kenya, 1993–1996

	Quantity (1,000,000 square meters equivalent)				Value in U.S.$ (million)			
	1993	1994	1995	1996	1993	1994	1995	1996
Shirts	3.8	7.9	7.8	4.6	8.9	20.6	20.1	12.1
Pillowcases	1.1	1.8	0.5	0.4	0.7	1.1	0.4	0.2
Total	4.9	9.7	8.3	5.0	9.6	21.7	20.5	12.3

Source: U.S. International Trade Commmission (1997: F-12, F-13).

how to allocate them. The first-come-first-served system that ensued increased the uncertainty created by the quota system for both exporters and importers. Table 4.8 shows U.S. imports of men's cotton nonknit shirts and cotton pillowcases from Kenya from 1993 to 1996. The volume of U.S. imports of shirts and pillowcases from Kenya in 1996 was only about 50 percent the level in 1994.

Perhaps more important, Kenya's exports of shirts and pillowcases to the United States fell to quantities far below the quota. In fact, Kenya's exports of pillowcases to the United States fell to zero in 1997, as shown in Table 4.9. Importers looked for more reliable sources, and factory owners in Kenya (mostly non-Kenyans with little vested interest in Kenya other than making the highest rate of return possible on their financial capital) wandered to other countries.

The direct negative impact of the U.S. quota on Kenya's textiles and clothing industry has been estimated to be about 10,000 jobs (out of about 15,000) and about thirty companies (out of about forty) (Phillips, 1996; Jacobs, 1997: 88–89). The Ministry of Trade in Kenya cautions, however, that determining the extent of the impact of the quota would require a careful study. The ministry's officials point to the fact that there was another important factor, import liberalization, that in the early to mid-1990s contributed to the decline of the textiles and clothing industry. Firms producing wholly or in part for the domestic market had been spoiled by protection, and some could not withstand the competition created by import liberalization.

Ironically, some of the competition for the apparel subsector came from the United States with the increase of exports of used clothes (known as *mitumba* in East Africa) to Kenya. U.S. exports of used apparel to Kenya increased by more than 500 percent in five years, from

Table 4.9 U.S. Quotas and Imports of Shirts and Pillowcases from Kenya (calendar years)

		1994	1995	1996	1997
Shirts	Quota (dozens)	360,000	387,000	416,025	447,227
	U.S. imports (dozens)	360,000	383,092	217,873	196,330
	% filled	100.0	98.99	52.37	43.90
Pillowcases	Quota (number)	2,600,000	2,795,000	3,004,625	3,229,972
	U.S. imports (number)	1,416,528	744,096	232,176	0
	% filled	54.48	26.62	7.73	0.00

Source: U.S. Department of Commerce, Office of Textiles and Apparel.

$696,000 in 1992 to $3.7 million in 1996 (U.S. International Trade Commission, 1997: 2–26). Thus, while the United States was pushing for protection against Kenyan shirts and pillowcases it was also pushing used clothes onto a now more open Kenyan market. As to be expected, this inconsistency gives those who do not understand the benefits of international trade something on which to base their argument for trade barriers in sub-Saharan Africa.

The imposition of the quota by the United States on a relatively poor country like Kenya raises doubts about how real the U.S. commitment is to support countries that are trying to liberalize their economies. The U.S. protectionist policy against Kenya was particularly damaging because it was not even reacting to an existing threat to its domestic market. Rather, it was reacting to Kenya's potential for developing its textiles and apparel industry in the future. It must be emphasized that the quota not only caused some firms to close but also dissuaded potential investors from investing in Kenya. The haste with which factory owners in Kenya closed their firms also raises doubts about the type of foreign investment attracted by short-term incentives. These incentives may only attract firms that are very mobile and very responsive to even small changes in market costs. Although these types of firms can easily respond to temporary tax holidays that a country may offer, one must be aware that they can also leave for another country just as quickly.

Outward-oriented policies must also be accompanied by financing arrangements that will enable domestic entrepreneurs to take advantage of the production and export incentives. Excessive reliance on (nomadic) foreign direct investment can breed uncertainty and can be a source of tension between "foreigners" and "natives," even when those investors create jobs. There are people in Kenya (some with influence on policies) who do not understand why there was such a big fuss about the U.S. quotas. They ask, "Who are we really trying to protect by fighting against these quotas? A few Kenyans who work in sweatshops or the foreign investors who are here to make a quick profit and run with it to other locations?"

Notes

1. For some commodities, such as coffee and cocoa, sub-Saharan African exports are relatively large proportions of world exports—approximately 20 percent and 60 percent, respectively.

2. In 1993 and 1994, Côte d'Ivoire and Ghana, on average, accounted for 23 percent and 11 percent, respectively, of world cocoa exports (UNCTAD, 1997a: 170, 173).

3. The percentages were calculated using data from UNCTAD (1997a: A.2, A.3).

4. The Cairns Group included Argentina, Australia, Brazil, Canada, Chile, Colombia, Fiji, Hungary, Indonesia, Malaysia, New Zealand, Philippines, Thailand, and Uruguay (OECD, 1994: 133). Note that the group included three OECD countries (Australia, Canada, and New Zealand).

5. For details, see one of the following: OECD (1995b), Ingco (1996), or Tangermann (1996).

6. See also Tangermann (1996: Table 1).

7. The Agreement on Agriculture requires a "minimum access commitment" for commodities subject to tariffication. Contracting members were required to establish access tariff quotas (reduced tariff rates on specified quantities) to allow up to 5 percent of domestic consumption by the year 2000. Given that some tariffs have been bound *higher* than the minimum level at which they would be prohibitive for some commodities, it is possible that even "access" tariff quotas for those commodities could still be prohibitive. As Tangermann (1996: 323) pointed out, "there is no commitment to import, but only commitment to charge no more than the specified reduced rates of tariffs on the products and quantities specified."

8. Countries have been given an option of using 1991–1992 as their base period instead of 1986–1990. However, the value of subsidies and volumes subsidized at the end of the implementation period must be the same as they would have been, had they used 1986–1990 as the base period (OECD, 1995b: 46).

9. For additional illustrations, see Anderson and Tyers (1990) and Valdés and Zietz (1980).

10. For details, see Anderson and Tyers (1990).

11. Production and export taxes on farmers have decreased in many sub-Saharan African countries since the late 1980s under the structural adjustment programs.

12. If the MFA annual quota growth rate (used as a base growth rate) was 6 percent, for example, the annual quota growth rates during the implementation period would be as follows: 1995–1997: 6.96 percent; 1998–2001: 8.70 percent; 2002–2004: 11.05 percent. Note that acceleration of the growth rate depends mainly on the initial MFA quota growth rate used as a base.

13. For details, see Smeets (1995).

14. The United States and China reached a trade pact in November 1999, which increases the latter's likelihood of being accepted into the WTO.

15. The U.S. House of Representatives passed the trade bill in July 1999. After defeating it in 1998, the U.S. Senate passed a more restrictive version of the bill in November 1999, as this book was in the final stages of production. It is possible that the two legislative houses will reconcile their versions of the trade bill in 2000 for President Bill Clinton to sign into law.

16. This is one of twelve requirements, some of which are very subjective.

17. It is important to note that the change in the "rules of origin" was a unilateral decision by the United States. It was not dictated by the agreement. However, the White House enacted the change to appease domestic producers and Senator Ernest Hollings (chair of the Senate Commerce Committee), who were opposed to the Agreement on Textiles and Clothing (Mammarella, 1994).

18. See note 15.

19. Mauritius is now preparing its labor force to move into the second phase of industrialization. This change involves diversifying within the clothing industry and also moving into service industries and technology-intensive industries.

20. In the 1980s and early 1990s, the state-owned textile facilities in Tanzania were barely operating owing to a lack of spare parts and poor management. A shortage of clothes ensued, as the government had set barriers to protect domestic production. When the shortage became severe, with no domestic solution in sight in the mid-1980s, the government allowed imports of relatively cheap "second-hand" clothes to alleviate the shortage and to make clothes accessible to the majority of the population, which is poor. Second-hand clothes, or what Tanzanian textile manufacturers refer to as "*so-called* second-hand clothes," have now become an integral part of Tanzania's apparel consumption and a challenge to domestic producers ("Tanzania's Textiles," 1995b: 2).

21. The Ministry of Commerce and Industry has since been split (in 1998) into two ministries—the Ministry of Industrial Development and the Ministry of Trade.

FIVE

◆

International Commodity Agreements

I nternational commodity agreements are arrangements in which
the countries exporting and importing a particular commodity
agree to control the supply of that commodity in the world market. These agreements are between governments. The primary objective of these agreements has been to stabilize and support prices
of primary products.

The focus of this chapter is on five international commodity
agreements that have had economic provisions to regulate the supply
of the respective commodity: the International Cocoa Agreement
(ICCA), International Coffee Agreement (ICA), International Natural Rubber Agreement (INRA), International Sugar Agreement
(ISA), and International Tin Agreement (ITA). Although only the
INRA currently has such economic provisions, such agreements are
still considered as a strategy to enhance the foreign currency earnings
of developing countries. As long as developing countries continue to
rely on primary products, this topic will continue to be important.

Sub-Saharan Africa's
Dependence on Primary Products

Many sub-Saharan African countries depend heavily on one or only a
few commodities for their export revenue. Table 5.1 shows the percentage of merchandise export revenue generated by one to three
leading export commodities in sub-Saharan African countries. For
many countries, a single mineral or agricultural crop is responsible
for more than 50 percent of their export revenue. Any sharp decreases or wild swings in commodity prices or output can have a detri-
mental effect not only on producers of those commodities but also on

Table 5.1   Average Annual Percentage of Merchandise Export Revenue Generated by 1 to 3 Leading Export Items— 1980–1990 or *1993–1994* (in italics)

Country		Percentage and Export Items
Angola	91	(petroleum 84, precious stones 7)
Benin	80	(cotton 58, petroleum 16, wheat flour 6)
Burkina Faso	98	(cotton 51, gold 31, live animals 16)
Burundi	90	(coffee 70, gold 12, tea 8)
Cameroon	*68*	*(crude petroleum 37, wood 24, cocoa 7)*
Central African Republic	74	(precious stones 38, wood 22, coffee 14)
Chad	86	(cotton 48, live animals 20, crude material 18)
Comoros	95	(spices 72, petroleum 15, uranium 8)
Congo, Democratic Republic of	74	(copper 47, petroleum 16, cobalt 11)
Congo, Republic of	*96*	*(crude petroleum 89, wood 7)*
Côte d'Ivoire	*61*	*(cocoa 38, coffee 10, wood 13)*
Equatorial Guinea	78	(wood 45, cocoa 33)
Ethiopia	81	(coffee 65, hides 16)
Gabon	*94*	*(crude petroleum 88, wood 6)*
Gambia	74	(precious stones 37, groundnuts 26, fisheries 11)
Ghana	*66*	*(cocoa 30, precious stones 19, aluminum 17)*
Guinea	90	(bauxite 82, precious stones 8)
Guinea-Bissau	75	(cashew nuts 58, fisheries 10, wood 7)
Kenya	*43*	*(tea 25, coffee 18)*
Lesotho	14	(wool)
Liberia	97	(iron ore 52, rubber 24, wood 21)
Madagascar	54	(spices 25, coffee 15, fisheries 14)
Malawi	86	(tobacco 68, tea 11, sugar 7)
Mali	79	(cotton 47, live animals 25, gold 7)
Mauritania	84	(iron ore 44, fisheries 32, live animals 8)
Mauritius	*25*	*(sugar)*
Mozambique	52	(shellfish 34, cashew nuts 11, cotton 7)
Niger	88	(uranium 73, live animals 15)
Nigeria	*94*	*(crude petroleum)*
Rwanda	85	(coffee 65, tea 20)
São Tomé and Principe	65	(cocoa 59, copra 6)
Senegal	*49*	*(fisheries 36, vegetable oils 13)*
Seychelles	*94*	*(fisheries)*
Sierra Leone	53	(precious stones 34, bauxite 19)
Somalia	90	(live animals 55, bananas 21, fisheries 14)
Sudan	61	(cotton 38, live animals 12, sesame 11)
Tanzania	56	(coffee 26, cotton 24, tea 6)
Togo	72	(fertilizer 48, cotton 17, coffee 7)
Uganda	84	(coffee)
Zambia	91	(copper 84, cobalt 7)
Zimbabwe	*31*	*(tobacco)*

Sources: Based on information available on UNCTAD's Country Profiles website, April 28, 1998: http://www.inicc.org/unctad/en/pressref/ldcs; and UNCTAD (1997a: 168–184).

the economies at large. These commodities generate revenue for producers as well as tax revenue for government expenditure.

The Rationale for and Objectives of International Commodity Agreements

Although some commodity agreements predate UNCTAD, it was UNCTAD's first secretary general, Raul Prebisch, who forcefully articulated the link between commodity export revenue and economic development. The hypothesis is that stable export revenues facilitate better planning for development, and rising export revenues augment imports of inputs and machinery. The full four-part hypothesis is that (1) a high degree of instability is associated with export earnings of developing countries that depend heavily on a few primary commodities, (2) instability in export earnings is transmitted into the rest of the economy, (3) overall economic instability slows economic growth, and (4) slow economic growth hinders economic development.[1]

Developing countries that depend on one or only a few export commodities are subject to wide fluctuations in their export revenues owing to a relative instability in output and/or in commodity prices. For developing countries with a high ratio of export revenue to GDP, export instability is transmitted into the economy at large.

Empirical evidence is inconclusive on how parts (1) and/or (2) in the hypothesis are linked with part (3). However, there is a general assumption that export instability will eventually lead to slow economic growth. The IMF established the Compensatory Financing Facility in 1963 to provide financial assistance to developing countries that experience shortfalls in their export earnings caused by external factors. Likewise, in 1975, the EU established STABEX (Stabilization of Export Earnings) under the first Lomé Convention for the same purpose (Herrmann et al., 1993; Lim, 1991).

As for link (4) in the hypothesis, economic growth (i.e., growth in GDP or GNP) is not a sufficient condition for economic development (the overall standard of living of the majority of the population). Nonetheless, over long periods it is a necessary condition. The provision of services like water, health, and education cannot be sustained without economic growth.

In addition to the instability of export earnings, Prebisch argued that the terms of trade were deteriorating for poor developing countries that were dependent on natural commodities. The main reasons for such deterioration are (1) the relatively lower price elasticity of demand and income elasticity of demand for primary products, as compared to manufactured products, which developing countries import; (2) the impact on prices of the different market structures, which are relatively more competitive for commodity markets, compared to those for manufactured goods, which, in relative terms, are rather oligopolistic;[2] (3) changing technology that increases substitution of synthetics for natural products (inputs) and minimizes the use of inputs in general; and (4) recycling.

Empirical evidence on the trend of the overall relative price of primary products in general has been mixed. It is apparent, however, that the terms of trade for almost all sub-Saharan African countries have slowly been declining over time, as shown in Table 5.2. The terms of trade for sub-Saharan Africa (excluding Nigeria and South Africa) declined by an annual average of 1 percent from 1975 to 1996 (World Bank, 1997c: 89). This decline has been mainly due to the decline in the relative prices of major, nonfuel primary commodities, such as cocoa and coffee (IMF, 1990).

Although developed countries also produce some primary commodities, they are not in the same predicament as developing countries, for three main reasons. First, for many natural commodities, developed countries are net importers. Some commodities such as cocoa and coffee are not produced at all in developed countries. Thus, a decrease in the relative price of these commodities is actually good news for importers and consumers in developed countries. Second, developed countries have diverse economies that can better absorb sharp changes in the prices of individual commodities. Third, domestic policies in developed countries, particularly agricultural policies, cushion producers against adverse price changes, as discussed in Chapter 4.

For developing countries, which are net exporters of these natural commodities, lower export revenues for a country's major commodity mean reduced incomes for producers (usually a large proportion of the workforce) and less government revenue. This shortfall can set off a vicious cycle, whereby shrinking government revenue causes investment in infrastructure and social services to fall, reducing further the overall production potential of the economy.

International commodity agreements have been viewed as one strategy to stabilize and support prices of commodities and, thus, to support developing countries. The primary objectives of these agreements include the following: (1) to stabilize (and support) prices, (2) to stabilize revenue, (3) to transfer income from importing (rich) countries to exporting (poor) countries, and (4) to maintain

Table 5.2 Terms of Trade—Average Annual Percentage Growth Rate

Country	1975–1984	1984–1994
Angola	NA	−4.8
Benin	−0.3	−2.8
Botswana	NA	12.7[a]
Burkina Faso	−0.7	−1.9
Burundi	−4.3	−5.3[a]
Cameroon	−2.9	−4.4
Cape Verde	7.6	0.0[a]
Central African Republic	3.9	−2.6
Chad	−2.8	0.2
Comoros	NA	0.8[a]
Congo, Democratic Republic of	3.7	−2.6
Congo, Republic of	3.7	−3.8
Côte d'Ivoire	−5.2	−3.4
Ethiopia	NA	−2.8
Gabon	7.5	−5.25
Gambia	−5.6	−2.04
Ghana	−1.4	−5.7
Guinea	NA	−4.9[a]
Guinea Bissau	5.0	−11.5[a]
Kenya	−3.8	−2.9
Lesotho	−2.5	−2.1[a]
Liberia	NA	−1.2
Madagascar	−2.9	−3.8
Malawi	−2.4	−2.9
Mali	1.5	−0.2
Mauritania	−3.6	−0.7
Mauritius	−5.3	4.9
Mozambique	NA	−0.2
Namibia	NA	1.3[a]
Niger	6.7	0.9
Nigeria	6.7	−6.0
Rwanda	2.0	−5.4
São Tomé and Principe	−4.6	−7.5[a]
Senegal	−1.3	−0.3
Seychelles	NA	−7.0[a]
Sierra Leone	2.1	−2.6
Somalia	2.4	−1.8
South Africa	−1.2	0.8[a]
Sudan	5.2	−1.4
Swaziland	−0.7	−1.7[a]
Tanzania	NA	−4.3
Togo	−2.1	−4.5
Uganda	NA	−7.7
Zambia	−8.5	−1.7
Zimbabwe	−1.0	−0.7[a]

Sources: The growth rates for the period 1984–1994 were calculated by the author using data from UNCTAD (1997a: 336–353). The rest of the growth rates are from World Bank (1997c: 89).

   a. 1985–1989.

a reliable supply of commodities. Secondary objectives include promoting consumption of respective commodities, helping developing countries to diversify their economies, supporting processing in developing countries, and collecting and disseminating information.

Operation of
International Commodity Agreements

Two main instruments have been used by international commodity agreements to try to achieve their primary objectives: buffer stock intervention and export controls. *Buffer stock* refers to supplies of a commodity that are purchased or sold by the coordinating body of the commodity agreement in order to regulate the supply of that commodity in the world market. The aim is to keep the world price of the commodity within the agreed price floor and ceiling. The funds that support the buffer stock arrangement are financed by all member countries, each one contributing according to its volume of exports or imports. The second instrument, *export controls,* works through quotas set for exporting countries so as to have the world price of a commodity fall within a specified price range. These instruments are sometimes supplemented by production policies to contain output growth rates.

International commodity agreements often exist without such economic provisions (or economic clauses). For example, the ICCA, the ICA, and the ISA currently exist without economic provisions to adjust prices. Only the INRA presently has a market intervention provision. The ITA had economic provisions that could not be sustained, and it collapsed in 1985.

Table 5.3 shows years in which the five agreements had economic provisions for adjusting prices.[3] It also indicates the level of the annual commodity average price in relation to the price range in force. As the figures in Table 5.3 show, even when the economic provision is in effect, it has not always been possible to keep commodity prices within the price floor and ceiling. Only the INRA can claim an excellent record in that respect.

Even in the absence of economic provisions, commodity organizations can continue to carry out other useful tasks. These include gathering and disseminating information, sponsoring research on consumption and production, facilitating discussions on the conditions of the market, and trying to negotiate new agreements that contain economic provisions. Exporting countries also continue to use the organization as a forum to try to organize themselves to limit

Table 5.3 Operation of International Commodity Agreements

Agreement (year of first agreement)	Intervention Instrument	Years with Economic Provision	Annual Commodity Average Price in Relation to the Price Range in Force		
			Below the Floor	Within the Range	Above the Ceiling
ITA (1953)	Buffer stock, supplemented by export controls	1956–1985 (29 years)		1956–1960, 1961–1963, 1967–1973, 1975–1976, and 1981–1985 (20 years)	1961, 1964–1966, 1973–1974, and 1977–1980 (9 years)
ISA (1954)	Export controls	1954–1961, 1969–1973, and 1978–1984 (20 years)	1955, 1959–1961, 1969, 1978–1979, and 1982–1984 (10 years)	1954, 1956, 1958, 1970, and 1971 (5 years)	1957, 1972–1973, 1980, and 1981 (5 years)
ICA (1962)	Export controls	1964–1971, 1980–1984, and 1987–1988 (15 years)[a]	1968 and 1988 (2 years)	1964–1967, 1970, 1980–1984, and 1987 (11 years)	1969 and 1971 (2 years)
ICCA (1972)	Buffer stock	1973–1979 and 1981–1989 (16 years)[a]	1981–1982 and 1984–1989 (8 years)	1983 (1 year)	1973–1979 (7 years)
INRA (1980)	Buffer stock	1980 to present[b]		1980 to present[b]	

Sources: The main sources are Gilbert (1996) and Raffaelli (1995). Other sources are Mshomba (1994) and the International Natural Rubber Organization, April 28, 1998 (http://www3.jaring.my/inro/dmip.html).
a. Coffee and cocoa years run from October 1 to September 30. For example, read 1964 as 1964/1965.
b. The current agreement was reached in 1995 and expires in 2000.

exports. For example, there have been a number of short-lived agreements of subsets of the coffee-exporting countries since economic provisions of the ICA were suspended in 1989 (Behrman, 1991, 1993; Taylor, 1993; McGee, 1995).

Participation in International Commodity Agreements

Producing countries participate in international commodity agreements for two main reasons: stability in export income and an increase in those incomes. For producing countries in which the covariance between world prices and export volume is zero or close to zero (a likely case for a small country), an international commodity agreement that stabilizes prices effectively stabilizes the country's export incomes as well (Newbery, 1993). Stability in export income may be a sufficient reason for a country to join a commodity agreement even if the average price and, therefore, the average income do not increase. In fact, risk-averse producing countries may even be willing to trade off average income for a reduction in the variance income. Thus, stability in export income is one reason why producing countries may participate in international commodity agreements.

Another reason is the possible support of average prices that would increase the average income. An international commodity agreement that is able to stabilize export income and at the same time increase average incomes will attract even more producing countries. Given that in practice international commodity agreements try to stabilize and support prices, it comes as no surprise that exporting countries are the ones who usually initiate the establishment of a commodity agreement. Many sub-Saharan African countries are members of various international commodity agreements, always as exporting members. The membership of sub-Saharan African countries in the ICA, the ICCA, the INRA, and the ISA is given in Table 5.4.

Why do importing (developed) countries also participate in these agreements? There are both political and economic reasons. First, some developed countries view their participation as a means to improve the North-South relationship (Kirthisingha, 1983). This was a particularly important factor in the 1960s. African countries were then gaining their independence and joining other developing countries in condemning what they considered to be an exploitative global economic system (rich countries exploiting poor countries).

Table 5.4   Membership of Sub-Saharan African Countries in International Commodity Agreements

Country	ICA 1994	ICCA 1993	INRA 1996	ISA 1992
Angola	X			
Burundi	X			
Cameroon	X	X		
Central African Republic	X			
Congo, Democratic Republic of	X			
Congo, Republic of	X			
Côte d'Ivoire	X	X	X	X
Equatorial Guinea	X			
Ethiopia	X			
Gabon	X	X		
Ghana	X	X		
Guinea	X			
Kenya	X			X
Madagascar	X			
Malawi	X			X
Mauritius				X
Nigeria	X	X	X	
Rwanda	X			
São Tomé and Principe		X		
Sierra Leone		X		
South Africa				X
Swaziland				X
Tanzania	X			
Togo	X	X		
Uganda	X			
Zambia	X			
Zimbabwe	X			X

Sources: International Coffee Organization (http://www.ico.org), International Cocoa Organization (http://www.icco.org), International Natural Rubber Organization (http://www3.jaring.my/inro/members.htm), and International Sugar Organization (http://www.sugarinfo.co.uk/ISO/ISOUpdate/ISOUp1.html).

Note: Dates in column heads indicate the year for which membership status was given.

Moreover, the British and French viewed commodity agreements as an opportunity to show support for their former colonies. The United States, likewise, wanted to secure an alliance with developing countries, especially Latin American countries, in its Cold War with the former Soviet Union. Germany (then West Germany) supported the establishment of the International Cocoa Organization, hoping for political support in its bid to have its headquarters in Hamburg,

Germany (Raffaelli, 1995: 150). The headquarters ended up in London.

There is no doubt that the participation of importing (developed) countries in commodity agreements is also explained by economic reasons. Some developed countries saw commodity agreements as a development policy to assist developing countries. Some feared that chaos in producing countries, presumably preventable by relatively stable commodity prices, could have an adverse impact on supply. Moreover, they figured price stabilization was not incompatible with a market system. They assumed that market forces would still determine price trends and that market intervention was mainly to prevent price shocks. At least they demanded that price stabilization be sensitive to market forces (Kirthisingha, 1983: 41–43).

Other explanations include the possibility of using international commodity agreements to push other policy agendas, such as those on illegal drugs and the environment.

Challenges Facing International Commodity Agreements

The operation of international commodity agreements faces many challenges. They include setting a price range, securing the participation of all major exporters and importers, increased production and substitution, compliance, and policy inconsistency. Other challenges, addressed in the next section, involve the effectiveness of the agreements and their cost.

Setting a Price Range

Two main problems are associated with setting a price range. First, exporting countries and importing countries have conflicting interests: Generally, exporting countries want a higher price range, and importing countries want a lower one. Raffaelli (1995: 169) reported that Côte d'Ivoire pulled out of the ICCA in 1980 mainly because it wanted a higher price floor—120 cents per pound instead of the designated 100 cents per pound. Côte d'Ivoire at that time accounted for about 25 percent of world exports of cocoa.

In early 1973 the quota system under the ICA was suspended temporarily owing to a disagreement between exporting and importing countries. Wanting to improve their terms of trade, coffee-producing countries pressed for higher coffee prices and reduced quotas. Consuming countries were adamantly opposed to such moves, and a compromise could not be reached until three years later.

The second problem in setting a price range is that forecasts for long-run market prices for commodities are unreliable and can vary. Yet a price range that is not in harmony with the long-run free market equilibrium cannot be sustained. With buffer stock stabilization, a price range above the free market price will deplete funds. For example, funds for cocoa stocks were rapidly exhausted in 1980 following the third ICCA, which set the price floor at 100 cents per pound and the intervention price (at the low end, i.e., the buffer stock purchasing price) at 110 cents per pound (Raffaelli, 1995: 168).[4] This intervention price was almost 40 cents per pound above the prevailing market price of cocoa (Gilbert, 1996: 6–9).

Even though commodity agreements invariably have provisions for price revision, price ranges are usually not revised in time. The exception is the INRA, which makes provision for automatic revision of the price range in response to the Daily Market Indicator Price and the sales and purchases of buffer stock.

Securing the Participation of All Major Exporters and Importers

Any single commodity is produced by several countries and consumed by an even larger number of countries. Cocoa and coffee are each produced in over fifty countries. Sugar is produced in many more countries—developing and developed alike. Persuading all key producing and consuming countries from such a large pool to join a commodity agreement is not an easy task, especially given the conflicting interests of different countries.

Rules and obligations set by international commodity agreements only bind members of respective agreements. Given that the success of a commodity agreement depends on compliance with the rules by producing and consuming countries, a designated price range has little significance if countries who can influence the world price are not parties to the agreement.

During the period between 1973/1974 and 1989/1990, only in 1983/1984 was the actual price of cocoa within the designated price range. The lack of participation by some key countries contributed to this poor record.[5] The United States, the largest importer of cocoa, has never been a member of the ICCA. In the 1980s, the United States imported about 23 percent of world exports of cocoa (UNCTAD, 1988b: 27–28). Côte d'Ivoire, by then the largest exporter of cocoa, accounting for about 25 percent of world cocoa exports, did not participate in the ICCA from 1980 to 1985.

The collapse of the ITA in 1985 was partly due to the lack of participation by important producers. Bolivia, Brazil, and China, which together accounted for almost 30 percent of world exports of tin (United Nations, 1990: 14), were not members of the ITA.

The relative success of the ICA, from 1962 to 1989, was due in part to the wide participation by exporting and importing countries. The two categories of membership represented more than 90 percent each of world coffee exports and world coffee imports. The same can be said of the continued success of the INRA. In 1998, exporting and importing members represented, respectively, 99 percent of world exports and 86 percent of world imports of natural rubber.

Increased Production and Substitution

Increased supply of and/or decreased demand for a commodity can undermine the operation of the respective commodity agreement. For example, the growing production of tin in Brazil from less than 1 percent of world production in 1953 (when the first ITA was reached) to almost 20 percent in 1985 (when the ITA collapsed) was a challenge to the ITA, especially given that Brazil did not join the agreement.

A similar scenario happened with respect to cocoa. In the 1980s, when the World Bank was encouraging sub-Saharan African countries to revitalize their agricultural export sector, it was also financing massive investments in cocoa production in new producing countries such as Indonesia and Malaysia. (It should be noted that the already established cocoa industry in Côte d'Ivoire also received a boost from the World Bank.) Between 1975 and 1979, Indonesia and Malaysia, in aggregate, produced an average annual output of 29 thousand tons of cocoa—less than about 2 percent of the world output. Only a few years later, between 1985 and 1989, their aggregate average annual output jumped to 210 thousand pounds—a little over 10 percent of the world output (UNCTAD, 1991: 176–177).[6] The induced competition from Southeast Asia must have contributed to the poor performance of the ICCA, since Malaysia and Indonesia did not join the agreement.

Ironically, the success of a commodity agreement can be the agreement's worst enemy in the long run. Higher prices for a commodity, which may be a result of a successful international commodity agreement, serve as an incentive for producers, members and nonmembers alike, to increase (or commence) production. Higher prices also encourage the search for and use of substitutes, such as the substitution of aluminum for tin, synthetic rubber for natural rubber, nonsugar sweeteners for sugar, tea for coffee, and milk fats for cocoa butter. The INRA, keenly aware of this problem, links the price of natural rubber to that of synthetic rubber.

Compliance

Getting countries to sign agreements is one thing; getting them to honor those agreements is another. Countries may purposefully export beyond their quotas or fail to pay their contributions to buffer stock funds. The pressure to sell beyond quotas intensified as economic crisis hit in the 1980s.

Policy Inconsistency

The goals of an international commodity agreement may not be consistent with domestic goals. Domestic policies may be moving production in the opposite direction of that in which a commodity agreement is moving. The following two examples, one from the EEC and the other from Côte d'Ivoire, will illustrate.

Although the EEC participated in the ISA (from 1953 to 1977) as an importer, its domestic policies limited imports and supported domestic production of sugar. Trade barriers and domestic support moved the EEC from being a net importer to a net exporter of sugar. In 1977 the EEC proposed its status be changed from an importing member to an exporting member. Furthermore, the EEC proposed quota provisions more favorable to the countries making up the EEC than those of exporting, developing countries (Raffaelli, 1995: 109–112). The proposal was rejected and the EEC, by then a large exporter of sugar, pulled out of the ISA.

Perhaps this example reflects the overall apparent hypocrisy of many developed countries in international commodity agreements. They have participated with demands that market forces be allowed to determine the path for the price trend. Yet they have continued to implement price-distorting policies to support their producers.[7]

As for Côte d'Ivoire (then also known as Ivory Coast), the contractionary production policy that occasionally supplemented the buffer instrument in the ICCA (ineffectively, it should be noted) was not consistent with Côte d'Ivoire's production goals of the 1970s and 1980s. In the early 1970s, when the first ICCA came into effect, Côte d'Ivoire was producing an annual average of 208 thousand tons of cocoa, that is, 14 percent of world production. It was then the third largest producer after Ghana and Nigeria. In 1981, when Côte d'Ivoire pulled out of the ICCA, it was already the largest producer of cocoa, producing 465 thousand tons a year, that is, 26 percent of the world output. When Côte d'Ivoire returned to the ICCA in 1986, its production was about 590 thousand tons a year, or 30 percent of the world output (UNCTAD, 1991: 176–191). In the early 1990s, when it appears that Côte d'Ivoire had reached its production capacity, the country started pushing for the formation in the International Cocoa Organization of a coordinating and monitoring committee on national production policies in order to limit production growth.

The two examples—the EEC and its sugar policy of protection and subsidies and Côte d'Ivoire and its cocoa production policy—suggest that domestic goals supersede those set by a commodity agreement. It is difficult for a commodity agreement to function effectively for an extended period of time when domestic policies of various countries have goals contrary to those of the agreement.

◆ ◆ ◆

In addition to these five challenges, there are others that are specific to the commodity in question and to the instruments used by a commodity agreement. The case at the end of this chapter, "The International Coffee Agreement," illustrates many of the challenges faced by international commodity agreements that use the quota system as their main instrument. These include establishing the criteria for setting quotas, the inflexibility of the quota system, and a two-tier market system in which exports to nonmember countries are sold at discounted prices compared to exports to members of the agreement. Nonetheless, it must be appreciated that some challenges brought out in the case—for example, different trends of demand for different types of coffee—are specific to coffee.

The main problem faced by agreements using buffer stock is insufficient funds. The problem is caused by a number of factors: setting contribution obligations too low, nonpayment of contributions by members (as in the case of the ICCA), and the use of buffer stock purchasing prices that are too high compared to the market price.

On that last point, for almost all of the 1980s the price floor for cocoa was above the market price, as shown in Table 5.3. The funds available to the ICCA could not last for such an extended period. The ITA faced the same predicament in its final years, although that reality cannot be deduced from the information in Table 5.3. Even though the price of tin was not below the price floor, from 1981 until the collapse of the ITA in 1985 the market price of tin was below the buffer stock purchasing price. Insufficiency of funds, itself a reflection of other problems, certainly contributed to the collapse of the ITA in 1985 and the suspension of the ICCA in 1990.

The Effectiveness and Costs of International Commodity Agreements

There are also questions relating to the effectiveness and costs of international commodity agreements. The discussion here will pose more questions than it answers. This is partly because the question of effectiveness itself is elusive. As Gilbert (1996: 16) pointed out: "There has never been a clear international consensus over whether the objectives of these agreements is the reduction of price variability or the achievement of higher prices." Moreover, international commodity agreements have not always kept prices within the price range even when economic provisions were in effect. In addition, even when the objective is stability, it is not clear whether it is the stability of prices or revenue that is sought. The two cannot be achieved simultaneously at times when instability in prices is mainly caused by changes in supply.

Such issues notwithstanding, the following questions merit consideration here: What is the impact of international commodity agreements on price variability and price level? What is the net economic welfare impact of price support on exporting (developing) countries? What costs are associated with international commodity agreements? It should be noted, however, that international commodity agreements have not lent themselves to reliable empirical studies. This is perhaps because of the sporadic nature of economic provisions, a failure to maintain prices within a determined range even when economic provisions are in effect, and a lack of clear objectives. Empirical studies have produced results that are, by and large, anecdotal.

1. *What is the impact of international commodity agreements on price variability and price level?* Anecdotal evidence provided by Kirthisingha (1983: 54–55) suggests that price variability for commodities with international agreements is not vastly different from that for similar commodities without international agreements. Other information from Gilbert (1996: 15–16) suggests that price variability during price intervention and post–price intervention periods for cocoa, coffee, sugar, and tin is more or less the same.

A more elaborate (but not necessarily more reliable) study by Herrmann et al. (1993: 133–164) suggested that the ICA managed to

increase the average price of coffee.[8] According to the study, in 1982
and 1983, the ICA on average raised the import price for importing
members by 30 percent, decreased the import price for nonimport-
ing members by 10 percent, and increased the export price for exporting members by 24 percent.[9]

Although the direction of change revealed in these results makes
perfect economic sense, their magnitudes must be taken as anecdotal. Herrmann et al. followed two main steps to derive their results.
First, they used supply and demand functions to estimate export and
import price elasticities. The sample period they used was 1966 to
1981. Second, they used the estimated price elasticities "to compute
prices and quantities on the world market in the hypothetical situation of not having an ICA" (139). The computed prices and quantities were then compared with the actual situation.

There is one major problem with the study. Export supply and
import demand are estimated using only two explanatory variables
each—price and the last period's production and price and the last
period's income, respectively. A lack of data may partly explain these
limited specifications. Nonetheless, other variables—such as prices
of related goods, domestic policies (and those of the World Bank, for
that matter), and even more important, the ICA itself—might also be
important determinants of export supply and import demand.

Regarding this last point, prior to 1982 the ICA had economic
provisions from 1964 to 1971 and in 1980 and 1981. If economic provisions in 1982 and 1983 had a significant impact on prices, as the results suggest, there is no reason to assume that prior economic provisions had no residual impact. These limitations notwithstanding, the
study by Herrmann et al. still sheds some light on the income distribution impact of international commodity agreements using a quota
system.

2. *What is the net economic welfare impact of price support on exporting
(developing) countries?* What is the net welfare impact of higher prices
for exporting countries, when the higher prices are attributed to international commodity agreements? In the case of a commodity
agreement using export quotas to limit supply, the allocation of the
quota rights within exporting countries can create rent seeking.

Suppose a country is given an export quota of 50,000 tons of coffee per year. Because of the export controls in place, those who are
able to obtain the right to export will be gaining more profits than
they would have gained otherwise. Thus, those who wish to export
engage in *rent seeking* or directly unproductive activities, such as corruption or lobbying, to influence the official distributing quota
rights. Needless to say, rent seeking occurs as a result of exporters'

acting in partnership with bureaucrats. Bowman et al. (1996: 399) showed "that rent-seeking losses can potentially outweigh any gains from higher prices caused by [international commodity agreements]."

Kenya met its coffee quota obligations by prohibiting the planting of new trees. However, this policy, according to two studies by McMahon (1987, 1988), resulted in large distribution effects that mostly hurt people in the lowest income classes who did not have coffee trees at the time.

It is important to remember that some producing countries join international commodity agreements to protect themselves against volatility in export incomes. Thus, any consideration of the net impact of the price support must also evaluate income stability.

3. *What are the costs associated with international commodity agreements?* This question is especially important when one considers the buffer stocks that require tying up funds for stockpiles. Assuming that the benefits of price stability exceed the costs of stabilization, what is the optimal price range that would maximize the net benefits? How are those benefits to be distributed? Negotiators of international commodity agreements are usually more preoccupied with more practical questions (the formula for the contribution of funds, the duration of the agreement, the price range, the geographical location of the stocks, and so on) than with reaching this more sophisticated level of inquiry. Still, these are important questions that require in-depth analysis.

The Integrated Programme for Commodities

The strongest support for internationally coordinated efforts came at UNCTAD IV in 1976 when the Integrated Programme for Commodities (IPC) was proposed. UNCTAD envisioned the establishment of a common fund to coordinate support for eighteen commodities: bananas, bauxite, cocoa, coffee, copper, cotton, hard fibers, iron ore, jute, manganese, meat, phosphates, rubber, sugar, tea, tin, tropical timber, and vegetable seeds and oil (Raffaelli, 1995: 23).

Efforts to establish a common fund for commodities met with resistance, however, from countries like the United States, which declined to participate. The United States questioned the ability of a common fund to fulfill the role envisioned by UNCTAD. Nonetheless, the idea for an Integrated Programme for Commodities appealed to many countries, particularly developing countries, which joined together to establish the Common Fund for Commodities (CFC).

The agreement establishing the CFC was concluded in 1980 and came into force in 1989. As of June 1998, the CFC had 106 member countries plus the European Community, the Organization of African Unity/African Economic Community (OAU/AEC), and the Common Market for Eastern and Southern Africa (COMESA). All sub-Saharan African countries except Liberia, Mauritius, Namibia, Seychelles, and South Africa were members.[10]

The CFC has two accounts. The First Account is for financing international buffer stocks and internationally coordinated national stocks. The Second Account is for financing research and development projects that are geared toward improving productivity, competitiveness, diversification, investment, marketing, and optimal use and management of natural resources (Common Fund for Commodities, 1997: 15, 59–63). Article 18.3 of the Agreement Establishing the Common Fund for Commodities describes measures of the Second Account:

> The measures shall be commodity development measures, aimed at improving the structural conditions in the markets and at enhancing the long-term competitiveness and prospects of particular commodities. Such measures shall include research and development, productivity improvements, marketing and measures designed to assist, as a rule by means of joint financing or through technical assistance, vertical diversification, whether undertaken alone, as in the cases of perishable commodities and other commodities whose problems cannot be adequately solved by stocking, or in addition to and in support of stocking activities. (Common Fund for Commodities, 1980: 11)

The strong skepticism of the United States about a common fund can be understood when one considers the envisioned function of the First Account. It is hard to imagine how the concept of an integrated approach toward buffer stock would work in practice, given the uniqueness of each commodity and the varying interests among and between importers and exporters. Individual commodity agreements have been having enough problems as it is. It is not surprising, therefore, that the First Account has not yet been activated.

The Second Account has been active since 1991. To be considered for assistance for a project for any commodity, a country can submit a project proposal to a respective International Commodity Body (ICB). The list of designated ICBs is given in Table 5.5. "ICBs are intergovernmental organizations that concentrate on specific

Table 5.5   Designated International Commodity Bodies

The International Cocoa Organization
The International Coffee Organization
The International Copper Study Group
The International Cotton Advisory Committee
The International Grains Council[a]
The International Jute Organization
The International Lead and Zinc Study Group
The International Natural Rubber Organization
The International Nickel Study Group
The International Olive Oil Council
The International Rubber Study Group
The International Sugar Organization
The International Tropical Timber Organization
Intergovernmental Group on Bananas[b]
Intergovernmental Group on Citrus Fruit[b]
Intergovernmental Sub-Committee on Fish Trade[b]
Intergovernmental Group on Grains[b]
Intergovernmental Group on Hard Fibres[b]
Intergovernmental Sub-Group on Hides and Skins[b]
Intergovernmental Group on Meat[b]
Intergovernmental Group on Oils, Oilseeds, and Fats[b]
Intergovernmental Group on Rice[b]
Intergovernmental Group on Tea[b]

Source: Common Fund for Commodities (1997: 26; 1998: 15).
a. Formerly the International Wheat Council.
b. Groups within the FAO.

commodities, mainly through consultations between consumers and producers and analyses of market developments" (Common Fund for Commodities, 1998: 6).

The ICB evaluates the proposal and, if the ICB makes a positive recommendation, then it formally sponsors the application to the CFC. The ICB also has the responsibility of monitoring the implementation of funded projects and disseminating information born out of the projects.

Most of the benefits of the projects accrue to the developing countries where those projects are implemented. It is important to note that projects must be commodity focused, not country focused, in order to be considered. The transferability of technology is an important consideration for project approval.

From 1991 to 1997, the CFC approved sixty-four projects with a total of U.S.$192.3 million, of which the fund financed 43 percent. The Secretariat of the CFC classified the sixty-four projects into three broad categories: research and development aimed at enhancing productivity—37 percent; processing, vertical diversification, marketing and quality testing—37 percent; and trade and market development—26 percent (Common Fund for Commodities, 1998: 6).

In 1996 the CFC Secretariat commissioned a study by outside experts on the functioning and future role of the CFC. The study concluded that the CFC still had an important role to play, especially in the economic development of the least developed countries, which are dependent on commodities. The report pointed out that the conditions that gave rise to the CFC—that is, commodity price instability, dependence on commodities by least developed countries, and the deterioration of the terms of trade for those countries—still existed and that the CFC is unique. It is the only international financing institution that specifically addresses commodity development and marketing issues in the global context with a focus on economic development in developing countries (Common Fund for Commodities, 1997: 45–54).

Table 5.6 shows the projects approved in 1996 and the primary beneficiaries of those projects. Considering the type of projects financed by the fund and the concentration of the benefits to developing countries, it is easy to accept the conclusion reached by the independent consultants commissioned by the CFC Secretariat.

Nonetheless, the apparent role of the CFC in development does not guarantee its future. Lately, some developed countries, notably Canada and France, have withdrawn from the CFC, thus limiting financial resources for the CFC. Developing countries must continue to lobby for the support of developed countries to finance the CFC. At the same time, developing countries must be willing to maintain it on their own, if necessary, even if that means it will operate on a level of support lower than what currently exists. However, this kind of commitment can only come from a clear understanding of the role of the CFC in development.

At an appropriate time in the future, it is important to conduct a qualitative and quantitative cost-benefit analysis of a sample of the CFC projects to determine, to the extent possible, the real impact of the CFC projects. It is currently too soon to conduct such a study. Projects like those financed by the CFC take several years to complete, and their results take even longer to be manifest. By the end of 1997, only nine projects (out of the sixty-four) had been completed.

Conclusion

It appears that there is still a need for international commodity agreements, but their future is not bright. Only the INRA currently

Table 5.6 Projects Approved by the Common Fund for Commodities in 1996

Project Title (Sponsoring ICB)	Project Executing Agency	Cost and Common Fund Grant (U.S.$)	Primary Beneficiaries
Development of Gourmet Coffee Potential (International Coffee Organization)	The International Trade Center	1,412,000 1,018,000	Brazil, Burundi, Ethiopia, Papua New Guinea, and Uganda
Study on Marketing and Trading Policies in Selected Coffee Producing Countries (International Coffee Organization)	World Bank	289,068 243,868	Angola, Cameroon, Ethiopia, Ghana, Guatemala, India, Madagascar, Togo, and the Democratic Republic of Congo
Integrated Management of Coffee Berry Borer (International Coffee Organization)	International Institute of Biological Control	5,467,000 2,968,000	Colombia, Ecuador, Guatemala, Honduras, India, Jamaica, and Mexico
Creation of Pilot Demonstration Plants and Training to Improve Olive Oil Quality (International Olive Oil Council)	Estación de Olivicultura y Elaiotechnia de Jaén	2,351,506 1,038,000	Algeria, Morocco, and Tunisia
Sustainable Productivity Improvement for Rice in Inland Valleys in West Africa (FAO Intergovernmental Group on Rice)	West Africa Rice Development Association	1,801,828 1,001,824	Burkina Faso, Côte d'Ivoire, and Nigeria

continues

Table 5.6 continued

Project Title (Sponsoring ICB)	Project Executing Agency	Cost and Common Fund Grant (U.S.$)	Primary Beneficiaries
Product and Market Development of Sisal and Henequen Products (FAO Intergovernmental Group on Hard Fibres)	United Nations Industrial Development Organization	5,387,785 2,569,823	Kenya and Tanzania
Development of Specific Applications of Jute-Based Non-Wovens to Enable Commercialization (International Jute Organization)	The Textiles Consultancy Ltd.	956,283 756,283	Footwear and floor-covering industries in the producing and European countries (project implemented in the U.K.)
The Use of Molecular Biology Techniques in Search for Varieties Resistant to Witches' Broom Disease in Cocoa (International Cocoa Organization)	Comissao Executive do Plano da Lavoura Cacauiera	3,196,936 816,197	South American and Caribbean countries
Cocoa Germplasm Utilization and Conservation: A Global Approach (International Cocoa Organization)	International Plant Genetic Resources	10,167,000 2,942,000	Initially cocoa breeders; ultimately cocoa growers
Transfer of Technology and Promotion of Demand: Zinc Die Casting, Phase II (International Lead and Zinc Study Group)	Zinc Development Association	156,154 139,879	China, India, Korea, Morocco, Peru, and Tunisia

continues

Table 5.6 continued

Transfer of Technology and Promotion of Demand: Zinc Hot Dip Galvanizing, Phase II (International Lead and Zinc Study Group)	Chambre Syndicale du Zinc et du Cadmium	216,838 184,813	China, India, Korea, Morocco, Peru, and Tunisia
Coconut Germplasm Utilization and Conservation to Promote Sustainable Coconut Production (FAO Intergovernmental Group on Oils, Oilseeds, and Fats)	International Plant Genetic Resources Institute	3,732,635 1,195,778	Coconut producers
Improvement of Marketability of Cotton Produced in Zones Affected by Stickiness (International Cotton Advisory Committee)	Sudan Cotton Company	2,059,988 1,101,093	Sudan

Source: Common Fund for Commodities (1997: 71–82).

operates with economic provisions. How the INRA has managed to maintain its economic provisions into the 1990s, whereas others have not, is a reflection to some extent of the salient features associated with each commodity. There are three main reasons why the INRA has been successful.

First, there are only about ten countries that export natural rubber. Six of them are members of the INRA. These exporting members include the "big three"—Thailand, Indonesia, and Malaysia—that together account for about 92 percent of the world exports of natural rubber. The remaining three exporting members—Côte d'Ivoire, Nigeria, and Sri Lanka—account for about 7 percent. Since there are so few of them, it is easier for the exporting members to iron out their differences. Moreover, exporting members have the strong Association of Natural Rubber Producing Countries (AN-RPC), which gives them some leverage in negotiating with importing members (Stubbs, 1984).[11]

Second, the participation of natural rubber importing countries has strong support from the multinational corporations in their respective automobile industries. Other commodity agreements do not enjoy such enthusiastic support.

Third, the INRA has a provision for automatic revision of the price range in response to the Daily Market Indicator Price and the sales and purchases of buffer stock. Moreover, the price of natural rubber is linked to the price of its competitor, synthetic rubber. The price range set by the INRA adjusts quickly to market trends. The fact that the INRA is "relatively innocuous," that is, that it has very little price-stabilizing effect, has helped it to survive (Gilbert, 1996: 15). Importing countries find it to be friendly to market forces and not very threatening.

Of course, the relative ineffectiveness of an international commodity agreement does not assure its future. If producers find it useless, they will pull out of the agreement.[12] On the other hand, if an international commodity agreement is effective in stabilizing and, more important, supporting prices, it may alienate importing countries. Moreover, it may be seen as interfering with the world market system.

The apparent success of the INRA notwithstanding, the future of international commodity agreements is not promising. The problems associated with commodity agreements, discussed in the previous section, and the apparent increased faith in the market system to solve economic problems contribute to this bleak picture. For example, there is an increasing belief that risks associated with price instability can be alleviated by using futures contracts rather than international intervention (Gilbert, 1985, 1996; Morgan et al., 1994).

A futures contract is a legal agreement to buy or sell, at some designated time in the future, a given amount of a clearly defined commodity at a rate agreed upon today. This contract can be reversed before its expiration. For example, someone who buys a September 2000 coffee futures contract in January 2000 can reverse his or her position in March 2000 by entering into a futures contract to sell the coffee he or she contracted to buy. Since futures contracts can either be delivered or traded, futures trading is very liquid. Futures trading also reduces the risks associated with price and production variability. In addition, it provides information about future prices (Morgan et al., 1994; Stoll and Whaley, 1993).

The bleak future of the international commodity agreements can also be understood, to some extent, in the context of the Cold War. The Cold War was a political conflict between nations and a conflict of ideology: the United States versus the USSR, capitalism versus communism, and market economic systems versus centrally planned economic systems. At the end of the Cold War, the USSR disintegrated, communism collapsed, and the ideology of the market system triumphed.

The United States, whose foreign policy was, by and large, dictated by the Cold War landscape, now has one less reason to participate in international commodity agreements. Developed countries in general, whose participation had always been lukewarm because of their fear that international commodity agreements interfere with market operations (regardless of what they practiced in their own countries), have felt vindicated.

Increasingly, the market system is seen as a panacea. It is expected to solve economic and social problems alike, be they poor education standards, health care problems, welfare problems, pollution, or income inequities. Welfare programs are cut in developed nations, and the poor are increasingly made to feel responsible for their situations. They are asked to believe in the miracle of the market system whose benefits will eventually trickle down to them.

Likewise, poor countries are told that the market system will solve their problems. Sub-Saharan African countries have been asked to study Asian countries for economic lessons on the miracles of opening economies to world market forces. When Asian countries started to undergo economic crises in 1997, responsibility was not attributed to the openness that may have made these countries vulnerable to world market forces. Instead, the prescription from the IMF was that more openness and freer markets were needed.

The point here is that unabated market systems have come to be demanded and accepted (though sometimes grudgingly) as the only road to prosperity. The motto seems to be "embrace unconditional market systems and thou shall be saved from the chains of poverty." The debate over efficiency and equity has subsided, with efficiency being given the higher priority (at times, the only priority) and/or the market system being expected to address both issues effectively. In this environment, international commodity agreements, which, in one sense, were meant to address the equity issue between developed and developing countries, do not have a bright future.

Purely from the point of view of efficiency, it is very difficult to defend international commodity agreements. They may distort prices and, thus, distort production and consumption and cause a deadweight loss. From the point of view of equity, they seem to be somewhat ineffective. The income per capita in sub-Saharan Africa as a ratio of the income per capita in the OECD countries has continued to decline. Similar observations can be made with other measures. Many countries are just as dependent on a few commodities for exports today as they were twenty-five years ago.[13] The terms of trade are still deteriorating for African countries.

In general, the economic situation that called for commodity agreements in the 1960s and 1970s is still present, especially for sub-Saharan Africa. On considering this situation, one can argue that international commodity agreements have been ineffective. Or one can consider the same situation and argue that international commodity agreements are still needed, as concluded by the CFC study cited earlier. Whatever one's conclusion, enthusiasm for commodity agreements is waning. Even some officials at UNCTAD, an institution with a well-deserved reputation for advocating for developing countries, are no longer quite comfortable with the term "international commodity agreements." They prefer terms such as *study groups* or *consultation groups* or similar terms that are market friendly and emphasize the changing role of international commodity agreements.

Likewise, some commercial attachés from sub-Saharan Africa privately contend that further pursuit of such agreements is a lost cause. Of course, they are neither oblivious to the problems facing sub-Saharan Africa nor against international commodity agreements per se. They are simply disillusioned by the dysfunctional nature of these agreements and see very little prospect in the revival of economic clauses. Accordingly, much of their economic diplomacy is now focused on debt relief, foreign direct investment, GATT and WTO agreements, and bilateral and multilateral preferential trade agreements, such as the Lomé Convention and regional economic cooperation. This may be a pragmatic use of the meager diplomatic resources available.

It thus appears that international commodity agreements with economic provisions are quickly becoming things of the past. This, of course, does not mean international commodity agreements will cease to exist altogether. They will continue to function at least as study groups. What were initially the secondary objectives of commodity agreements—collecting and disseminating information, sponsoring research on consumption and production, helping developing countries diversify their economies, and supporting processing in developing countries—will likely increasingly become the primary objectives.

One can also expect sporadic short-lived agreements by subsets of producers to control exports, as has been demonstrated by the ICA. Likewise, the CFC may not completely give up on the functions of its First Account, namely, financing international buffer stocks and internationally coordinated national stocks. However, over time, reality will likely force the CFC and international commodity agreements increasingly to adopt as their primary objective that of the CFC's Second Account: to finance research and development projects that are geared toward improving productivity, competitiveness, diversification, investment, marketing, and optimal use and management of natural resources.

Case: The International Coffee Agreement[14]

The International Coffee Agreement (ICA) was established in 1962. Its operation is administered by the International Coffee Organization (ICO). The main objective of the ICA is to support and stabilize coffee prices. The ICA has tried to achieve this goal by regulating coffee supplies through an export quota scheme.

Basic Information About Coffee

Coffee is a perennial evergreen tree (shrub) that normally bears fruit once a year. There are two main botanical species of coffee: *Coffea Arabica*, known as coffee arabica, and *Coffea Canephora*, known as coffee robusta. Arabica accounts for 75 to 80 percent of the world production of coffee, and robusta accounts for the rest. Coffee grows best in tropical climates. The only significant producing area outside of the tropics is Parana in Brazil, which lies around 25° South (Marshall, 1983).

The gestation period is about four to five years for coffee arabica and two to three years for coffee robusta. Coffee trees reach maturity in their sixth or seventh year and have a productive life span of thirty to forty years.

In the world market, coffee is divided into four different types according to its natural quality. In descending order of quality, the types are Colombian Milds, Other Milds, Brazilian and Other Arabicas, and Robustas. Most coffee is exported as green coffee and only a small proportion as roasted or soluble coffee.[15]

About 90 percent of the world's output of coffee is exported and consumed in developed countries. The three major importers—the European Union, the United States, and Japan—import about 70 percent of the world's supply (EU 40 percent, United States 24 percent, and Japan 6 percent).

Volatility of the Price of Coffee

In a free world market environment, the price of coffee has the potential to rise and fall dramatically from year to year and also within the coffee year. There are four main causes of annual price instability (Fisher, 1972):

1. Supply variability due to exogenous factors such as frost, drought, heavy rains that may prevent harvesting, the botanical cyclical production pattern, and pests and diseases;
2. Price inelasticity of supply, especially in the short run;
3. Price inelasticity of demand; and
4. Speculation influences.

The price of coffee can also be quite volatile within the coffee year since a large part of the world's output is harvested at about the same time, the summer and early fall. As Fisher (1972) pointed out, this seasonal price instability is exacerbated by poor storage facilities, an urgent need for export revenues, inefficient marketing systems in producing countries, exporters' uncertainty about political stability, and pessimism about the price of coffee in the future.

The Importance of Coffee to Developing Countries

Almost all coffee that enters commercial channels in the world market is produced in developing countries. Most of the coffee in the world is produced by small farmers. Being labor intensive, coffee production is an important source of employment in developing countries.

Coffee is second only to oil as a source of export revenue in developing countries. In many coffee-producing countries, coffee is a very important or the most important source of foreign exchange (see Table 5.1). This high degree of dependence coupled with the volatility of world prices of coffee causes these countries to have relatively unstable export earnings. The importance of coffee to developing countries was a significant factor in the formation of the International Coffee Agreement.

The Evolution of the International Coffee Agreement

In the first quarter of the twentieth century, the state of São Paulo in Brazil produced over 75 percent of the world's coffee. The state government acted as a monopsony (a single buyer of all coffee produced in São Paulo) as well as a monopoly (a single seller of coffee produced in São Paulo to importers). The state government also restricted new planting. In the early 1930s, the Brazilian federal government took control of coffee policy. It began to destroy marketable coffee as an additional measure to increase coffee prices or to maintain high coffee prices.

The high prices caused by the Brazilian coffee policy gave an incentive to Colombia and other Latin American countries to expand their coffee production. However, the outbreak of World War II in 1939 diminished demand for coffee. This crisis brought the United States and fourteen Latin American countries together to form the Inter-American Coffee Agreement in 1940. The United States was the only importing member country of the agreement. Coffee prices were regulated by setting export quotas to the United States and nonmember countries. At that time, the United States was importing more than two-thirds of the world's coffee. Although the United States was opposed to commodity regulation, it yielded to this agreement to ensure Latin America's alliance during the war.[16] In 1945, at the end of the war, the United States pulled out of the agreement and returned to its position in favor of the free market. The Inter-American Coffee Agreement was dissolved in 1948.

After the war, there was a dramatic increase in demand for coffee and, consequently, a sharp increase in coffee prices, which peaked in 1954. The high prices encouraged extensive coffee production in Latin American countries and in Africa.

The supply of coffee rose in the mid-1950s, pushing prices down and renewing interest among producing countries to control exports. A producers' cartel known as the Mexico Agreement was formed in 1957. It included seven countries: Brazil, Colombia, Costa Rica, El Salvador, Guatemala, Mexico, and Nicaragua. By the end of 1960, the agreement included other Latin American countries and African countries.[17] None of the importing countries were members of the agreement except those that were representing their colonies.

The 1962 International Coffee Agreement

In spite of the agreement of producing countries to restrict exports and thus increase coffee prices, production rose and prices hit bottom in 1961–1962. During this period, the United States revised its policy and decided to join the coffee agreement. The change of policy by the U.S. government is explained by the following interrelated factors (Lucier, 1988; Bates, 1997):

1. Fear of economic chaos in Latin America;
2. "Cold War" fears, exacerbated by the Cuban revolution, and the perception that alliance with Latin American countries would prevent the spread of communism;
3. The perception that a coffee agreement, rather than being merely a commodity policy, would be a development policy for poor countries;
4. Confidence that an effective agreement could be achieved; and
5. Support by the coffee industry in the United States. The U.S. coffee traders and roasters were concerned mainly with the potential for the economic collapse of producing countries. Moreover, large processors were able to use their support for the agreement to secure rebates from dominant producers and increase their competitiveness over small roasters.

In 1962, twenty-two importing countries (including the United States) and forty-six exporting countries formed the International Coffee Agreement, which went into effect in 1963. The main objectives of the agreement were to support the price of coffee and reduce price instability. Other objectives were to increase and stabilize export earnings and to assure adequate supplies of coffee. The primary instrument to be used to achieve these objectives was export quotas. The agreement covered green, roasted, and soluble coffee.

Individual country basic export quotas were set using historical shares of exports. This historical share formula of allocating quotas was favored by Brazil and Colombia, who had large market shares. In 1965 the ICA set a price range within which coffee prices were to fluctuate. This price range and the quotas were adjusted periodically according to market conditions. Quotas were changed largely on a pro rata system and, to a much lesser extent, on a selectivity system.

To enforce compliance with the agreement, all export quotas had to be accompanied by certificates of origin. In addition to requiring certificates of origin, in 1967 the ICO started to issue export stamps that were also to accompany export quotas. The number of export stamps issued to each exporting member depended on a country's quota.

The export restrictions set by the ICA did not cover the volume of exports from producing members to nonmembers. A resolution passed in 1966 did, however, limit quantities of imports by importing members from nonmembers. The major importing members imported mainly green coffee and only a small proportion of roasted or soluble coffee.[18]

The 1968 International Coffee Agreement

A second agreement came into effect in 1968. The main difference between this and the previous one was that the new one added a resolution for mandatory contributions by exporting members into a "diversification fund."[19] The fund was then allocated by the ICO to exporting members according to their contribution and need. Individual member countries, however, maintained autonomy over their domestic policies on the allocation of resources.

A dispute between two superpowers in the coffee industry, the United States (the largest importer) and Brazil (the largest exporter), posed a serious threat to the 1968 ICA. In the 1960s Brazil encouraged processing of green coffee into soluble coffee, thus adding value to its exports. The Brazilian processors had an advantage over their U.S. competitors because they could buy low quality green beans (which were not exported) at a lower price. They also saved on transportation costs by exporting soluble coffee rather than green coffee.[20] The share of Brazilian soluble coffee in the U.S. market rose from 1 percent in 1965 to 14 percent in 1967 (Fisher, 1972).

In the United States, coffee processors complained that Brazilians had an unfair advantage and demanded measures that would reduce Brazil's competitiveness. Pressured by green coffee brokers and processors, the U.S. government demanded that Brazil "voluntarily" reduce its exports of soluble coffee. A bilateral agreement could not be reached, and the ICO was subsequently drawn into the negotiations. The controversy was resolved by requiring Brazil to sell low quality green coffee to the U.S. processors (Lucier, 1988). This requirement increased the supply of cheap unprocessed coffee to the U.S. processors.

In the early 1970s, another divisive conflict arose. Wanting to improve their terms of trade, coffee-producing countries pressed for higher coffee prices and reduced quotas. Consuming countries were adamantly opposed to such moves. The disagreement between producers and consumers led to the suspension of the economic provision of the ICA in 1973.

The 1976 International Coffee Agreement

In 1976 a third agreement was reached. However, the 1975 frost in Brazil reduced the supply of coffee (relative to demand) for four consecutive years. Thus, the quota system did not resume until 1980.

Under this agreement, 70 percent of the quota was determined by the countries' share of exports in 1968–1972, and the remaining 30 percent was based on the countries' volume of inventory (Lucier, 1988).

The 1983 International Coffee Agreement and the Suspension of the Quota System in 1989

The 1983 agreement was similar to the previous ones. Quotas were suspended in 1986 owing to a severe drought in Brazil that reduced the world supply of coffee. The quota system resumed in October 1987. Negotiations for a new agreement started in 1988. Three main impediments to the renewal of the 1983 Coffee Agreement, according to Brandt (1991), were:

1. Disagreement over shares of export quotas;
2. Inflexibility of the quota system, which prevented importing countries from obtaining optimal amounts of the types of coffee they wanted; and
3. The two-tier market system, in which exports to nonmember countries were sold at discounted prices compared to exports to the members of the agreement, as seen in Figure 5.1. Note that nonmembers generally received discounted prices only when quotas were in effect.

The first impediment could be characterized as a dispute primarily among producers and the next two as disputes between producers and consumers. However, the conflicts were much more complex because of each country's own situation and vested interests.

The dispute among producing countries over shares of export quotas had its roots in the first agreement. Export quotas were determined using historical data on exports. All quotas set under subsequent

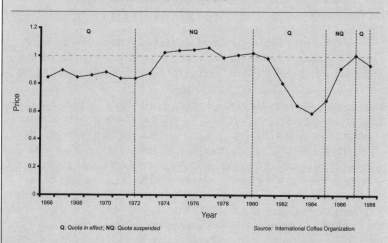

Figure 5.1   The Price of Coffee to Nonmembers as a Ratio of the Price of Coffee to Members

Q: *Quota in effect*; NQ: *Quota suspended*   *Source:* International Coffee Organization

agreements were directly tied to this formula, which was favored by Colombia and Brazil. Small producers, particularly African countries, wanted a more flexible formula that would take into account production growth rates. They also argued for increased export quotas for their countries owing to the importance of coffee in their economies.

The second main problem, the inability of the quota system to accommodate changes in demand for different types of coffee, was a constant frustration to consuming countries. Importers, especially in the United States, wanted a selective system that increased or decreased producing countries' quotas according to price indicators for different types of coffee. According to Ralph Ives, a U.S. delegate to the ICA, the United States wanted to see increased supplies of high quality mild arabica, whose prices had gone up as a result of artificial shortages created by the rigid quota system. Ives explained that the price of mild arabicas was 40 cents per pound higher than the price of robustas in September 1988, compared to a price difference of 10 cents in September 1987 (phone interview with Ralph Ives by the author, fall 1993).

The German Coffee Association expressed its concern about the rigidity of the quota system as follows:

> The main problem with the present agreement is that the distribution of export quotas does not comply with market trends. A shortage of quality coffees that are in demand is artificially created, and an excess of poorer qualities is offered. Political power relations among the producing countries are

> preventing a lasting change in quota distribution. (Quoted in
> Brandt, [1991: 86], taken from Deutscher Kaffee-Verband, *In-
> ternationales Kaffeeabkommen,* Bonn, 7 February 1990: 5.)

Adopting a selective system of quotas would mean increasing quotas for Colombian milds and other milds and reducing quotas for the
robusta and Brazilian arabica. Brazil, the major coffee producer, vigorously opposed this type of quota system.

Finally, the two-tier market system was another serious problem
for importing member countries. The ICO resolutions that had been
adopted between 1983 and 1988 to reduce discounted prices to nonmembers had not been effective. Nonmember countries were buying
coffee from producer member countries at a price less than 50 percent
of the price paid by importing members.[21] This price disparity opened
many doors for the triangular transshipment of coffee, sometimes referred to as "tourist coffee."

Ralph Ives described the problem to the author as follows:

> The huge profits that could be made by selling nonmember
> coffee on the member market provoked substantial smuggling.
> ICO data indicate that the diversion of smuggled coffee to the
> member market was around 5 to 6 million bags—about 10
> percent of the total annual quota for the member market. But
> not only was a large quantity smuggled, the quality of the cof-
> fee was being switched. High quality coffee destined for non-
> members was exchanged for poor quality coffee purchased
> for the member market. Firms that refused to take part in
> these illegal operations were placed at a competitive disadvan-
> tage to those that did participate.

Coffee traders and roasters in the United States and other countries echoed the same complaints, arguing that consumers in the United
States were, in effect, being taxed to support a black market in coffee.

The chief negotiator for the United States in the coffee talks, Jon
Rosenbaum, warned that any proposed new agreement that did not
solve the two-tier market would not get U.S. support. Since no agreeable compromise could be reached on this and the other two issues,
negotiations collapsed, and economic provisions of the ICA were suspended in July 1989. Exporting countries, led by Brazil, responded with
a sales frenzy that caused the price of coffee to fall by more than 25
percent within just a few days.

The last ICA was reached in 1994 without economic provisions
and without the United States. There have been numerous attempts by
the Association of Coffee Producing Countries (with Brazil typically

taking the lead) to boost coffee prices (Behrman, 1991, 1993; Taylor, 1993; McGee, 1995). These efforts, however, have all been short lived and have tended to put more distance between producing and consuming countries.

Notes

1. See Lim (1991: 5–53) for an analysis of the first three parts.

2. For any product, prices are higher in an oligopolistic market than in a perfectly competitive market.

3. It should be noted that various initiatives to control exports took place prior to the years indicated in Table 5.3.

4. The price ceiling was set at 160 cents per pound, and the upper intervention price was set at 150 cents per pound.

5. For details about the International Cocoa Agreement, see Raffaelli (1995: 136–180).

6. The forecast by UNCTAD (1991: 188–189) suggested that Indonesia and Malaysia will account for 20 percent of the world output of cocoa by the mid-2000s.

7. Although it seems that developed countries deceived developing countries, many developing countries, on their part, deceived their own producers. Developing countries continued to speak for the poor farmers in their countries. Most of them, especially in sub-Saharan Africa, nevertheless continued to impose a heavy tax burden on those farmers by administering relatively low government-controlled domestic prices and subsidizing the operation of inefficient marketing boards. It is tempting to say that taxing farmers was a production policy consistent with the objectives of a given commodity agreement to limit output. There is no apparent consistent difference between agricultural price policies for different export crops, however, to suggest that those without international commodity agreements were spared the tax burden.

8. Alternatively, see Herrmann (1986).

9. The last number was calculated by the author using data on volume and export earnings in table 6.1 in Herrmann et al. (1993).

10. Since 1996 there have been discussions between the Secretariat of the CFC and South Africa on possible membership of the latter in the CFC.

11. The ANRPC predated the INRA. In spite of their leverage, exporting countries seek the cooperation of consuming countries, both for financial contributions to cover the costs of stocking and for the political harmony of the agreement.

12. Negotiations for the third INRA were protracted for more than two years (1993–1995), partly owing to the dissatisfaction of the exporting members (Gilbert, 1996: 16).

13. See African Development Bank Group (1982: 17–19) for the percentage shares of major commodities in total value of exports for African countries for 1972 through 1980.

14. This is a condensed version of the author's study, *The Uncertainty of the International Coffee Agreement*, originally published as Pew Case Study in International Affairs 159. Copyright 1994 by The Pew Charitable Trusts, Georgetown University, Washington, D.C. Reprinted by permission.

15. The following definitions are given by the International Coffee Organization. *Green coffee* means all coffee in the dry form before roasting. *Roasted coffee* means green coffee roasted to any degree; to find the equivalent of roasted coffee to green coffee, multiply the net weight of roasted coffee by 1.19. *Soluble coffee* means the dried, water-soluble solids derived from roasted coffee; to find the equivalent of soluble coffee to green coffee, multiply the net weight of soluble coffee by 2.6.

16. The United States had twelve votes, and the other nations (all of them producers) combined had twenty-four votes. This protected U.S. interests, as there was a provision that allowed an unlimited increase in import quotas by a one-third vote (Fisher, 1972).

17. African countries that were not yet independent were represented by their colonialists: Portugal, France, Great Britain, and Belgium. These colonial powers participated in the agreement as exporters and not as consumers.

18. Quotas are set in terms of green coffee. However, an exporting country could sell its coffee as roasted or soluble coffee, using the formula in Note 15 to determine its equivalent amount in green coffee.

19. The provision for the diversification fund was removed in 1976.

20. About two-thirds of the weight is lost in the processing of green coffee into soluble coffee.

21. See Herrmann (1986) or Herrmann et al. (1993).

SIX

◆

Regional Economic Integration

R *egional economic integration* refers to special economic arrangements between countries in a given geographical area. It implies differential treatment in trade for member countries in comparison with treatment for nonmember countries.

Some have argued that sub-Saharan Africa is "short-changed" in the world market and that one way of addressing the situation is for African countries to forge closer ties among themselves. African politicians voice strong support for economic integration as an effective strategy for trade and development in sub-Saharan Africa. Most academic and institutional researchers likewise agree with this strategy.[1] Part of what makes economic integration in Africa an interesting subject for research, however, is the wide gap between the rhetorical support of politicians and the real state of economic integration.

Stages of Economic Integration

Economic integration can be divided into five progressive stages: preferential trading arrangements, a free trade area, a customs union, a common market, and an economic union.

Preferential Trading Arrangements

Under this lowest level of integration, member countries agree to lower trade barriers between themselves. Each country sets its own trade policies vis-à-vis nonmembers, though a most-favored-nation clause usually precludes preferential treatment by any member country to a nonmember. An example is the Preferential Trade Area (PTA) for eastern and southern African states before it became

175

COMESA in 1994. Note that even the objectives of the PTA went beyond typical preferential trading arrangements, for example, by engaging in sector policy coordination, monetary and financial cooperation, and coordinated development programs (UNCTAD, 1996: 57568). COMESA hopes to achieve a free trade area by the year 2000.

A Free Trade Area

At this next level of economic integration, members remove barriers on intragroup trade for all goods or on an agreed subset of goods. In arrangements that are similar to preferential trading arrangements, member states set their own national barriers on trade with nonmembers. The rather misleading names and overly ambitious goals of regional economic blocs in sub-Saharan Africa notwithstanding, almost all of them are either at the first stage of integration (preferential trading arrangements) or at the infancy level of a free trade area.

Since member countries under preferential trading arrangements or free trade areas are allowed to set their own external barriers, there is the potential for exporters to transship their goods to avoid high tariffs. Transshipment involves two steps. First, a product is exported from a nonmember country to a member country that has relatively low external protection. Second, the product is reexported to another member country that has higher external protection. For example, suppose Eritrea has lower tariffs than Ethiopia on a product imported from Italy. Suppose also that under the PTA group to which Eritrea and Ethiopia belong, there are no tariffs on intra-PTA trade on this product. The disparity in external tariffs creates an incentive to export the product from Italy to Ethiopia through Eritrea.

Preferential trading or free trade agreements usually try to avoid the transshipment problem by including a "rules of origin" provision. For example, COMESA rules of origin stipulate that for goods to qualify for preferential tariff treatment, they must meet two conditions. First, the goods must be imported directly from another member state in which they were produced. Second, if the exporting country used inputs imported from nonmembers, the cost, insurance, and freight (CIF) value of the inputs must not exceed 60 percent of the total cost of materials used in production, or the ex-factory value added must be at least 45 percent.[2] For products deemed important for the economic development of member states, the value-added requirement is set at 25 percent.

The Economic Community of West African States (ECOWAS) has eliminated trade barriers for some products and reduced them for others. The ECOWAS rules of origin are similar to those of COMESA. In addition, for goods to be considered to have originated from ECOWAS member states, ECOWAS citizens must own at least 25 percent of the equity capital of the enterprises producing the goods.

A Customs Union

In a customs union, member countries not only remove trade barriers among themselves but also maintain common trade barriers for goods imported from nonmembers. The East African Community (EAC) was a customs union that existed from 1967 to 1977.[3] The three members of the Mano River Union (MRU)—Guinea, Liberia, and Sierra Leone—established a common external tariff in 1977; however, political instability and civil war in the region in the 1990s have paralyzed the MRU (UNCTAD, 1997c: 12). The Central African Customs and Economic Union (Union douanière et économique de l'Afrique Centrale, UDEAC) has been a customs union since its inception in 1966 (UNCTAD, 1996: 43–50).[4] Even though the Southern African Customs Union (SACU), with its roots in colonial times, was established primarily as a mechanism to distribute revenue among members (Mayer and Zarenda, 1994; McCarthy, 1992), it serves as the best example of a customs union in sub-Saharan Africa. Except for agricultural products, the movement of goods within the SACU countries is duty free, and member countries have a common external tariff.

According to COMESA's timetable of integration, it plans to implement a customs union by the year 2004. After failing to achieve a customs union by 1990 as was originally stipulated, ECOWAS set the year 2000 as its new target date. Given the sluggishness in implementing its agreements, it is safe to predict that ECOWAS will not achieve a free trade area, let alone a customs union, by the year 2000 (ECOWAS Secretariat, 1993: Article 35).

A Common Market

This stage of integration extends the customs union by allowing free movement of factors of production, labor, and capital within the bloc. ECOWAS has shown significant progress in intraregional immigration and may serve as a model for other regions. A protocol on the free movement of persons and right of residence was adopted in 1979. The implementation was divided into three phases: (1) right of entry and abolition of visas, (2) right of residence, and (3) right of establishment. Phases 1 and 2 came into force in 1980 and 1986, respectively. The protocol has been in its third phase of implementation since 1991 (UNCTAD, 1996: 27). The East African Co-operation, comprising Kenya, Tanzania, and Uganda, was established in 1996 and renamed the East African Community in 1999 (twenty-two years after the collapse of the first East African Community). It is also making headway in intraregional immigration.

Although regional economic blocs in sub-Saharan Africa have a common market as one of their stated objectives, most of them have not reached this stage of integration. Target dates have come and gone, only for new ones to be set. The OAU in 1980 in its Lagos Plan of Action set the year 2000 as the time by which an African Common Market would be established. Ten years into the Lagos Plan of Action, it was obvious that Africa would not even come close to the realization of this level of integration by the turn of the century. The Abuja Treaty, which entered into force in 1994 (UNCTAD, 1997c: 10), set a new target year for an African Common Market—2022 (Organization of African Unity, 1991: Article 6).[5]

An Economic Union

An economic union comprises all features of a common market plus unification of fiscal and monetary policies. The Abuja Treaty envisions an African Economic Union with a single African currency within five years of establishing an African Common Market.

During the colonial era, African countries were unified by the colonial currencies and institutions (O'Connell, 1997). For example, Kenya, Tanzania, and Uganda had a common currency until 1965, when each country introduced its own currency. Most of the former French colonies have continued monetary integration established during the colonial period by using the CFA franc, tied to the French franc, as their currency.

Likewise, after their independence Botswana, Lesotho, and Swaziland chose to peg their currencies to the South African rand, under the Rand Monetary Agreement (RMA) reached in 1974. Botswana left the RMA a year later. In 1986, the RMA was replaced by the Common Monetary Agreement (CMA), which had the same monetary arrangements. The RMA and CMA were applicable to Namibia, and Namibia joined the CMA formally in 1990 following its independence.

The Static and Dynamic
Impact of Economic Integration

The potential impact of economic integration (leaving out factors within regional groups that may augment or diminish the potential), like that of any other partial movement toward free trade, can be divided into two types, static and dynamic. The *static impact* refers to the change in equilibrium of the market price and quantity before and after the movement toward free trade. The *dynamic impact* refers to other changes in the economy, such as efficiency, investment, and industrialization, that are associated with economic integration.

The static impact of economic integration, as expected, is similar to the static impact of the GSP program, as discussed in two sections in Chapter 3, "The Potential Impact of the GSP Program" and "The Benefits to Preference-Giving Countries." Economic integration causes trade creation or trade diversion. *Trade creation* takes place when economic integration leads a product source to shift from high-cost domestic producers to low-cost producers in a member country. *Trade diversion* occurs when integration causes a product source to shift from a low-cost nonmember country to a high-cost member country. As discussed and demonstrated in "The Benefits to Preference-Giving Countries" in Chapter 3, trade creation is a movement toward free trade. Trade creation produces an unequivocal net welfare gain. (See Figure 3.1.) Trade diversion, on the other hand, may cause a net welfare gain or a net welfare loss. (See Figure 3.2.)

The dynamic impact of economic integration includes increased competition, increased investment, economies of scale, political and economic leverage, and political stability.

1. *Increased competition.* Economic integration exposes domestic producers to competition from their counterparts in the region. This leads to more efficiency in the long run. Increased competition moves resources into line with comparative advantage and also forces producers to find ways to cut costs. In general, the higher the level of integration, the higher the level of competition.

2. *Increased investment.* The free market generated within the region is an incentive to domestic and foreign investors to invest in the region.

3. *Economies of scale.* Economies of scale, a likely impact of economic integration, are also closely connected to the growth in market size. A firm experiences economies of scale when its long-run average

cost of production falls as it produces more (internal economies) or as more firms enter the industry (external economies).

Economic integration enlarges the markets for products and inputs, thus allowing firms to expand production. Increased production allows for more specialization of labor, the use of better equipment, and the acquisition of inputs at a discount price, all of which bring forth internal economies of scale.

Expanded markets also attract new firms. This may, in turn, bring external economies of scale by increasing the speed at which new techniques are generated and diffused throughout the industry, enhancing the lobbying power of the industry against government regulations, and attracting suppliers of inputs to locate into the region. Two studies by Romer (1986, 1987) suggest positive externalities from investment. That is, capital accumulation by one firm improves not only its own productivity but also that of other related firms through diffusion of technology.

4. *Political and economic leverage.* Multilateral negotiations rarely reflect democratic equality in the sense of one country, one vote. Votes are usually distributed to countries in direct relationship to the economic power of a country or region. Economic integration unites countries to speak as a group in negotiations with other countries or regions and, thus, increases their leverage in such negotiations.

5. *Political stability.* Economic integration is not performed in a political vacuum. In fact, as Asante (1997: 26) argued, "[economic] integration is political as well as economic in both its objectives and procedures." Economic integration and political stability support one another. A successful integration, even if economic in nature, will tend to forge political stability in the region. Likewise, political stability enhances economic integration.

The Association of Southeast Asian Nations (ASEAN) was formed in 1967 by Indonesia, Malaysia, the Philippines, Thailand, and Singapore, primarily to bring political stability to the subregion. The initial primary objective of the members of this regional group was to reduce conflicts among themselves and forge unity against the threats of their communist neighbors, Vietnam, the (former) USSR, and China. In fact, the threat of outside forces, although requiring a reallocation of resources to address, solidified the unity of ASEAN members. The political stability achieved within the ASEAN countries allowed devotion to economic cooperation and development (Simon, 1982; Leifer, 1989).

The ECOWAS Monitoring Group (ECOMOG) has also achieved some success in reducing the level of political instability in the west African region. Most notable was ECOMOG's leadership in containing the civil war in Liberia throughout most of the 1990s and in restoring a democratically elected president of Sierra Leone, Ahmad Kabbal, to power on March 10, 1998. Kabbal had been overthrown on May 25, 1997, in a coup d'état led by Major Johnny Paul Koroma.

Regional Economic Groups in Sub-Saharan Africa

Economic integration has always been accepted by African leaders as a strategy for trade and development. As such, efforts to sustain regional economic groups carved out under colonialism and to establish new ones have always been a part of sub-Saharan African economic and political history. There are at least twelve regional economic groups in sub-Saharan Africa. Some groups are subsets of others, as shown in Figures 6.1, 6.2, and 6.3. The four regional economic groups in sub-Saharan Africa with the largest memberships are COMESA and the Southern African Development Community (SADC) in eastern and southern Africa, ECOWAS in western Africa, and the Economic Community of Central African States (ECCAS) in central Africa. All sub-Saharan African countries belong to at least

Figure 6.1   Regional Economic Blocs in Eastern and Southern Africa

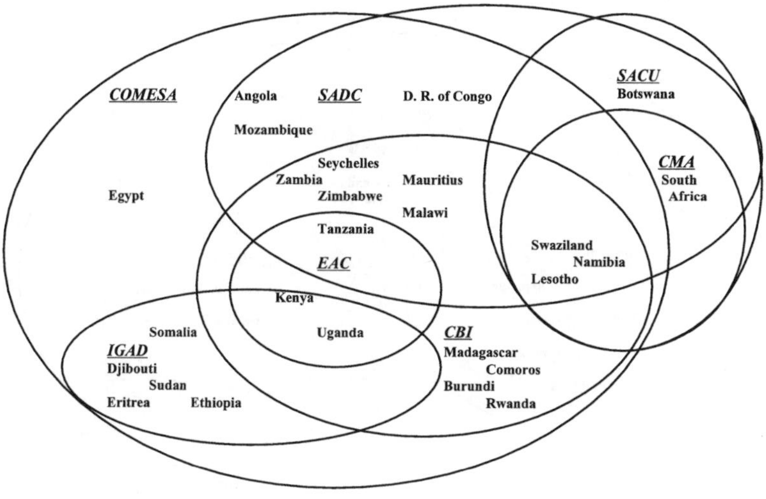

Figure 6.2   Regional Economic Blocs in West Africa

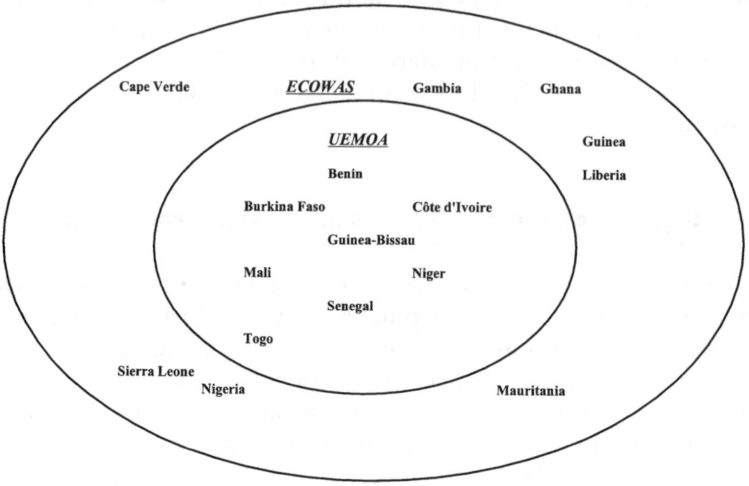

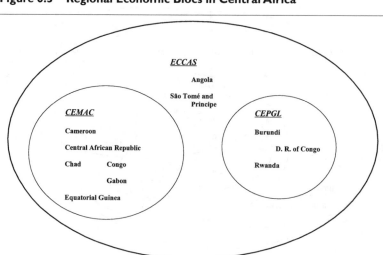

one of these regional groups. Other regional economic blocs in-
clude Cross Border Initiative (CBI), Economic and Monetary Com-
munity of Central Africa (CEMAC), Economic Community of the
Great Lakes Countries (CEPGL), Intergovernmental Authority on
Development (IGAD), and West African Monetary and Economic
Union (UEMOA).

Figure 6.3   Regional Economic Blocs in Central Africa

Common Market for Eastern and Southern Africa (COMESA)

As noted earlier, COMESA, despite its name, is *not* a common market. COMESA is nonetheless the largest regional economic group in Africa. The region extends from Egypt (which joined in June 1998) in the north to Swaziland and Namibia in the south. In mid-1998, COMESA had twenty-four member states (as shown in Figure 6.1). However, since then, Lesotho and Mozambique have withdrawn from COMESA, and in July 1999 Tanzania announced its intention to leave COMESA in the year 2000. Somalia has also become a de facto nonmember for lack of a representative government. The membership of COMESA could go down to twenty countries by the end of the year 2000. Table 6.1 shows some key indicators for twenty-one of the twenty-four countries. (Figures were not available for Lesotho, Namibia, and Swaziland.)

Like most other regional groups in sub-Saharan Africa, COMESA has a very diverse membership in terms of GNP per capita, GNP per capita growth rate, and trade indicators, as shown in Table 6.1. For example, from 1994 to 1996, Kenya and Zimbabwe alone contributed about two-thirds of all intraregional exports (for the twenty-one member states listed); a number of other countries contributed negligible amounts.

COMESA has its roots in the PTA that was established in 1981 by nine countries—Comoros, Djibouti, Ethiopia, Kenya, Malawi, Mauritius, Somalia, Uganda, and Zambia (UNCTAD, 1996: 58). The treaty establishing the PTA went into force in 1982.

The main objective of the PTA was to promote economic cooperation among its member states. The PTA established three instruments to support intra-PTA trade: the PTA Clearing House (1984), the PTA Bank (1988), and the PTA travelers checks (1988). The main function of the PTA Clearing House was to promote "the use of national currencies in the settlement of all transactions among member States" (UNCTAD, 1996: 62).

All three PTA instruments have been underutilized for various reasons. For example, the utilization of the PTA Clearing House has, in some years, been as low as 10 percent of the intra-PTA trade. This underutilization has been due to (1) a lack of information and understanding of its operation; (2) bilateral payment arrangements among member states, whereby payments are handled outside of the Clearing House mechanism; (3) insistence by some member states on payments in hard currency; and (4) exchange controls in some member states (Kumar, 1989; UNCTAD, 1996: 60–64). The liberal-

Table 6.1   COMESA Countries—Basic Indicators and Trade Performance[a]

| Country | GNP Per Capita | | Annual Average Percentage of Intra-regional Exports, 1994–1996[b] | Annual Average Percentage of Intra-regional Imports, 1994–1996[b] |
	1995 (U.S.$)	Annual Average Percentage Growth, 1985–1995		
Angola	410	–6.1	0.00	0.90
Burundi	160	–1.3	0.79	1.97
Comoros	470	–1.5[c]	0.00	0.98
Congo, Democratic Republic of	120	–8.9[c]	0.77	4.93
Djibouti	NA	NA	5.78	2.56
Egypt	790	1.1	2.47	8.26
Ethiopia[d]	100	–0.3	0.98	5.91
Kenya	280	0.1	41.06	3.44
Madagascar	230	–2.2	1.40	0.34
Malawi	170	–0.7	2.56	8.13
Mauritius	3,380	5.4	3.84	3.14
Mozambique	80	3.6	1.02	5.66
Rwanda	180	–5.4	0.12	5.49
Seychelles	6,620	3.5[c]	0.02	0.61
Somalia	NA	NA	0.09	7.40
Sudan	NA	NA	0.00	3.27
Tanzania	120	1.0	6.52	14.76
Uganda	240	2.7	0.72	12.89
Zambia	400	–0.8	6.61	5.32
Zimbabwe	540	–0.6	25.24	4.02

Sources: World Bank (1997b, 1997c); IMF (1997).
a. Does not include Lesotho, Namibia, and Swaziland.
b. Numbers may not add up to 100 because of rounding.
c. These figures are for 1986–1996.
d. Export and import figures for Ethiopia include Eritrea.

ization of financial markets (including foreign exchange markets), which happened in the early 1990s under structural adjustment programs, has also eroded the earlier uniqueness of these three instruments (COMESA, 1994: 43–45).

A clause in the treaty establishing the PTA allowed any eastern or southern African country that shared borders with a member country to be allowed into the PTA. (Exceptions were made for island countries and for Swaziland and Lesotho, which were surrounded by

Table 6.2 Average COMESA Tariff Rates, Average National Customs Tariff Rates, and the Former as a Percentage of the Latter, November 1997

Country	(1) COMESA Rates	(2) National Rates	(3) $(1)/(2) \times 100$
Angola	27	27	100
Burundi	16	39	41
Comoros	5	28	18
Democratic Republic of Congo	18	18	100
Eritrea	30	65	46
Ethiopia	29	29	100
Kenya	7	23	30
Lesotho	30	30	100
Madagascar	7	18	39
Malawi	6	20	30
Mauritius	11	35	31
Mozambique	20	20	100
Namibia	30	30	100
Rwanda	18	46	39
Sudan	10	48	21
Swaziland	30	30	100
Tanzania	24	24	100
Uganda	2	12	17
Zambia	6	15	40
Zimbabwe	9	47	19

Source: COMESA (1998).

South Africa.) Likewise, the treaty provided for a gradual reduction of tariffs and a target date of 1992 for achieving a free trade area. Although the membership of the PTA grew rapidly, the reduction of tariffs was slow and varied between member countries. The reduction of nontariff barriers has been even slower.

In 1993, the PTA pushed back the 1992 target date for a free trade area to the year 2000. In addition, it established COMESA, which officially replaced the PTA in 1994. It is highly unlikely that COMESA will meet its target of a free trade area by the year 2000. An 80 percent tariff reduction, using 1982 as the base year (which is when the PTA treaty entered into force), was scheduled to be completed by 1996; as of 1998, only 5 countries—Comoros, Eritrea, Sudan, Uganda, and Zimbabwe—had accomplished this reduction. Nonetheless, COMESA reports show that average COMESA tariff rates are considerably lower than average national tariff rates for the majority of the member states, as seen in Table 6.2.

COMESA is scheduled to reach its objective of becoming a customs union by the year 2004. Should that be achieved, the common external tariffs will be 0 percent, 5 percent, 15 percent, and 30 percent, respectively, on capital goods, raw materials, intermediate goods, and final goods. The year 2004 target date is, however, rather optimistic, given the slow movement toward a free trade area and the large number of member states.

A customs union, by virtue of having common external tariffs, negotiates trade agreements with nonmembers as a single body. Given the political and economic heterogeneity of the COMESA member states, such unity will be almost impossible to achieve within the proposed time frame. Unity appears even more remote considering the membership of COMESA countries in other regional economic groups. There is, for example, an important divide between COMESA and SADC, although as of mid-1998 twelve countries were members of both entities (see Figure 6.1) (Mandaza et al., 1994).

In the early 1990s, PTA/COMESA wanted to merge with SADC. SADC strongly opposed such a merger. One would have hoped the two economic blocs would have worked to complement each other. Instead, there has been increasing duplication, rivalry, and competition for donor support. In 1994 SADC encouraged its members to withdraw from PTA/COMESA; it also wanted the trade functions of the PTA to be incorporated into SADC. There was fear that PTA/COMESA would collapse if such a withdrawal were to take place.

In a strategic move to protect themselves in case that collapse happened, in 1996 Djibouti, Eritrea, Ethiopia, Kenya, Somalia, Sudan, and Uganda (seven of the twelve countries that are members of COMESA but not SADC) transformed their regional cooperation. Their Intergovernmental Authority on Drought and Development (IGADD), which had focused on food security and desertification control, became the Intergovernmental Authority on Development (IGAD). Its mandate was expanded to include regional economic cooperation, similar to that of COMESA (IGAD Secretariat, 1996). Of course, such division challenges COMESA's unity.

Unity is even further constrained by the fact that Namibia and Swaziland, members of SACU, cannot sign off on COMESA trade policy without the approval of South Africa (also a member of SACU). SACU does not pose a significant challenge to SADC, however, since the former is a subset of the latter. Although South Africa, which joined SADC in 1994, has also been invited to join COMESA, it has declined to do so thus far. COMESA's membership did expand in June 1998, however, when Egypt was admitted. Egypt had originally applied to join the PTA (years before South Africa joined SADC) but had not been accepted. Some officials with the Ministry of Eastern African and Regional Cooperation in Kenya observe that Egypt has been admitted into COMESA in the hope that South Africa will be enticed to join COMESA and/or to balance the power between COMESA and SADC.

Southern African Development Community (SADC)

SADC was established in 1992 as a successor to the Southern African Development Coordination Conference (SADCC). SADCC was born out of the 1980 Lusaka Declaration of nine countries—Angola, Botswana, Lesotho, Malawi, Mozambique, Swaziland, Tanzania, Zambia, and Zimbabwe. SADCC was rooted in the efforts of the frontline states (Angola, Botswana, Mozambique, Tanzania, and Zambia) to bring political freedom to Zimbabwe (then Rhodesia) and Namibia. Namibia joined SADCC in 1990 (as its tenth member) immediately following its independence.

The main objectives of SADCC were to reduce economic dependence, especially (but not only) on South Africa; create genuine and equitable regional integration; promote national, interstate, and regional policies; and secure international cooperation within the framework of the strategy for economic liberation (Mehrotra, 1991; UNCTAD, 1996: 69). In addition to pursuing these objectives, SADCC functioned effectively as a political forum, particularly against South Africa's apartheid regime.

Political changes in southern Africa in the late 1980s and early 1990s led SADCC to formalize itself into a legal entity "with effective capacity to lead the region into deeper integration" (UNCTAD, 1996: 69). The Formalization Exercise led to the creation of SADC in 1992. South Africa joined SADC in 1994. In the next three years, Mauritius, Seychelles, and the Democratic Republic of Congo also joined SADC to bring the number of member states to fourteen. Table 6.3 shows some indicators for ten of the fourteen member states. In this group of ten, South Africa and Zimbabwe have contributed approximately 90 percent of the intraregional exports.

SADC has identified distinct sectors of cooperation and has assigned member countries the role of coordinating them as outlined in the following list—Angola: energy; Botswana: (1) agricultural research and (2) livestock production and animal disease control; Lesotho: (1) environment and land management and (2) water; Malawi: inland fisheries, forestry, and wildlife; Mauritius: tourism; Mozambique: (1) culture and information and (2) transport and

Table 6.3 SADC Countries—Basic Indicators and Trade Performance[a]

Country	GNP Per Capita 1995 (U.S.$)	Annual Average Percentage Growth, 1985–1995	Annual Average Percentage of Intra-regional Exports, 1994–1996[b]	Annual Average Percentage of Intra-regional Imports, 1994–1996[b]
Angola	410	–6.1	0.06	3.80
Congo, Democratic Republic of	120	–8.9[c]	2.70	6.23
Malawi	170	–0.7	2.36	8.60
Mauritius	3,380	5.4	0.40	6.00
Mozambique	80	3.6	1.06	17.79
Seychelles	6,620	3.5[c]	0.03	0.97
South Africa	3,160	–1.1	72.30	13.10
Tanzania	120	1.0	0.57	5.43
Zambia	400	–0.8	2.65	7.95
Zimbabwe	540	–0.6	17.88	30.11

Sources: World Bank (1997b, 1997c); IMF (1997).
a. Does not include Botswana, Lesotho, Namibia, and Swaziland.
b. Numbers may not add up to 100 because of rounding.
c. These figures are for 1986–1996.

communications; Namibia: marine fisheries and resources; South Africa: (1) health and (2) finance investment; Swaziland: human resources development; Tanzania: industry and trade; Zambia: (1) mining and (2) employment and labor; and Zimbabwe: food, agriculture, and natural resources. The Democratic Republic of Congo and Seychelles, the newest members, have yet to be assigned sectors to coordinate.

Clearly, there is overlap in the coordination of responsibilities for these sectors. The disaggregation of the areas of cooperation and the apparently agreeable distribution of responsibilities among member states have allowed SADC to identify projects of mutual interest. This, in turn, has made SADC relatively successful in securing foreign funds for its projects.

Nonetheless, SADC's overdependence on foreign funds is its weakness. On average, 85 percent of the financial need for SADC projects is sought from foreign sources. Implementation of projects thus depends on the endorsement of foreign financiers.

Economic Community of West African States (ECOWAS)

The initiatives to establish a west African economic community date back to the mid-1960s. However, it was the signing of an economic cooperation treaty between Nigeria and Togo in 1972 that gave impetus to the idea of economic integration (UNCTAD, 1996: 16). Nigeria (an anglophone country) and Togo (a francophone country) had managed to overcome their considerable differences in economic size and colonial history to reach such a treaty. In addition, Nigeria and Togo sent missions to other states with the possibility of forming a regional economic community (Greer, 1992). Following these initiatives and regional meetings, ECOWAS was created by fifteen nations in 1975. The sixteenth member, Cape Verde, joined in 1977. See Table 6.4 for a complete list of member states and some key indicators. In this group of sixteen member countries, Nigeria and Côte d'Ivoire contributed nearly 80 percent of the intraregional exports in the 1994–1996 period.

The main objective of ECOWAS is to "promote co-operation and integration, leading to the establishment of an economic union in West Africa" (ECOWAS Secretariat, 1993: Article 3). The original schedule for integration in ECOWAS called for a customs union by the year 1990. However, delays in reducing tariff barriers forced a revision of the schedule. Reductions of tariff barriers for industrial products did not even begin until 1990. The revised schedule sets the year 2000 as the new target date for a customs union to be achieved.

Reductions of tariff barriers for member countries in intraregional trade were determined on the basis of the country's level of industrial and infrastructural development and the country's dependence on tariff revenue. Member states were put in three groups. The countries in group 1—Burkina Faso, Cape Verde, the Gambia, Guinea Bissau, Mali, Mauritania, and Niger—had ten years, from 1990, to eliminate tariff barriers. Group 2 countries—Benin, Guinea, Sierra Leone, and Togo—had eight years to eliminate tariff barriers. Group 3 countries—Côte d'Ivoire, Ghana, Nigeria, and Senegal— had six years. None of these countries has met or will meet the deadline.

The large differences in economic development and trade performance, as suggested by Table 6.4, also led ECOWAS members to propose a scheme to compensate for the loss of revenue from the importation of industrial products (ECOWAS Secretariat, 1993: Article

Table 6.4 ECOWAS Countries—Basic Indicators and Trade Performance

Country	GNP Per Capita		Annual Average Percentage of Intra-regional Exports, 1994–1996[a]	Annual Average Percentage of Intra-regional Imports, 1994–1996[a]
	1995 (U.S.$)	Annual Average Percentage Growth, 1985–1995		
Benin	370	–0.3	0.46	2.59
Burkina Faso	230	–0.2	0.47	7.27
Cape Verde	960	11.2[b]	0.00	0.17
Côte d'Ivoire	660	–2.0[b]	35.56	20.68
Gambia	320	1.0[b]	0.24	1.39
Ghana	390	1.4	10.55	22.74
Guinea	550	1.4	0.25	4.55
Guinea Bissau	250	2.0	0.02	0.32
Liberia	NA	NA	0.14	0.92
Mali	250	0.8	0.42	0.91
Mauritania	460	0.5	1.58	0.32
Niger	220	–2.2[b]	0.32	2.23
Nigeria	260	1.2	41.41	8.70
Senegal	600	–0.5[b]	5.88	5.00
Sierra Leone	180	–3.6	0.02	1.74
Togo	310	–2.7	2.68	11.50

Sources: World Bank (1997b, 1997c); IMF (1997).
a. Numbers may not add up to 100 because of rounding.
b. These figures are for 1986–1996.

36). There is no evidence that this scheme has worked or that it can work effectively. If anything, it may have increased any preexisting disagreements between the relatively more advanced countries and the least developed ones in the region.

It also appears that there has been increased division between the francophone countries and the other states following further consolidation of the former. The West African Economic Community (Communauté économique de l'Afrique de l'Ouest—CEAO), to which all francophone countries in ECOWAS (except Togo) belonged, was replaced by a more ambitious West African Monetary and Economic Union (Union économique et monétaire ouest-africaine—UEMOA) in 1994.[6] All former members of CEAO, except Mauritania, have joined UEMOA. Togo, which was not a member of

CEAO, has also joined UEMOA (UNCTAD, 1997c: 10). Guinea Bissau, a nonfrancophone, has also joined UEMOA.

Officials in the Ministry of Trade in Ghana and business firms in Ghana complain that goods from their country face discriminatory barriers in UEMOA countries. That is, they face trade barriers that are not applied on intra-UEMOA trade. Apparently, these complaints have fallen on deaf ears. As of mid-1998, Ghana was contemplating the possibility of requesting observer status in UEMOA. Whether such a strategy by Ghana would enhance or weaken ECOWAS is hard to predict.

Amid these divisions, ECOMOG has been relatively successful in intervening in civil wars in the region. Of course, the civil wars and political conflicts themselves within the region are a major distraction to economic integration. These conflicts not only divert resources away from economic integration efforts but also initiate economic embargos within the region. For example, fifteen ECOWAS countries imposed an economic blockade against Sierra Leone (also a member of ECOWAS) as a way to force the rebel leader, Koroma, to surrender power to the civilian leader, Kabbal.

Economic Community of Central African States (ECCAS)

ECCAS was established in 1983 by the ten countries listed in Table 6.5 plus Angola (UNCTAD, 1996: 39–40). Angola maintained observer status until 1998, when it formally joined the group. The disparity in economic and trade indicators observed in other regional blocs is present here, as well. For example, Cameroon alone contributed over 80 percent of the region's exports in the 1994–1996 period but only imported about 4.5 percent of the other countries' exports to the region.[7]

If integration had been progressively established according to the implementation schedule, ECCAS would have been a customs union in the year 2000. However, ECCAS has yet to form a free trade area. The civil wars within countries in the region have added to the delay in integration. There are also divisions within ECCAS that mirror those in ECOWAS. The six CFA countries—Cameroon, Central African Republic, Chad, Congo, Equatorial Guinea, and Gabon—have their own subgroup, the Economic and Monetary Community of Central Africa (Communauté économique et monétaire de l'Afrique Centrale—CEMAC).[8] Another subgroup within ECCAS is the Economic Community of the Great Lakes Countries (Commu-

Table 6.5 ECCAS Countries—Basic Indicators and Trade Performance[a]

| Country | GNP Per Capita | | Annual Average Percentage of Intra-regional Exports, 1994–1996[b] | Annual Average Percentage of Intra-regional Imports, 1994–1996[b] |
	1995 (U.S.$)	Annual Average Percentage Growth, 1985–1995		
Burundi	160	–1.3	1.97	1.38
Cameroon	650	–6.6	82.25	0.79
Central African Republic	340	–2.4	4.38	9.86
Chad	180	0.6	4.38	26.63
Congo, Democratic Republic of	120	–8.9[c]	5.70	8.68
Congo, Republic of	680	–3.2	3.95	0.59
Equatorial Guinea	380	2.3[c]	0.00	18.35
Gabon	3,490	–8.2	0.66	29.19
Rwanda	180	–5.4	0.43	3.55
São Tomé and Principe	350	–0.3[c]	0.00	0.98

Sources: World Bank (1997b, 1997c); IMF (1997).
a. Does not include Angola. Angola joined ECCAS in February 1998.
b. Numbers may not add up to 100 because of rounding.
c. These figures are for 1986–1996.

nauté economique des pays des Grands Lacs—CEPGL), consisting of Burundi, the Democratic Republic of Congo, and Rwanda.

Challenges Facing the Pursuit of Economic Integration in Sub-Saharan Africa

Many Africanists advocate for regional economic integration as an effective strategy for trade and development in sub-Saharan Africa. The process of forging integration in sub-Saharan Africa involves many interrelated challenges. Some of these, such as overdependence on foreign funds and a lack of political commitment, are found in sub-Saharan African countries generally and are not unique to economic integration. The discussion here, however, focuses on the manifestation of these problems in economic integration.

The Movement Toward Economic Integration

It is perhaps easier to argue that the readiness to accept economic integration as a strategy for development is an asset and not a problem. However, given that this strategy is seemingly unquestioned and is accepted categorically, governments may neglect to conduct in-depth evaluations of the potential impact of joining a regional bloc. It seems that many countries in sub-Saharan Africa join any and all regional economic blocs to which they have access, without carefully assessing the costs and benefits involved.

As seen in Figures 6.1 through 6.3, some countries belong to more than three economic blocs, thus creating a multiplicity of intergovernmental organizations. Figures 6.1, 6.2, and 6.3, respectively, show the membership of eastern and southern African countries in seven regional blocs; the membership of western African states in two regional blocs; and the membership of central African states in three regional blocs. Note that if the three figures were to be combined, Figures 6.1 and 6.2 would intersect with Figure 6.3.

Theoretical models and empirical studies confirm that moving toward free trade is beneficial to participating countries. Thus, one could conclude that decisions to form (or join) regional economic blocs, even if done without full consideration of costs and benefits, are still beneficial. The problem, however, is that such regional blocs may lack the commitment and clear direction usually borne out of careful evaluation. Such evaluation, often prompted by critical disagreement, can be preempted by nonchalant political unanimity.

In 1996, the parliament of Tanzania unanimously accepted the reestablishment of economic cooperation between Kenya, Tanzania, and Uganda. When the author spoke later with some members of parliament about specific potential effects of such cooperation on their constituencies, it was apparent that they had not considered these problems, and some had even started to question the decision to reestablish such cooperation.

It appears that economic integration is as popular in the 1990s as import substitution was in the 1970s. As argued in Chapter 2, many sub-Saharan African countries did not have carefully designed programs for import substitution, in spite of the overwhelming support for the strategy. Many policies were implemented in the name of import substitution even when they were effectively working against it. Although import substitution, as an economic strategy, is not on par with economic integration, the latter suffers from a lack of commitment and clear direction just as the former did. It appears that politicians and government officials like the idea of economic integration. Nevertheless, many do not have a clear understanding of the political and financial commitment necessary to achieve meaningful integration.

Not all politicians vote for integration because of the positive impact it might have. Rather, some vote for it because they think the impact of integration is far removed from their constituencies. Some vote for it not because of the perceived relevance of integration but rather because they predict that integration will not actually happen or because they assume that integration will not have much impact. In other words, some have a very cavalier attitude and simply "go with the crowd." Worse still, some policymakers may be in favor of integration only for their own personal benefits, such as international travel and generous per diems that can be obtained even in an ailing regional bloc.

The point here is not that disagreement about regional integration is necessarily good for integration. Rather, an uninformed, quick, unanimous decision to join a regional bloc can be less effective than a delayed, challenged, and carefully considered decision to do so. Since regional integration seems to be accepted at face value, many politicians and governments in sub-Saharan Africa do not engage in effective debate and analysis.

Lack of Political Commitment

It is one thing to decide to establish or join a regional economic bloc. It is quite another actually to implement policies and allocate resources that would bring about integration. Agreements are reached, but some countries do not honor them, even though they are party to the agreements. In many regional groups the functions of the secretariats are severely constrained because member states do not pay their dues on time (UNCTAD, 1992: 2, 1996: 9).

The main reason for the lack of political commitment goes beyond economic integration. Many sub-Saharan African countries lack political accountability. Political and government leaders are held accountable neither for their statements nor for the agreements they sign. At the launching of the Secretariat for East African Co-operation on March 14, 1996, President Daniel Arap Moi of Kenya spoke not only of creating a customs union but also of forming a federation. Although such a vision is neither new nor totally unrealistic, it is unlikely that anyone took his statements seriously. A leader who has not manifested a genuine intention to listen to and bring together opposition parties in his own country can hardly be taken seriously in suggesting a politically unified East Africa.

Oftentimes government leaders commit their countries to agreements without having to justify such decisions to their public (Asante, 1997: 80). Furthermore, they are not held accountable internally for failing to implement such decisions. In some cases, governments are held accountable externally by the institutions that administer the agreements. That is the situation, for example, with WTO agreements. Regional blocs in sub-Saharan Africa, however, take painstaking precautions not to offend any country, so punitive measures for those who fail (or refuse) to honor agreements are minor and infrequent. Moreover, some regional blocs take too much pride in the number of their members to worry about the commitment of those members. As such, countries are held accountable neither internally nor externally.

To elaborate, a country may agree to reduce tariffs on intragroup trade, only to say a few months later, sometimes with the blessing of the Secretariat, that it cannot do so because such an action will reduce its revenues. Countries set group objectives without linking them to national policies (Asante, 1997: 74–75). Countries join a multitude of regional groups within the same region and with similar objectives, thus duplicating activities and increasing the financial burden to themselves. (In fact, this is one reason why many countries cannot afford to pay budgetary contributions.) Still, usually no one holds the governments in these countries accountable for such costly and unproductive decisions.

Overdependence on Foreign Donors

One of the potential dynamic consequences of regional economic integration is the political and economic leverage it can accord African countries in multilateral negotiations. This potential is compromised, however, by too much dependence on foreign donors or, as they are often called, foreign partners.

Over 85 percent of financial resources for SADC projects come from foreign sources. Part of the rivalry between regional groups such as COMESA and SADC or between ECOWAS and its subgroup, UEMOA, is over foreign donors. For example, all UEMOA member states, except one, are francophone countries and, as such, are in a better position to secure more financial support from France.

IGADD was restructured into IGAD in part to attract foreign partners. The restructuring itself was done with guidance from foreign partners. Some of IGAD's technical meetings are held in the country that chairs IGAD's foreign forum (Italy was the chair in 1998), and paid for by the foreign partners. This situation is not atypical of other regional groups in sub-Saharan Africa, but such a setting is not conducive to providing leverage for Africans. It does not allow self-determination, which is often considered the ultimate objective of economic integration in Africa. Projects are proposed not only by assessing the needs in the region but also by determining which ones have a higher probability of being funded by foreign partners.

The dependence on or the anticipation of foreign funds may explain, in part, why some countries join many regional blocs and why regional groups set unrealistic schedules. They join many regional groups to be sure they get a piece of every "pie" coming from foreign donors into the region. Groups set unrealistic schedules to impress donors and to qualify for funds.

Sub-Saharan Africa needs assistance and should get assistance from the rest of the world when it is truly for economic development. However, for a development strategy principally grounded in self-determination, African countries should have ownership—responsibility both for the costs and direction—of the programs in their regional blocs. Undoubtedly, this approach would significantly scale down the size of the secretariat units and the number of projects. Such an approach might not necessarily undermine the speed of genuine integration in Sub-Saharan Africa. In fact, it might enhance it by eliminating from regional groups those opportunistic countries that join only to tap foreign funds.

Foreign Countries' Dominance

As the saying goes, "it takes two to tango." Developed countries also often play a role in the ongoing overdependence of sub-Saharan African countries on foreign funds. The scramble for African resources by developed countries did not end with political independence for African countries.

Some developed countries continue to devise strategies that would maintain the pattern of trade created by colonialism, whereby sub-Saharan African countries export unprocessed primary products and import manufactured products. (This is not to say that trade between sub-Saharan Africa and the rest of the world is not also dictated by the market forces of supply and demand.) These strategies are usually hard to resist because they are coated with sweeteners such as "assistance funds." African leaders who focus only on the short run have a difficult time avoiding such temptations.

Some argue that France has weakened ECOWAS with its controlling support of its former colonies in West Africa. Member states of CEAO and its successor, UEMOA, find it more comfortable to rely on their former master, France, than to work on building economic cooperation with their anglophone neighbors.

As discussed in Chapter 4, in 1998 some members of the U.S. Congress proposed H.R. 1432, the African Growth and Opportunity Act, which was designed to encourage more trade between the United States and sub-Saharan Africa. Although the bill did not pass Congress, it is interesting to note that it proposed the establishment of a U.S.–sub-Saharan African free trade area.[9] Sub-Saharan Africa is not in a position to establish a free trade area with the United States when neither SSA as a region nor SSA subregional groups have yet succeeded in achieving that level of integration. Indeed, the schedule for economic integration in Africa as envisioned by the Abuja Treaty targets the achievement of a free trade area for the continent by the year 2016. Considering the trend of economic integration in subregional groups, this projection itself is very ambitious, let alone trying to integrate the whole SSA region with the United States.

Nonetheless, the assistance (though meager) stipulated in the bill made it irresistible to many countries. In addition, the bill appeared to represent an important departure from an "aid" strategy to a "trade" strategy. Many African diplomats in Washington, D.C., testified in favor of the bill. Offers of free trade partnership from developed countries, however, may divert (rather than direct) efforts in sub-Saharan Africa from subregional and continental economic cooperation. This happens especially as each country (or each subregional group, for that matter) attempts to draw attention to itself for the most assistance.

If sub-Saharan African countries were honest with themselves and the United States, they would have expressed their appreciation for the initiative and affirmed their belief in economic integration while explaining that it was too soon to discuss a free trade area with the United States. They would also have pursued the fact that the U.S. offer of "partnership" did not include north Africa, whereas the goal of the Organization of African Unity is to integrate the entire continent.

The European Union, which already has strong trade links to Africa, is preparing a summit with Africa for the year 2000. Undoubtedly, the focus of summits such as this one will be on important issues such as trade and investment. However, African countries must be careful to avoid gazing at the EU and other such bodies, waiting for assistance, rather than working diligently to build economic cooperation among themselves.

Unrealistic Schedules

Making implementation projections is an important part of programming. However, such schedules must be realistic, and commitments to keep to the schedule must be binding. The preceding discussion shows how far ECOWAS, COMESA, and the Lagos Plan of Action are from their projections.

Some countries "commit" to a schedule to reduce trade barriers either without any real intention of doing so or before they evaluate the impact of such reductions. There are countries whose intragroup imports are less than 5 percent of their total imports who claim that reducing tariffs on intragroup trade would have a severe impact on their government revenue. This is one of the excuses given by COMESA and ECOWAS countries for failing to bring tariffs down to the scheduled levels. Even if this excuse were valid, it would still leave one wondering why the revenue problem could not have been anticipated before the agreement was reached. Perhaps, as already noted, it is because some agreements are reached primarily as a strategy to draw financial support from donors.

Fear of Uneven Distribution of Benefits

As seen in Tables 6.1, 6.3, 6.4, and 6.5, countries in each regional group vary considerably in basic economic indicators. Foroutan (1992) described economic differences among sub-Saharan African countries as the major obstacle to realizing trade and factor market integration. These economic differences cause concern that the benefits of integration will gravitate toward those countries whose manufacturing sectors are relatively more developed, such as Kenya, Mauritius, and Zimbabwe in COMESA; South Africa and Zimbabwe in SADC; Côte d'Ivoire, Ghana, Nigeria, and Senegal in ECOWAS; and Cameroon in ECCAS. These concerns have given rise to two phenomena that have undermined the integration process itself: compensation schemes and selective liberalization schemes.

First, regarding compensation schemes, ECOWAS stipulates that member countries will be compensated for their loss of import duties resulting from the reduction of tariffs on processed and industrial products (ECOWAS Secretariat, 1993: Articles 36 and 48).[10] Although such compensation schemes may sound altruistic, they do not work (except to the extent that they restrain integration, thereby removing the need to have them). Determining an agreeable and effective formula for contributions into and an allocation of the compensation fund is nearly impossible. More important, focus on the loss of import revenues neglects the positive impact of reduced tariffs to consumers and on the efficient allocation of resources. Even if losses of tariff revenues on intragroup trade indeed cannot be sustained, then countries should reduce tariffs more gradually rather than setting ambitious tariff reduction schedules that are sure to be ignored or compensatory schemes that are sure to fail.

There are those who believe that integration efforts need to include arrangements for *equalizing* the gains from regionalization (Asante, 1997: 67). However, the gains from regionalization to each member country depend on many factors, one of which is the domestic investment environment and policies. Economic integration is an incentive to domestic and foreign investors to invest in the region. To which countries investors commit their resources, however, depends on such factors as the infrastructure, human skills available, domestic policies, and political conditions in each country, to list a few. A country with a corrupt civil service and judiciary system, for example, may not be able to attract investment. In fact, it may lose its investors to other member states. It would be inappropriate to compensate such countries for losing investors even when such a loss is connected to integration. Such compensation, in this situation, would be subsidizing corruption.

This does not mean that more developed countries in a regional group cannot or should not assist the least developed countries. They can assist through such means as proportionately higher contributions to regional development banks or to the secretariats' costs. Such contributions can be determined in terms of GDP or GDP per capita, but they should not be tied directly to the volume or value of trade. Regional development banks can also give priority to responsible governments and/or nongovernmental organizations of relatively poor countries in issuing loans.

Essentially, support programs should not be tied directly to trade nor should they be used to decide bureaucratically where firms should be located. Decisions on specialization and location of firms should be left to individual investors (the stakeholders). Direct interference with trade or production decisions limits the very benefits expected to be derived from economic integration—increased competition and efficiency.

In addition to compensatory schemes, the fear of uneven distribution of the gains of integration has been an excuse for a second phenomenon—selective and limited liberalization schemes. The fear is that member countries with more advanced manufacturing sectors will benefit at the expense of member countries with less advanced manufacturing sectors. As a result, the movement toward free trade for CEAO, CEPGL, ECCAS, and ECOWAS, for example, has mainly focused on unprocessed products (UNCTAD, 1996). Tariff reductions on manufactured products and primary products that have undergone industrial processing have been held back, and they lag far behind.

This selective approach, however, reduces the potential for economic integration. There is considerable homogeneity in primary products in the regional groups. Free trade limited to these products does not produce significant intraregional trade. Moreover, such a selective approach breeds suspicion among some countries that feel they are resented for their relative success.

An official with the Kenyan Ministry of East African Co-operation and Regional Integration contends that "some of the so-called fears" of unequal distribution of benefits are simply jealousy—"jealousy that my neighbor is going to develop faster than I will" (interview by the author, Nairobi, Kenya, July 7, 1998). The argument is that some of Kenya's exports to its neighboring countries, for example, do not displace production in those countries but rather compete with imports from nonmember countries.

Some believe that part of the solution to the wide differences in economic development between countries is to assign certain industries to certain countries so that no country is left too far behind. This recommendation often comes packaged as part of a regional industrial development strategy. For example, ECCAS's industrial policy calls for the establishment of large industrial units and an industrial development center but does not allow industrial competition among its member nations (UNCTAD, 1996: 42). By limiting competition, these restrictions limit the potential benefits of integration.

Political Instability

Even though progressive political reforms have taken place in many countries in sub-Saharan Africa during the 1990s, wars and political insecurity are still pervasive in some parts of the region. Angola, the Democratic Republic of Congo, Guinea Bissau, Liberia, Rwanda, Sierra Leone, Somalia, and Sudan are some of the countries entering the twenty-first century still experiencing major internal conflicts. CEPGL has been paralyzed by conflicts in the Great Lakes region. ECOWAS, through its peacekeeping force, ECOMOG, has had to direct resources and attention to wars in Liberia and Sierra Leone.

Conclusion

The Swahili saying *"umoja ni nguvu, utengano ni udhaifu"* means "unity is strength; division is weakness." Standing together on the same platform does not in itself, however, constitute unity.

It is clear that the prerequisite for real progress in economic integration in sub-Saharan Africa is real political commitment. How to bring about such commitment is anyone's guess. Some countries are too overburdened with internal conflicts and other domestic challenges such as severe poverty, famine, and the debt crisis to be diligent in their pursuit of economic integration. Some African leaders (not unlike some leaders in other parts of the world) are blinded by their own selfishness or corruption or are simply not able to think carefully about the future.

Perhaps it does not take the vision and commitment of every African president for economic integration on the continent to thrive. The liberation efforts for southern Africa in the 1970s and 1980s were kept alive by a few totally committed leaders, including Julius Nyerere, Kenneth Kaunda, and Samora Michel. For better or worse, the initiative and operation of the ECOWAS Monitoring Group have primarily been the result of Nigeria's leadership and commitment (Nwokedi, 1992). Economic integration lacks such leadership.

Whatever leadership emerges, it is important to be sure that economic integration is used as a strategy toward free trade and development. The leadership must be careful that import substitution policies, which generally work against free trade, do not find their way into economic integration efforts. They have to be careful because it is very easy to argue that sub-Saharan Africa is too dependent on developed countries. In the 1960s and 1970s, SSA countries tried to reduce this dependence by implementing an import substitution strategy. They did not succeed, though it was not until the 1980s and 1990s that outward-looking structural adjustment programs started to replace import substitution policies at the national level.

It would be ironic if the modest efforts toward economic integration made in the spirit of outward orientation would allow import substitution policies to find new life. This would amount to transferring import substitution policies from the national to the regional level. Of course, it should be noted that import substitution policies at the regional level are not as harmful as import substitution policies at the national level. This is because the regional level at least allows for increased competition and a more efficient allocation of resources as intra-regional trade develops.

Table 6.6   Intraregional Trade as a Percentage of Total Exports of Each Region

Region	1970	1980	1985	1990	1993	1994
COMESA[a]	9.6	12.1	5.5	7.5	7.8	7.7
ECCAS	2.4	1.5	2.1	2.1	2.4	2.4
ECOWAS	3.0	10.2	5.3	7.9	10.0	10.7
SADC[b]	2.6	0.5	1.5	2.6	7.0	8.0

Source: UNCTAD (1997a: 34–35).
a. Data unavailable for Namibia and Swaziland.
b. Data unavailable for Botswana, Lesotho, and Swaziland.

Table 6.6 shows the official intraregional trade as a percentage of total exports of each of the four main regional blocs in sub-Saharan Africa. Of course, given the widespread unofficial regional trade in SSA, particularly in the 1980s, the actual level of intraregional trade is higher than what is shown in Table 6.6.

The official intraregional trade as a percentage of total exports for ECCAS has been relatively low and stable. The percentage for ECOWAS countries increased following the establishment of ECOWAS in 1975, from 3 percent in 1970 to an average of 10 percent in the early 1990s. As for COMESA and SADC, it is difficult to discern the trend in their percentages since some of the changes are a factor of the changes in membership.

Also hard to discern is the relationship between reducing absolute tariffs on intraregional trade, on the one hand, and intraregional trade as a percentage of total exports of the region, on the other hand. Many assume the relationship is necessarily positive. The percentage of intraregional trade may not increase, however, if reductions of trade barriers are also extended to other countries outside the bloc. In addition, even tariff reductions on intraregional trade alone may increase the region's trade with the rest of the world. In either of these cases, the percentage of intraregional trade as a percentage of total exports of the region is indeterminate a priori, that is, it may increase, stay the same, or decrease.

Suppose, for example, that Ghana exports its cotton textiles to countries outside ECOWAS. Reductions in trade barriers within ECOWAS that enable Ghana to import more cotton, say from Benin, will also increase Ghana's exports of textiles to non-ECOWAS countries. Depending on the value added to cotton, it is possible for intraregional trade as a percentage of total exports of the region to fall.

One objective of economic integration is to reduce trade costs. Since this is done discriminately, it may lead to trade diversion from OECD markets to African markets. Many politicians and academics consider such trade diversion to be good in itself because it represents (or symbolizes) self-reliance. A lack of growth in intraregional trade as a percentage of the region's total exports may suggest the absence of trade diversion; as such, it is often presented as disappointing.

Considering the static impact of economic integration, however, trade diversion may cause a net welfare loss. In addition, the reduction of tariffs within a group may not only increase intraregional trade; such a reduction may also increase trade between members of the group and the rest of the world, as already illustrated. Furthermore, sub-Saharan African countries have limited potential for increased intraregional trade in the short run owing to limited demand for each other's exports (Foroutan, 1992). This level of demand is largely due to the considerable homogeneity in primary products in the regional groups. The manufacturing sector, which has the potential of producing differentiated products and, thus, allowing intraindustry trade, is still very small for most of the countries in SSA.

Therefore, although the low growth in the percentages shown in Table 6.6 suggests a limited reduction in trade barriers, trade liberalization must be measured in its true sense—the reduction in policy-induced costs of trading. Assessing the level of integration in terms of intraregional trade may place undue emphasis on the short-run impact of economic integration, which is likely to be minimal in SSA.

Economic integration is a step toward free trade. The objective is not to break ties with the OECD countries but rather to take advantage of economies of scale that may help sub-Saharan African countries develop their manufacturing sectors. Eventually this may indeed result in more intraregional trade.

There are those who point to the adoption of the classical model as the reason for the poor return on economic cooperation in sub-Saharan Africa (Aly, 1994). Undoubtedly, the classical model has its limitations in developed countries, not to mention developing countries. Markets are not as competitive, and prices are not as flexible as the classical model assumes. Needless to say, there are market failures associated with externalities. Moreover, income distribution considerations may call for government programs and regulations to adapt and complement the classical model. The classical model, however, is often simply a convenient villain.

For example, Aly (1994) argued that the classical integration process (outward-looking integration) in developing countries is irrelevant because developing countries lack well-developed manufacturing sectors. Aly contended further that classical integration is likely to do more harm than good to member countries because of the disparity in economic development between member countries.

It is presently difficult to associate the poor return on integration in sub-Saharan Africa (assuming that has been adequately documented to be the case) with anything but the limited degree to which integration has actually taken place. The lack of a well-developed manufacturing sector does not render the classical model irrelevant unless integration prevents the growth of the manufacturing sector where it should occur, considering relative costs of production.

Regarding economic development, whatever asymmetry exists between African countries, the asymmetry is even greater when African countries are compared to developed countries. Should African countries discourage trade with developed countries? Differences in economic development do not necessarily render trade a zero-sum game.

Although it is important to be aware of the shortcomings of the classical model, it cannot be disqualified categorically. In the 1960s and 1970s there were policymakers in Africa who ignored producer price incentives to subsistence farmers, naively thinking that the classical model (price incentives, in this case) was irrelevant to such farmers. That premise was subsequently well established to be wrong. What Aly called classical integration has not yet actually happened in most regional blocs in sub-Saharan Africa, and when it happens it will certainly not work like magic. Effective integration goes far beyond reducing tariffs. It includes the development of human capital, infrastructure, financial systems, effective property and antitrust laws, and other areas that affect integration. All these require thoughtful involvement of the government in the economy.

Perhaps a major problem, as alluded to throughout this chapter, is that most of the government decisions are not guided. Consider, for example, the high propensity to join many regional blocs and the plethora of intergovernmental organizations within and between overlapping regional blocs. This situation turns what would have been classical integration into a labyrinth of bureaucracy and duplication. There are no signs that the propensity for duplication will change soon, and this is not because countries do not know what ought to be done. Although there is a call from within to rationalize intergovernmental organizations, the political will and courage to do so are lacking.

This may change, however, with an increase in political accountability. If democracy and the private sector continue to grow, it is likely that the political system and economic institutions that unfold will generate serious and healthy political and economic debate and hold leaders accountable.

Notes

1. Several studies have made important contributions to the study of economic integration in Africa. See, for example, Aly (1994), Asante (1997), Oyejide et al. (1997), and several studies by UNCTAD (1992; 1996; 1997c).

2. In other words, if the value added of a product is at least 45 percent of the product's total value at the point of leaving the factory, it satisfies the rules of origin, regardless of where the materials are from.

3. In November 1999, the former members of the EAC (Kenya, Tanzania, and Uganda) agreed to reestablish a customs union within four years.

4. UDEAC is presently CEMAC—the Economic and Monetary Community of Central Africa.

5. The Abuja Treaty, which established the African Economic Community, was signed in 1991 in Abuja, Nigeria, by the fifty-one member states of the OAU.

6. Members of CEAO were Benin, Burkina Faso, Côte d'Ivoire, Mali, Mauritania, Niger, and Senegal.

7. On average, Cameroon contributed 82.25 percent of the region's exports. The other countries contributed 17.75 percent. Cameroon imported 0.79 percent of the region's total exports. That means it imported 4.45 percent ($0.79 \div 17.25$) of the other countries' exports to the region.

8. The Economic and Monetary Community of Central African States was formed in 1994 to replace UDEAC. The membership did not change.

9. The U.S. House of Representatives passed the trade bill in July 1999. After defeating it in 1998, the U.S. Senate passed a more restrictive version of the bill in November 1999, as this book was in the final stages of production. It is possible that the two legislative houses will reconcile their versions of the trade bill in the year 2000 for President Bill Clinton to sign the final bill into law.

10. There is no compensation for losses of revenue resulting from the importation of ECOWAS-originating unprocessed goods and traditional handicraft.

SEVEN

◆

Conclusion

International trade is neither an enemy of sub-Saharan Africa nor a panacea. Sub-Saharan African trade with the rest of the world has been characterized, however, by many internal and external impediments that have reduced the benefits from trade. Inefficient and unsustainable domestic policies such as overvalued domestic currencies, negative real interest rates, and low producer prices for farmers were the norm in many countries in the 1970s and 1980s. These policies reduced exports, diminished the quantity and quality of investment, reduced agricultural production, and increased the propensity for corruption.

Likewise, trade policies in OECD countries have hardly been as generous to African exports as one might be led to assume from programs such as the GSP. Developed countries decided to exclude the agricultural sector and the textiles and clothing industry from GATT and continued to increase domestic subsidies and protection in those sectors. The free trade rhetoric in developed countries often gives way to the political power of domestic groups threatened by more competitive foreign producers. For example, the proposed African Growth and Opportunity Act, which called for liberalization of trade between the United States and sub-Saharan Africa, was strongly supported by the Clinton administration yet stalled by the powerful textile producer constituency in the United States.

There is reason to be cautiously optimistic, however, about the future growth of trade and its contribution to development in sub-Saharan Africa. Economic reforms in many sub-Saharan African countries have reduced bureaucratic and policy-induced impediments to the growth of the export sector and to the private sector in general. Political reforms in many sub-Saharan African countries have allowed some measure of freedom of expression and a relatively secure environment to challenge the government. Although corruption is still a major problem in many countries, it is at least being openly challenged these days. Associations of manufacturers are becoming more autonomous and able to pursue their interests with the government or in spite of the government.

Although the benefits of the GSP program have so far been minuscule, they could increase in the future, despite the reduced margin of preference—that is, the reduced difference between the most-favored-nation tariff and the GSP tariff. An increase in benefits could come from an expansion of product coverage, the reduction of non-tariff barriers in OECD countries, and economic reforms in sub-Saharan African countries that have the potential to increase these countries' exports and the ability to utilize the program.

The completion of the Uruguay Round of GATT and the establishment of the World Trade Organization have set the agricultural sector and the textiles and clothing industry en route to trade liberalization. With appropriate technological assistance, sub-Saharan Africa stands a good chance of developing these sectors significantly.

OECD countries are beginning to respect sub-Saharan African countries as trading partners instead of viewing them simply as poor countries in need of help. The African Growth and Opportunity Act was an effort to develop sustainable trade relations with sub-Saharan Africa. As one African diplomat in Washington, D.C., commented, there was hardly anything in the proposed U.S. trade bill that the United States as a world power could not have done without engaging Africans. He saw the significance of the bill in the rare respect the United States was showing to sub-Saharan Africa. Likewise, the Lomé Convention, which will be renegotiated in the year 2000, may reflect a new respect for sub-Saharan African (and Caribbean and Pacific) countries as trading partners who offer some measure of reciprocity.

Economic integration in SSA faces many challenges, but none that cannot be overcome. More important, the growth of the private sector and the search by manufacturers for markets will inevitably force a reduction of trade barriers between neighboring countries, thus enhancing economic integration. Moreover, associations of manufacturers and other business associations are gradually becoming more involved in formulating and shaping economic integration in SSA. Their increased participation will restrain governments from making empty declarations and will help hold government leaders accountable for their commitments.

These positive trends are only the beginning. There is still much more that must be done, internally and externally, for sub-Saharan

Africa to realize fully and to increase the benefits associated with trade.

Governments must be clear about their short-run and long-run objectives and be sure to assess the costs and benefits of various strategies for achieving them. The end does not always justify the means. Consider the experience of many sub-Saharan African countries in the 1970s and 1980s. The goal of increasing investment did not justify the negative real interest rates, and it was not achieved by them. The goals of subsidizing imports of essential inputs and preventing inflation did not justify the overvaluation of domestic currency, and they were not achieved by it. The goal of bringing equity did not justify governments' direct involvement in production, distribution, marketing, and price controls, and it was not achieved by such involvement. In fact, the means used to try to achieve these objectives produced opposite results: reduced loanable funds and a lower quality and growth rate in investment; less foreign currency and a reduced ability to import; increased inflation as prices generally reflected the parallel market exchange rate; and increased bureaucracy, favoritism, and corruption.

Since the late 1980s, many sub-Saharan African countries have been implementing structural adjustment programs that have increasingly allowed market forces to determine prices and the allocation of resources. Of course, the structural adjustment programs must be assessed objectively and not embraced simply because they seem to be the antithesis of the old policies. Given sub-Saharan Africa's unsuccessful prior policies, it is easy for one to assess new policies in terms of the old ones, rather than to assess the new ones in terms of their own merit and the objectives sought.

Countries should not necessarily do away with their objectives just because the means to attain them have failed. Many objectives pursued in the 1970s are still valid today for sub-Saharan Africa. In addition, it was not always policies pursued to achieve those objectives that were wrong per se. A major problem was the single-mindedness with which those policies were implemented. For example, subsidies for borrowers and importers were not balanced with the reality of the availability of loanable funds and foreign currency, respectively. An overall negative real interest rate cannot be justified by a desire to subsidize a particular investment; nor can an overvalued domestic currency be justified by a desire to subsidize particular imports. Economies cannot sustain subsidies to all borrowers and/or all importers. At the same time, a total elimination of subsidies cannot be justified in the name of a free market. It may be necessary to subsidize some types of investments, especially those with external benefits, such as those that help to develop human capital.

It is important that sub-Saharan African countries avoid the tendency to compartmentalize economic problems. This tendency often leads to narrowly focused, ineffective, and uncoordinated programs. The objective of increasing investment and exports, for example, may not be achieved by simply establishing investment promotion centers and/or creating export processing zones. For these investment programs to be successful, they need an environment with effective educational and training programs, public investment programs in infrastructure (roads, railways, energy, water, and telecommunications), and a reliable judicial system.

Sub-Saharan African countries must also be clear about the potential impact of the international programs they seek and support. Not everything that glitters is gold. For example, domestic agricultural subsidies in OECD countries that have resulted in depressed world prices of agricultural products may seem good to net importers of food, as many SSA countries are. In reality, some of those countries are net food importers in part because of these OECD policies. SSA countries must remember that higher world prices of agricultural products would encourage their own farmers to produce more, with the potential for these countries to become net exporters of food.

In addition, SSA countries must put into place domestic programs to take advantage of international agreements. For example, although the GSP program can be useful, thus far it has produced only minimal benefits for sub-Saharan Africa. This is the result of the inability of SSA to take full advantage of the program as well as of limitations within the GSP programs themselves.

The decision of many sub-Saharan African countries to sign off on the agreements of the Uruguay Round and to be members of the World Trade Organization was a strategic one. Although they did not fully understand the agreements, they knew it would have been much harder to join the WTO later. Now that they have benefited from a number of workshops by the WTO and they understand the agreements better, sub-Saharan African countries must put into place interinstitutional committees on the WTO. The objective of these committees, as suggested by UNCTAD, would be to coordinate trade information and national policy for implementation of the multilateral agreements, maximize the benefits from the agreements, and prepare effectively for future trade negotiations.

Kenya has had a committee on the WTO since 1995. Initially, it was called the Inter-Ministerial Committee, composed of participants from government ministries. In 1997, the committee was expanded to include participants from the business sector, professional associations, and research institutions. It was also renamed the National Committee on WTO. It is too early to assess the operation and effectiveness of this committee. However, it appears to be a good model for other sub-Saharan African countries to follow.

World trade will increasingly be guided by the rules of the WTO and the spirit of free trade. As a result, international commodity agreements with economic provisions to control supply and prices will increasingly lose ground. Moreover, these agreements have not worked effectively in the past. Nonetheless, sub-Saharan African countries should support the role that commodity agreements play as study groups. These study groups collect and disseminate information, sponsor research on consumption and production, help developing countries diversify their economies, and support processing in developing countries. Sub-Saharan Africa should likewise support the CFC in its role in financing research and development projects geared toward improving productivity, competitiveness, diversification, investment, marketing, and the optimal use and management of natural resources.

The need for CFC-sponsored research projects may diminish over time if sub-Saharan Africa is able to establish effective economic integration in the region. Such research projects could be proposed, funded, and implemented by regional groups as these blocs develop.

Of course, economic integration faces many obstacles, including an overdependence on foreign donors, the dominance of foreign countries, fear of an uneven distribution of benefits, and political instability. Certainly political commitment has not yet matched the political rhetoric. The competition for foreign assistance sometimes brings unhealthy rivalry between member countries in one economic bloc or between economic blocs. In seeking assistance, sub-Saharan African countries must be more consistent in using an "us" strategy rather than a "me" strategy, to overcome the history of "divide and rule."

Developed countries, for their part, must practice what they preach, particularly free trade. Trade has not been "free" in developed countries in sectors in which developing countries have a comparative advantage, such as textiles and agriculture. The long history of protecting these sectors and the lack of real implementation of the Agreement on Agriculture and the Agreement on Textiles and Clothing reveal hypocrisy and a lack of genuine interest in the welfare of developing countries.

The U.S. African Growth and Opportunity Act, which proposes a freer market for textiles and clothing from sub-Saharan Africa, was stalled by U.S. domestic producers. This happened even though (1) the bill could be a significant boost to a country like Kenya, whose per capita GNP in 1997 was one-ninetieth that of the United States; (2) the projected loss of jobs in the U.S. textiles and clothing industry is only one in every one thousand; and (3) the projected net gain to the U.S. economy for each job lost would be $70,000 to $143,000.

In spite, or perhaps because, of the WTO, the political pressures for protection in developed countries will grow. Sub-Saharan African countries must expand their economic diplomacy beyond working with government officials and politicians in OECD countries. They must collaborate with business associations in OECD countries that are against protection. For example, in the United States, the International Mass Retail Association and U.S. Association of Importers of Textiles and Apparel support free trade treatment for U.S. imports of textiles and apparel from sub-Saharan Africa. To achieve collaboration with such associations, African embassies and consulates in OECD countries desperately need additional resources (staff and technological linkages) for their economic divisions.

The private sector in sub-Saharan African countries must also be aware that the "good" or "bad" old days when the government took charge of everything for or against private firms are over. Associations of manufacturers must work together, especially given how limited their resources are. They must also work with their governments and business associations in OECD countries to effect favorable policy changes in those countries. For example, the Mauritius-U.S. Business Association, consisting of private firms in both countries, added support for the U.S. African Growth and Opportunity Act.

Sub-Saharan African countries can and should use trade to their best possible advantage. This means they should coordinate their domestic policies to position themselves better to capitalize on opportunities available through the WTO and other international organizations. They should also work to make greater opportunities for themselves by preparing effectively for future trade negotiations. It also means that at the regional level they should refocus their efforts to develop their regional blocs and achieve greater economic integration.

Abbreviations

ACP	African, Caribbean, and Pacific countries
AEC	African Economic Community
AMS	Aggregate Measure of Support
ANRPC	Association of Natural Rubber Producing Countries
ASEAN	Association of Southeast Asian Nations
CAP	Common Agricultural Program
CBI	Cross Border Initiative
CEAO	Communauté économique de l'Afrique de l'Ouest (West African Economic Community)
CEMAC	Communauté économique et monétaire de l'Afrique Centrale (Economic and Monetary Community of Central Africa)
CEPGL	Communauté économique des pays des Grands Lacs (Economic Community of the Great Lakes Countries)
CFA	Communauté Financiére Africaine
CFC	Common Fund for Commodities
CIF	cost, insurance, and freight
CMA	Common Monetary Agreement
COMESA	Common Market for Eastern and Southern Africa
CSE	consumer subsidy equivalent
DC	developed country
EAC	East African Community
EC	European Community
ECCAS	Economic Community of Central African States
ECOMOG	ECOWAS Monitoring Group
ECOWAS	Economic Community of West African States
EEC	European Economic Community

EPZ	Export Processing Zones
EU	European Union
FAO	Food and Agriculture Organization
G7	Group of Seven
GAPEX	General Agricultural Products Exports (Tanzania)
GATT	General Agreement on Tariffs and Trade
GDFI	gross domestic fixed investment
GDP	gross domestic product
GNP	gross national product
GSP	Generalized System of Preferences
HFCS	high-fructose corn syrup
ICA	International Coffee Agreement
ICB	International Commodity Body
ICCA	International Cocoa Agreement
IGAD	Intergovernmental Authority on Development
IGADD	Intergovernmental Authority on Drought and Development
IMF	International Monetary Fund
INRA	International Natural Rubber Agreement
IPC	Integrated Programme for Commodities
ISA	International Sugar Agreement
ITA	International Tin Agreement
ITO	International Trade Organization
LDC	less developed country
LLDC	least developed country
LTA	Long Term Arrangement
MFA	Multi-Fiber Arrangement
MFN	most favored nation
MRU	Mano River Union
NAC	nominal assistance coefficient
NMC	National Milling Corporation (Tanzania)
NTB	nontariff barrier
NTM	nontariff measure
OAPs	offshore assembly provisions
OAU	Organization of African Unity
OECD	Organization for Economic Cooperation and Development
PI	private investment
PPP	purchasing power parity
PRC	People's Republic of China
PSE	producer subsidy equivalent
PTA	Preferential Trade Area
RMA	Rand Monetary Agreement

SACU	Southern African Customs Union
SADC	Southern African Development Community
SADCC	Southern African Development Coordination Conference
SITC	Standard International Trade Classification
SSA	sub-Saharan Africa
STA	short term arrangement
STABEX	Stabilization of Export Earnings
UDEAC	Union douanière et économique de l'Afrique Centrale (Central African Customs and Economic Union)
UEMOA	Union économique et monétaire ouest-africaine (West African Monetary and Economic Union)
UGFCC	United Ghana Farmers' Cooperative Council
UNCTAD	United Nations Conference on Trade and Development
WTO	World Trade Organization

References

African Development Bank Group
    1982   *Selected Statistics on Regional Member Countries.* Abidjan: African Development Bank.

Ake, Claude
    1991   *A Political Economy of Africa.* New York: Longman.
    1996   *Democracy and Development in Africa.* Washington, D.C.: Brookings Institution.

Alam, M. Shahid
    1989   "The South Korean 'Miracle': Examining the Mix of Government and Markets." *Journal of Developing Areas* 23, 2: 233–257.
    1991   "Trade Orientation and Macroeconomic Performance in LDCs: An Empirical Study." *Economic Development and Cultural Change* 39, 4: 839–848.

Aly, Ahmad
    1994   *Economic Cooperation in Africa.* Boulder: Lynne Rienner.

Amjadi, A., et al.
    1996   *Did External Barriers Cause the Marginalization of Sub-Saharan Africa in World Trade?* World Bank Discussion Paper 348. Washington, D.C.: World Bank.

Amjadi, A., and A. Yeats
    1995   *Nontariff Barriers Africa Faces: What Did the Uruguay Round Accomplish, and What Remains to Be Done?* Policy Research Working Paper 1439. Washington, D.C.: World Bank.

Anderson, Kym, and Rod Tyers
    1990   "How Developing Countries Could Gain from Agricultural Trade Liberalization in the Uruguay Round." In *Agricultural Trade Liberalization: Implications for Developing Countries,* edited by Ian Goldin and Odin Knudsen, 41–75. Paris: OECD.

Ansu, Yaw
    1997   "Macroeconomic Aspects of Multiple Exchange Rate Regimes: The Case of Ghana." In *Parallel Exchange Rates in Developing Countries,* edited by Miguel Kiguel et al., 188–220. New York: St. Martin's Press.

Aron, Janine, and Ibrahim Elbadawi
  1997   "The Parallel Market Premium and Exchange Rate Unification:
           A Macroeconomic Analysis for Zambia." In *Parallel Exchange
           Rates in Developing Countries*, edited by Miguel Kiguel et al.,
           291–332. New York: St. Martin's Press.
Asante, S.K.B.
  1997   *Regionalism and Africa's Development—Expectations, Reality and Chal-
           lenges.* New York: St. Martin's Press.
Baldwin, Robert, and Tracy Murray
  1977   "MFN Tariff Reductions and Developing Country Trade Benefits
           Under the GSP." *Economic Journal* 87: 30–46.
  1986   "MFN Tariff Reductions and Developing Country Trade Benefits
           Under the GSP." *Economic Journal* 96: 537–539.
Bank of Tanzania
  1982   *Tanzania: Twenty Years of Independence: 1961–1981.* Dar-es-Salaam:
           Bank of Tanzania.
Bates, Robert H.
  1981   *Markets and States in Tropical Africa—The Political Basis of Agricul-
           tural Policies.* Los Angeles: University of California Press.
  1994   "The Impulse to Reform in Africa." In *Economic Change and Politi-
           cal Liberalization in Sub-Saharan Africa*, edited by Jennifer A.
           Widner, 13–28. Baltimore: The Johns Hopkins University
           Press.
  1997   *The International Coffee Organization: An International Institution.*
           Occasional Paper 16, Bureau of Economic Studies, Macalester
           College, St. Paul, Minn.
Behrmann, Neil
  1991   "New Coffee Pact Is Sought in Bid to Lift Market." *Wall Street Jour-
           nal,* September 21, A6C.
  1993   "Some Analysts Say New Coffee Producer Cartel Formed in Brazil
           Is Doomed to Ultimate Failure." *Wall Street Journal,* September
           27, C12.
Bienen, Henry
  1990   "The Politics of Trade Liberalization in Africa." *Economic Develop-
           ment and Cultural Change* 38, 4: 713–732.
Biggs, Tyler, et al.
  1996   *Africa Can Compete! Export Opportunities and Challenges for Garments
           and Home Products in the European Market.* World Bank Discus-
           sion Paper 300, Africa Technical Department Series. Washing-
           ton, D.C.: World Bank.
Blejer, Mario, and Mohsin Khan
  1984   "Government Policy and Private Investment in Developing Coun-
           tries." *IMF Staff Papers* 31, 2: 379–403.
Boahen, A. Adu
  1987   *African Perspectives on Colonialism.* Baltimore: The Johns Hopkins
           University Press.
Bouton, Lawrence, and Mariusz A. Sumlinski
  1996   *Trends in Private Investment in Developing Countries: Statistics for
           1970–95.* International Finance Corporation, Discussion Pa-
           per 31. Washington, D.C.: World Bank.

Bowman, Mary, et al.
1996   "Rent Seeking and International Commodity Agreements: The Case of Coffee." *Economic Development and Cultural Change* 44, 2: 379–404.

Brandt, Hartmut
1991   *The Formulation of a New Coffee Agreement*. Berlin: German Development Institute.

Brown, Drasulla
1987   "General Equilibrium Effects of the U.S. Generalized System of Preferences." *Southern Economic Journal* 54, 1: 27–47.
1989   "A Computational Analysis of Japan's Generalized System of Preferences." *Journal of Development Economics* 30: 103–128.

Burkett, Elinor
1997   "God Created Me to Be a Slave: Mauritania's 90,000 Slaves Don't Rebel." *New York Times Magazine*, October 12, 56–60.

Caprio, Gerard, and Daniela Klingebiel
1996   "Bank Insolvency: Bad Luck, Bad Policy, or Bad Banking?" In *Annual World Bank Conference on Development Economics 1996*, edited by Michael Bruno and Boris Pleskovic. 79–104. Washington, D.C.: World Bank.

Clark, Don, and Simonetta Zarrilli
1992   "Non-Tariff Measures and Industrial Nation Imports of GSP-Covered Products." *Southern Economic Journal* 59, 2: 284–293.

Cline, William
1990   *The Future of World Trade in Textiles and Apparel*. Rev. ed. Washington, D.C.: Institute for International Economics.

COMESA [Common Market for Eastern and Southern Africa]
1994   *Report of the First Meeting of the COMESA Council of Ministers*, COMESA/CM/I/5. Lusaka: COMESA Center.
1998   *On the Threshold of a Free Trade Area*. Lusaka: COMESA Centre.

Common Fund for Commodities
1980   *Agreement Establishing the Common Fund for Commodities*. Amsterdam: Common Fund for Commodities.
1997   *Annual Report 1996*. Amsterdam: Common Fund for Commodities.
1998   *Some Notes on the Common Fund for Commodities*. Amsterdam: Common Fund for Commodities.

Craig, Peter
1992   "Mauritius, a Success Story of the 1980s, Is Looking for Investors to Participate in Next Development Phase." *Business America* 113, 6: 28–31.

Cuddington, John T.
1987   "Capital Flight." *European Economic Review* 31, 1/2: 382–388.

Darrat, Ali F.
1986   "Trade and Development: The Asian Experience." *The Cato Journal* 6, 2: 695–699.

Davenport, Michael
1992   "Africa and the Unimportance of Being Preferred." *Journal of Common Market Studies* 30, 2: 233–251.

DeRosa, Dean
   1991   "Protection in Sub-Saharan Africa Hinders Exports." *Finance and Development* 28, 3: 42–45.
Dercon, Stefan
   1996   "Risk, Crop Choice, and Savings: Evidence from Tanzania." *Economic Development and Cultural Change* 44, 3: 485–513.
DeVault, James
   1996a   "Political Pressure and the U.S. Generalized System of Preferences." *Eastern Economic Journal* 22, 1: 35–46.
   1996b   "Competitive Need Limits and the U.S. Generalized System of Preference." *Contemporary Economic Policy* 14, 4: 58–66.
Dollar, David
   1992   "Outward-oriented Developing Economies Really Do Grow More Rapidly: Evidence from 95 LDCs, 1976–1985." *Economic Development and Cultural Change* 40, 3: 523–544.
ECOWAS [Economic Community of West African States] Secretariat
   1993   *Economic Community of West African States (ECOWAS)—Revised Treaty.* Accra: Sampsco Press.
Edwards, Sebastian
   1993   "Openness, Trade Liberalization, and Growth in Developing Countries." *Journal of Economic Literature* 31, 3: 1358–1393.
Elbadawi, Ibrahim
   1997   "The Parallel Market Premium for Foreign Exchange and Macroeconomic Policy in Sudan." In *Parallel Exchange Rates in Developing Countries,* edited by Miguel Kiguel et al., 221–246. New York: St. Martin's Press.
Esfahani, Hadi
   1991   "Exports, Imports and Economic Growth in Semi-Industrialized Countries." *Journal of Development Economics* 35, 1: 93–116.
Export Processing Zones Authority
   1998   *Export Processing Zones in Kenya: Information for Potential Investors.* Nairobi, Kenya: Export Processing Zones Authority.
Faini, Riccardo
   1994   "The Output and Inflationary Impact of Devaluation in Developing Countries: Theory and Empirical Evidence from Five African Low-Income Countries." In *From Adjustment to Development in Africa: Conflict, Controversy, Convergence, Consensus?* edited by Giovanni A. Cornia and Gerald K. Helleiner, 334–352. New York: St. Martin's Press.
Fisher, Bart
   1972   *The International Coffee Agreement: A Study in Coffee Diplomacy.* New York: Praeger Publishers.
Foroutan, Faezeh
   1992   "Regional Integration in Sub-Saharan Africa." In *New Dimensions in Regional Integration,* edited by Jaime de Melo and Arvind Panagariya, 234–271. Cambridge: Centre for Economic Policy Research, Cambridge University Press.
Fry, Maxwell
   1993   *Financial Repression and Economic Growth.* International Finance Group Working Paper IFGWP-93–07, University of Birmingham, Britain.

Galbis, Vicente
  1979   "Money, Investment, and Growth in Latin America, 1961–1973."
          Economic Development and Cultural Change 27, 3: 423–443.
Gardner, Bruce
  1990   "Origin and Evolution of U.S. Farm Policies." In *Agricultural Pro-
          tectionism in the Industrialized World,* edited by Fred H. Sander-
          son, 19–63. Washington, D.C.: Resources for the Future.
GATT [General Agreement on Tariffs and Trade] Secretariat
  1994   "The Final Act of the Uruguay Round: A Summary." *International
          Trade Forum* 1: 4–21.
Gilbert, Christopher
  1985   "Futures Trading and the Welfare Evaluation of Commodity
          Price Stabilization." *Economic Journal* 95: 637–661.
  1996   "International Commodity Agreements: An Obituary Notice."
          World Development 24, 1: 1–19.
Goldberg, Jeffrey
  1997   "Their Africa Problem and Ours." *New York Times Magazine,*
          March 2, Section 6, 33–39, 59, 62, 75–77.
Grabowski, Richard
  1994   "Import Substitution, Export Promotion, and the State in Eco-
          nomic Development." *Journal Of Developing Areas* 28, 4:
          535–554.
Greenfield, Jim, et al.
  1996   "The Uruguay Round Agreement on Agriculture: Food Security
          Implications for Developing Countries." *Food Policy* 21, 4/5:
          365–375.
Greer, Thomas
  1992   "The Economic Community of West African States: Status, Prob-
          lems and Prospects for Change." *International Marketing Review*
          9, 3: 25–39.
Haberler, G.
  1964   "Comparative Advantage, Agricultural Production and Interna-
          tional Trade." *The International Journal of Agrarian Affairs*
          (May): 130–149.
Harrison, Ann
  1996   "Openness and Growth: A Time-Series, Cross-Country Analysis
          for Developing Countries." *Journal of Development Economics* 48:
          419–447.
Hastings, N.A.J., and K.A.B. Msimangira
  1992   "Manufacturing Management in Development Countries with
          Particular Reference to the Tanzanian Textile Industry." *Inter-
          national Journal of Public Sector Management* 5, 2: 7–14.
Hathaway, Dale, and Merlinda Ingco
  1996   "Agricultural Liberalization and the Uruguay Round." In *The
          Uruguay Round and the Developing Countries,* edited by Will Mar-
          tin and L. Alan Winters, 30–58. Cambridge: Cambridge Uni-
          versity Press.
Hecht, David
  1997   "Virtual Slavery." *The New Republic* 216 (May 12): 9–10.

Helleiner, Gerald K.
  1986   "Outward Orientation, Import Instability and African Economic Growth: An Empirical Investigation." In *Theory and Reality in Development*, edited by Sanjaya Lall and Frances Stewart, 139–153. Hampshire, England: Macmillan.
  1990   "Trade Strategy in Medium-term Adjustment." *World Development* 18, 6: 879–897.
Hermes, Niels, and Robert Lensink
  1992   "The Magnitude and Determinants of Capital Flight: The Case for Six Sub-Saharan African Countries." *Economist-Leiden* 140, 4: 515–530.
Herrmann, Roland
  1986   "Free Riders and the Redistributive Effects of International Commodity Agreements: The Case of Coffee." *Journal of Policy Modeling* 8, 2: 597–621.
Herrmann, Roland, et al.
  1993   *International Commodity Policy: A Quantitative Analysis*. London: Routledge.
Heston, Alan, and Robert Summers
  1996   "International Price and Quantity Comparisons: Potentials and Pitfalls." *American Economic Review* 86, 2: 20–24.
Hillman, Jimmye S.
  1991   *Technical Barriers to Agricultural Trade*. Boulder: Westview Press.
Hirschman, Albert
  1958   *The Strategy of Economic Development*. New Haven: Yale University Press.
Hopkins, Raymond
  1993   "Developing Countries in the Uruguay Round: Bargaining Under Uncertainty and Inequality." In *World Agriculture and the GATT*, edited by William Avery, 143–163. Boulder: Lynne Rienner.
"How Africa Should Industrialize," 1995 *Business Africa*, March 16–31, 1–3.
Hufbauer, Gary, and Kimberly Elliott
  1994   *Measuring the Costs of Protection in the United States*. Washington, D.C.: Institute for International Economics.
IGAD [Intergovernmental Authority on Development] Secretariat
  1996   *IGAD Forges Regional Cooperation in the Horn of Africa: Summit of Heads of State and Government to Launch Revitalized IGAD*. Nairobi: The Regal Press Kenya.
IMF [International Monetary Fund]
  1990   *Primary Commodities: Market Developments and Outlook*. Washington, D.C.: International Monetary Fund.
  1997   *Direction of Trade Statistics Yearbook*. Washington, D.C.: International Monetary Fund.
  1997   *Government Finance Statistics Yearbook*. Washington, D.C.: International Monetary Fund.
Ingco, Merlinda
  1996   "Tariffication in the Uruguay Round: How Much Liberalisation?" *The World Economy* 19, 4: 425–446.
Ingrassia, Lawrence
  1993   "Developing Countries Feel Shortchanged by GATT." *Wall Street Journal*, December 15, A6.

International Labour Organization
    1984   *Rural Development and Women in Africa.* Geneva: International Labour Office.

Jackson, John
    1994   "Dispute Settlement Procedures." In *The New World Trading System: Readings,* 117–124. Paris: OECD.

Jacobs, Brenda
    1995   "U.S. Trade Liberalization Takes the Slow Boat." *Bobbin* 36, 7: 14–18.
    1997   "H.R. 1432 Could Propel Sub-Saharan Sourcing." *Bobbin* 38, 11: 88–89.

Jansen, Doris J.
    1991   "Zambia." In *The Political Economy of Agricultural Pricing Policy: Africa and the Mediterranean,* Vol. 3, edited by Anne Krueger et al., 268–327. Baltimore: The Johns Hopkins University Press.

Jung, Woo S., and Peyton J. Marshall
    1985   "Exports, Growth and Causality in Developing Countries." *Journal of Development Economics* 18, 2: 1–12.

Kaufmann, Daniel, and Stephen O'Connell
    1997   "Exchange Controls and the Parallel Premium in Tanzania." In *Parallel Exchange Rates in Developing Countries,* edited by Miguel Kiguel et al., 247–290. New York: St. Martin's Press.

Kirthisingha, P. N.
    1983   "International Commodity Agreements." *International Journal of Social Economics* 10, 3: 40–65.

Krueger, Anne, et al.
    1988   "Agricultural Incentives in Developing Countries: Measuring the Effect of Sectoral and Economywide Policies." *World Bank Economic Review* 2, 3: 255–271.

Kumar, Umesh
    1989   "Trade Liberalization and Payments Arrangements Under the PTA Treaty: An Experiment in Collective Self-Reliance." *Journal of World Trade* 23, 5: 93–121.

Laird, S., and A. Yeats
    1990   *Quantitative Methods for Trade-Barrier Analysis.* New York: New York University Press.

Lancaster, Carol
    1999   *So Much to Do So Little Done.* Chicago: The Century Foundation, The University of Chicago Press.

Landau, Daniel
    1990   "The Pattern of Economic Policies in LDCs: A Public Choice Explanation." *The Cato Journal* 10, 2: 573–601.

Langhammer, Rolf, and André Sapir
    1987   *Economic Impact of Generalized Tariff Preferences.* Brookfield, Vt.: Trade Policy Research Centre, Gower Publishing.

Leifer, Michael
    1989   *ASEAN and the Security of South-East Asia.* London: Routledge.

Lim, David
    1991   *Export Instability and Compensatory Financing.* London: Routledge.

Lindauer, David, and Ann Velenchik
  1994   "Can Africa Labor Compete?" In *Asia and Africa: Legacies and Op-
          portunities in Development*, edited by David Lindauer and
          Michael Roemer, 269–304. San Francisco: Institute for Con-
          temporary Studies.
Lofchie, Michael F.
  1994   "The Politics of Agricultural Policy." In *Beyond Capitalism vs. So-
          cialism in Kenya and Tanzania*, edited by Joel D. Barkan,
          129–173. Boulder: Lynne Rienner.
Lucier, Richard
  1988   *The International Political Economy of Coffee*. New York: Praeger Pub-
          lishers.
MacPhee, Craig
  1989   *A Synthesis of the GSP Study Programme*. UNCTAD/ITP/19. Geneva:
          UNCTAD.
MacPhee, Craig, and Victor Oguledo
  1991   "The Trade Effects of the U.S. Generalized System of Prefer-
          ences." *Atlantic Economic Journal* 19, 4: 19–26.
MacPhee, Craig, and David Rosenbaum
  1989   "The Asymmetric Effects of Reversible Tariff Changes Under the
          United States GSP." *Southern Economic Journal* 56, 1: 105–125.
Mammarella, James
  1994   "Retailers Reverse Field on GATT." *Discount Store News* 33, 20: 3,
          63.
Mandaza, Ibbo, et al.
  1994   *THE JOINT PTA/SADC STUDY on Harmonisation, Rationalisation
          and Coordination of the Activities of the Preferential Trade Area for
          Eastern and Southern African States (PTA) and the Southern African
          Development Community (SADC)*. Harare, Zimbabwe: COMESA/
          SADC.
Marriott, Cherie
  1995   "Moving into Top Gear to Boost Exports." *Asiamoney* (July/Au-
          gust): 32–33.
Marshall, C. F.
  1983   *The World Coffee Trade*. Cambridge: Woodhead-Faulkner.
"Master and Slave in Mauritania," 1996 *Economist* 340 (September 21): 44.
Mataya, Charles, and Michele Veeman
  1996   "The Behavior of Private and Public Investment in Malawi."
          Canadian Journal of Economics 29: 438–442.
Mayer, Marina, and Harry Zarenda
  1994   *The Southern African Customs Union: A Review of Costs and Benefits*.
          Policy Working Paper 19. Development Bank of Southern
          Africa, Halfway House, South Africa.
Mbelle, Ammon, and Thomas Sterner
  1991   "Foreign Exchange and Industrial Development: A Frontier Pro-
          duction Function Analysis of Two Tanzanian Industries." *World
          Development* 19, 4: 341–347.
McCarthy, Colin
  1992   "The Southern African Customs Union in a Changing Economic
          and Political Environment." *Journal of World Trade* 26, 4: 5–24.

McFarquhar, A.M.M., and G.B. Aneuryn Evans
1972   *Employment Creation in Primary Production in Less Developed Coun-*
        tries: Case Studies of Employment Potential in the Coffee Sectors of
        Brazil and Kenya. Paris: Development Centre of the Organiza-
        tion for Economic Cooperation and Development.
McGee, Suzanne
1995   "Coffee Soars After Accord on Restricting Exports." *Wall Street*
        Journal, July 27, C14.
McKinnon, Ronald I.
1973   *Money and Capital in Economic Development.* Washington, D.C.:
        Brookings Institution.
McMahon, Gary
1987   "Does a Small Developing Country Benefit from International
        Commodity Agreements?" *Economic Development and Cultural*
        Change 35, 2: 409–423.
1988   "The Income Distribution Effects of the Kenyan Coffee Market-
        ing System." *Journal of Development Economics* 31, 2: 297–326.
Mehrotra, Santosh
1991   "Southern Africa Development Coordination Conference
        (SADCC): Evaluating Recent Trends in Regional Coopera-
        tion." *International Studies* 28, 4: 389–408.
Morgan, C. W., et al.
1994   "Price Instability and Commodity Futures Markets." *World Devel-*
        opment 22, 11: 1729–1736.
Morisset, Jacques
1993   "Does Financial Liberalization Really Improve Private Investment
        in Developing Countries?" *Journal of Development Economics* 40:
        133–150.
Mshomba, Richard E.
1993   "The Magnitude of Coffee Arabica Smuggled from Northern Tan-
        zania into Kenya." *Eastern Africa Economic Review* 9, 1: 165–175.
1994   *The Uncertainty of the International Coffee Agreement.* Washington, D.C.:
        Institute for the Study of Diplomacy, Georgetown University.
1997   "African Responsibility for Economic Problems." *ISSUE: A Journal*
        of Opinion 25, 1: 50–53.
Newbery, David
1993   "Implications of Imperfect Risk Markets for Agricultural Taxa-
        tion." In *The Economics of Rural Organization: Theory, Practice,*
        and Policy, edited by Karla Hoff et al., 406–435. New York: Ox-
        ford University Press.
Ng, F., and A. Yeats
1996   *Open Economies Work Better! Did Africa's Protectionist Policies Cause Its*
        Marginalization in World Trade? Policy Research Working Paper
        1636. Washington, D.C.: World Bank.
Ngugi, D. N., et al.
1990   *East African Agriculture.* 3d ed. London: Macmillan Education.
Nwokedi, Emeka
1992   *Regional Integration and Regional Security: ECOMOG, Nigeria and the*
        Liberia Crisis. Talence Cedex, France: Centre d'Etude d'Afrique
        Noire.

O'Connell, Stephen
  1997   "Macroeconomic Harmonization, Trade Reform, and Regional
          Trade in Sub-Saharan Africa." In *Regional Integration and Trade
          Liberalization in Sub-Saharan Africa,* edited by Ademola Oyejide
          et al., 89–158. New York: St. Martin's Press.
OECD [Organization for Economic Cooperation and Development]
  1983   *The Generalized System of Preferences: Review of the First Decade.* Paris:
          OECD.
  1994   *Agricultural Policies, Markets and Trade: Monitoring and Outlook
          1994.* Paris: OECD.
  1995a   *Agricultural Policies, Markets and Trade: Monitoring and Outlook
          1995.* Paris: OECD.
  1995b   *The Uruguay Round: A Preliminary Evaluation of the Impacts of the
          Agreement on Agriculture in the OECD Countries.* Paris: OECD.
  1997   *Agricultural Policies in OECD Countries: Measurement of Support and
          Background Information 1997.* Paris: OECD.
Organization of African Unity
  1991   *Treaty Establishing the African Economic Community.* Centre for
          Southern African Studies, University of the Western Cape, Bell-
          ville, South Africa.
Oshikoya, Temitope W.
  1994   "Macroeconomic Determinants of Domestic Private Investment
          in Africa: An Empirical Analysis." *Economic Development and Cul-
          tural Change* 42, 3: 573–596.
Oyejide, Ademola, et al.
  1997   *Regional Integration and Trade Liberalization in Sub-Saharan Africa.*
          New York: St. Martin's Press.
Perlez, Jane
  1990   "Mauritius Thrives as Textiles Boom." *New York Times Current
          Events Edition,* September 10, D4.
Phillips, Michael
  1996   "U.S. Rethinks Trade Policy with Africa." *Wall Street Journal,* July
          15, A2.
Pinto, Brian
  1991   "Black Markets for Foreign Exchange, Real Exchange Rates and
          Inflation." *Journal of International Economics* 30: 121–135.
Pomfret, Richard
  1986a   "MFN Tariff Reductions and Developing Country Trade Benefits
          Under the GSP: A Comment." *Economic Journal* 96: 534–536.
  1986b   "The Effects of Trade Preferences for Developing Countries."
          Southern Economic Journal 53, 1: 18–26.
Raby, Geoff
  1994   "Introduction." In *The New World Trading System: Readings,* 13–25,
          Paris: OECD.
Raffaelli, Marcelo
  1995   *Rise and Demise of Commodity Agreements.* Cambridge: Woodhead
          Publishing.
Raghavan, Chakravarthi
  1990   *Recolonization: GATT, the Uruguay Round & the Third World.*
          Penang, Malaysia: Zed Books.

Raj, Dev
  1990   *Economic Development: Critical Analysis of GSP*. New Delhi: Anmol
         Publications.
Republic of Kenya
  1998   *Economic Survey 1998*. Nairobi: Ministry of Planning and National
         Development.
Richardson, Richard, and Osman Ahmed
  1987   "Challenge for Africa's Private Sector." *Challenge* (January-Febru-
         ary): 16–25.
Riddell, Roger
  1993   "The Future of the Manufacturing Sector in Sub-Saharan Africa."
         In *Hemmed In—Responses to Africa's Economic Decline*, edited by
         Thomas Callaghy and John Ravenhill, 215–247. New York: Co-
         lumbia University Press.
Roach, Loretta
  1995   "IMRA Calls for GSP Renewal." *Discount Merchandiser* 35, 6: 16.
Rodrik, Dani
  1992   "The Limits of Trade Policy Reform in Developing Countries."
         Journal of Economic Perspectives 6, 1: 87–105.
Romer, Paul
  1986   "Increasing Returns and Long-Run Growth." *Journal of Political
         Economy* 94, 5: 1002–1037.
  1987   "Crazy Explanations for the Productivity Slowdown." In *Macroeco-
         nomic Annual*, edited by Stanley Fisher, 163–202. Cambridge:
         MIT Press.
Runge, C. Ford
  1993   "Beyond the Uruguay Round: Emerging Issues in Agricultural
         Trade Policy." In *World Agriculture and the GATT*, edited by
         William Avery, 181–213. Boulder: Lynne Rienner.
Samboma, J. Lahai
  1994   "Africa Must Renegotiate GATT." *New African* (April): 25.
Sanderson, Fred H., ed.
  1990   *Agricultural Protectionism in the Industrialized World*. Washington,
         D.C.: Resources for the Future.
Sapir, A., and L. Lundberg
  1984   "The U.S. Generalized System of Preferences and Its Impact." In
         The Structure and Evolution of Recent U.S. Trade Policy, an NBER
         Conference Report, edited by Richard Baldwin and Anne
         Krueger, 195–231. Chicago: University of Chicago Press.
Schmidt-Hebbel, Klaus, et al.
  1996   "Saving and Investment: Paradigms, Puzzles, and Policies." *The
         World Bank Research Observer* 11, 1: 87–117.
Schmitz, Hubert
  1984   "Industrialization Strategies in Less Developed Countries: Some
         Lessons of Historical Experience." *Journal of Development Studies*
         21, 1: 1–21.
Shipton, Parker
  1991   "Time and Money in the Western Sahel: A Clash of Cultures in
         Gambian Rural Finance." In *Markets in Developing Countries:
         Parallel, Fragmented and Black*, edited by Michael Roemer and

Christine Jones, 113–139. San Francisco: The International Center for Economic Growth and the Harvard Institute for International Development, ICS Press.

Simon, Sheldon
1982   *The ASEAN States and Regional Security*. Stanford, Calif.: Hoover Institution Press, Stanford University.

Singleton, John
1997   *The World Textile Industry*. London: Routledge.

Smeets, Maarten
1995   "Main Features of the Uruguay Round Agreement on Textiles and Clothing, and Implications for the Trading System." *Journal of World Trade* 29, 5: 97–109.

Solow, Robert M.
1957   "Technical Change and the Aggregate Production Function." *Review of Economics and Statistics* 39: 312–320.

Sorsa, Piritta
1996   "Sub-Saharan African Own Commitments in the Uruguay Round—Myth or Reality?" *The World Economy* 19, 3: 287–305.

Stoll, Hans, and Robert Whaley
1993   *Futures and Options: Theory and Applications*. Cincinnati: South-Western Publishing.

Stryker, J. Dirck
1991   "Ghana." In *The Political Economy of Agricultural Pricing Policy: Africa and the Mediterranean*, Vol. 3, edited by Anne Krueger et al., 79–121. Baltimore: The Johns Hopkins University Press.

Stubbs, Richard
1984   "The International Natural Rubber Agreement: Its Negotiation and Operation." *Journal of World Trade Law* 18, 1: 16–31.

Summers, Robert, and Alan Heston
1988   "A New Set of International Comparisons of Real Product and Price Levels Estimates for 130 Countries, 1950–1985." *Review of Income and Wealth* 34: 1–25.

Tangermann, Stefan
1994   "An Assessment of the Agreement on Agriculture." In *The New World Trading System*, 143–151. Paris: OECD.
1996   "Implementation of the Uruguay Round Agreement on Agriculture: Issues and Prospects." *Journal of Agricultural Economics* 47, 3: 315–337.

Tanzania, United Republic of
1991   *Speech by the Minister for Finance Hon. Steven A. Kibona (MP) Introducing to the National Assembly the Estimates of Government Revenue and Expenditure for Financial Year 1991/92 on the 13th of June, 1991*. Dar-es-Salaam: Government Printer.

"Tanzania's Textiles Collapse," 1995 *Business Africa*, March 16–31, 2.

Taylor, Jeffrey
1993   "Coffee Prices Increase as Brazil Makes Progress Toward Adhering to Export-limiting Accord." *Wall Street Journal*, November 19, C14.

Truett, Dale B., and Lila J. Truett
1992   "Nonprimary Exports of African LDCs: Have Trade Preferences Helped?" *Journal of Developing Areas* 26: 457–474.

"U.N. Agency Opposed to EU Ban on Mozambican Fish"
  1998   Panafrican News Agency, March 3, http://www.africanews.org/
          PANA/news/19980227/feat.8.html.
UNCTAD [United Nations Conference on Trade and Development]
  1988a   *Handbook of Trade Control Measures of Developing Countries, 1987,*
          and *Handbook Supplement, 1987.* New York: United Nations.
  1988b   *International Cocoa Agreement, 1986.* New York: United Nations.
  1991   *Prospects for the World Cocoa Market Until the Year 2005.* New York:
          United Nations.
  1992   *Regional and Subregional Economic Integration and Cooperation
          Among Developing Countries: Adjusting to Changing Realities—The
          Case of Africa.* UNCTAD/ECDC/228. Geneva: United Nations.
  1994   *Trade and Development Report, 1994.* New York: United Nations.
  1995a   *Handbook of International Trade and Development Statistics 1994.*
          New York: United Nations.
  1995b   *The Least Developed Countries 1995 Report.* New York: United Na-
          tions.
  1995c   *Review of the Implementation, Maintenance, Improvement and Utiliza-
          tion of the Generalized System of Preferences, Rules of Origin and Tech-
          nical Assistance.* TD/B/SCP/12. Geneva: UNCTAD.
  1996   *Handbook of Economic Integration and Cooperation Groupings of Devel-
          oping Countries.* Vol. 1: *Regional and Subregional Economic Integra-
          tion Groupings.* New York: United Nations.
  1997a   *Handbook of International Trade and Development Statistics 1995.*
          New York: United Nations.
  1997b   *The Least Developed Countries 1997 Report.* New York: United Na-
          tions.
  1997c   *Regional Experiences in the Economic Integration Process of Developing
          Countries.* UNCTAD/ITCD/TSB/1. Geneva: United Nations.
United Nations
  1990   *Terms of Reference of the International Tin Study Group.* New York:
          United Nations.
  1992   *GSP Graduation, International Trade, and Investment in the Asia and
          Pacific Region.* New York: United Nations.
Upton, Martin
  1996   *The Economics of Tropical Farming Systems.* Cambridge: Cambridge
          University Press.
U.S. Bureau of the Census
  1976   *The Statistical History of the United States from Colonial Times to the
          Present.* Washington, D.C.: U.S. Bureau of the Census.
U.S. House of Representatives
  1998   *H.R. 1432—African Growth and Opportunity Act.* Washington, D.C.:
          U.S. House of Representatives.
U.S. International Trade Commission
  1991   *A Guide to the U.S. Generalized System of Preferences.* Washington,
          D.C.: Office of the U.S. Trade Representative.
  1993   *Operation of the Trade Agreements Program.* Washington, D.C.: U.S.
          International Trade Commission.
  1994   *The Year in Trade: Operation of the Trade Agreements Program.* USITC
          Publication 2769. Washington, D.C.: U.S. International Trade
          Commission.

1997   *Likely Impact of Providing Quota-Free and Duty-Free Entry to Textiles and Apparel from Sub-Saharan Africa.* USITC Publication 3056. Washington, D.C.: U.S. International Trade Commission.

Valdés, Alberto, and Joachim Zietz
1980   *Agricultural Protection in OECD Countries: Its Cost to Less-Developed Countries.* Research Report 21. Washington, D.C.: International Food Policy Research Institute.

Vietta, Gérard, and Carmel Cahill
1991   "The Resistance to Agricultural Reform." *The OECD Observer* 171: 4–8.

Westlake, Michael J.
1994   *Economic Management of Administered Agricultural Pricing and Payment Systems in Africa: A Practical Guide.* FAO Economic and Social Development Paper 119. Rome: FAO.

Wilde, John C. de
1984   *Agriculture, Marketing, and Pricing in Sub-Saharan Africa.* Los Angeles: African Studies Center and African Studies Association.

World Bank
1985   *World Development Report 1985.* New York: Oxford University Press.
1987   *World Development Report 1987.* New York: Oxford University Press.
1988   *World Development Report 1988.* New York: Oxford University Press.
1990   *World Tables 1989/1990.* Washington, D.C.: World Bank.
1993   *World Development Report 1993.* New York: Oxford University Press.
1994a   *Adjustment in Africa: Reforms, Results, and the Road Ahead.* New York: Oxford University Press.
1994b   *Global Economic Perspective and the Developing Countries.* New York: Oxford University Press.
1994c   *World Development Report 1994.* New York: Oxford University Press.
1995   *World Tables 1995.* Washington, D.C.: World Bank.
1997a   *World Development Indicators 1997.* Washington, D.C.: World Bank.
1997b   *World Development Report 1997.* New York: Oxford University Press.
1997c   *African Development Indicators 1997.* Washington, D.C.: World Bank.
1999   *World Development Report 1998/99.* New York: Oxford University Press.

Yeats, A., et al.
1997   *Did Domestic Policies Marginalize Africa in International Trade?* Washington, D.C.: World Bank.

Yoffie, David, and Jane Kenney Austin
1983   *Textiles and the Multi-Fiber Arrangement.* Case 383–164. Boston: Harvard Business School.

"Zimbabwe: Populism Awry," 1998 *Economist* 346, 8052 (January 24–30): 43.

Index

Abuja Treaty (1994), 178, 197, 205(n4)
Ad valorem tariff, 101, 102(table)
African Common Market, 178
African Economic Community, 205(n4)
African Economic Union, 178
African Growth and Opportunity Act (U.S.), 125–126, 128, 197, 208, 211–212
Aggregate measure of support (AMS), 103–104
Agreement on Agriculture (GATT-WTO; 1995), 100(table), 211; countries/products affected by, 108, 109(table); effects of, 105, 108, 109(table), 110–111; market access in, 99, 100–103, 105, 137(n7); protections affecting, 98, 99, 101–103, 105, 106, 116; SSA regional factors influencing, 111–116. *See also under individual countries*
Agreement on Textiles and Clothing (GATT-WTO; 1995), 122–124, 134, 138(n15), 211. *See also under individual countries*
Agricultural exports, 54(n11), 94, 95, 137(nn 1, 2), 210; and Agreement on Agriculture, 108, 109(table); government control of, 33, 50, 83; listed, 94–95, 139, 140(table). *See also* Agricultural subsidies; Cash crops; Food exports

Agricultural imports, 94, 95, 108, 109(table), 110
Agricultural marketing, 33–34, 50, 52, 53, 173(n7)
Agricultural output, 32, 36, 112–113
Agricultural policies, 13, 31–36, 54(n11), 83, 94–95; case study of, 50–53; in developed countries, 83, 95–99, 129; and marketing, 33–34; and monopolies, 33, 36, 50
Agricultural prices, 32, 33–34, 207, 210; in Agreement on Agriculture, 106–107, 108, 110, 114; controls on, 32, 33, 35, 36, 55(n15), 173(n7)
Agricultural subsidies, 54(n14), 83, 95–96; in Agreement on Agriculture, 100(table), 103–104, 129; export, 95, 96, 104–105, 106, 109(table), 112, 137(n8)
Agricultural taxes, 32, 33, 34, 54(n14), 138(n11), 173(n7); in Agreement on Agriculture, 98, 114
Alam, M. Shahid, 47
Aluminum, 140(table)
Aly, Ahmad, 203–204
Amjadi, A., 82
AMS. *See* Aggregate measure of support
Angola, 2(table), 7(table), 9(table), 27(table); and Agreement on Agriculture, 109(table); in commodity agreements, 140(table), 143(table), 147(table), 159(table); and GSP, 75(table), 90(n5); and regional economic integration,

231

About the Book

This in-depth analysis of the role of international trade in Africa focuses on four central issues: the trade policies of the sub-Saharan African countries; the impact of GATT and its successor, the World Trade Organization; the impact of specific GATT/WTO agreements and the changing role of commodity agreements; and the viability of regional economic integration as a strategy for trade and development.

Mshomba combines rigorous theoretical analysis with an empirical approach that gives attention to the experiences of individual countries and particular institutional settings. Avoiding generalizations, he identifies the winners and losers resulting from various policy decisions. In his concluding discussion, he tackles the controversial question of whether international trade is a barrier to development in Africa or, instead, has the potential to raise the standard of living on the continent.

Richard E. Mshomba is associate professor of economics at La Salle University.